THE HID

FIONA DAVISON stu_____ord
and joined the RHS in _____ib-
itions. She appears frequ_____out
garden history and has written numerous articles and features on
the subject.

———·———

'Delightful... *The Hidden Horticulturists* pulsates with the extraordinary energy and excitement of the time.' *Daily Mail*

'The chance discovery by the author, the RHS's chief librarian, of a
notebook led to this excellent page-turner.' 'Top Ten Gardening
Books of the Year', *Sunday Telegraph*

'This book by the head librarian of the RHS is a cracker... A highly
original piece of research into the lives of jobbing gardeners in
the early 19th century, with plenty of fascinating social background.' Tim Richardson, *Gardens Illustrated*

'The rise and progress of the Victorian head gardener is a tale of
ever-increasing professionalism in a developing world of technological progress, artistic revolution and endless plant novelties...
It's time their story was told.' *Country Life*

'The story of a cadre of promising young men who qualified as gardeners in the early 19th century... What is refreshing is that nearly
all the names unearthed will be unfamiliar, even to garden historians... Davison has conducted deep research into the later careers of
most of these gardeners, discovering what happened to them after
they left Chiswick. The result is a revealing insight into the lives
of aspiring working men in this period.' *Literary Review*

THE HIDDEN HORTICULTURISTS

THE WORKING-CLASS MEN WHO
SHAPED BRITAIN'S GARDENS

Fiona Davison

Atlantic Books
London

First published in Great Britain in 2019 by Atlantic Books,
an imprint of Atlantic Books Ltd.

This paperback edition first published in
Great Britain in 2022 by Atlantic Books.

Copyright © Fiona Davison, 2019

The moral right of Fiona Davison to be identified as
the author of this work has been asserted by her in accordance
with the Copyright, Designs and Patents Act of 1988.

All rights reserved. No part of this publication may be
reproduced, stored in a retrieval system, or transmitted in any
form or by any means, electronic, mechanical, photocopying,
recording, or otherwise, without the prior permission of both
the copyright owner and the above publisher of this book.

1 3 5 7 9 8 6 4 2

A CIP catalogue record for this book
is available from the British Library.

All illustrations are from the RHS Lindley
Collections, except where noted.

E-book ISBN: 978-1-78649-509-9
Paperback ISBN: 978-178649-508-2

Printed in Great Britain

Atlantic Books
An Imprint of Atlantic Books Ltd
Ormond House
26–27 Boswell Street
London
WC1N 3JZ

www.atlantic-books.co.uk

MIX
Paper from
responsible sources
FSC® C171272
FSC
www.fsc.org

FOR PATRICK, LIAM AND JOEL

Contents

Acknowledgements

WRITING A BOOK IN MY SPARE TIME INEVITABLY means that I have relied very heavily on the support of lots of people. I could never even have contemplated a project like this without access to digitized collections from a number of libraries and archives across the globe. The availability and accessibility of these collections relies on the dedicated labour of countless skilled and committed staff members and volunteers, and every researcher owes them an enormous debt.

I am especially grateful to the archive staff at Royal Botanic Gardens Kew and Royal Botanic Garden Edinburgh, who sent through so many digital files of scanned correspondence and minutes. Leonie Paterson and Graham Hardy were particularly helpful and I really enjoyed the opportunity to visit them to see the site of James Barnet's home. My colleagues in the RHS Libraries team have also been very supportive (as, of course, they are to hundreds of researchers every year), helping to track down images and sources. It has been a treat to witness their expertise and enthusiasm from 'the other side of the fence'. Dr Brent Elliott has provided invaluable support in reading and meticulously checking early proofs – any remaining errors that have managed to slip through are, of course, my own responsibility. I have relied heavily on his pioneering work on Victorian gardening. I have also drawn upon the genealogical research expertise of my mother, Ann Thornham, in particular her determination to track down the runaway Annie Slowe, long after I had given up on her.

I also have to thank London Broncos Rugby League Club for use of their clubhouse to work in, on many evenings whilst I waited for my son Joel to finish training. This is what the strange woman in the corner with the laptop was up to.

This project would never have made it into book form without the faith and encouragement of Rebecca Winfield of Luxton Associates, who has expertly guided me through the mysteries of the publishing world. James Nightingale and the team at Atlantic Books have been great to work with as a first-time author, and I am delighted that this is a co-publication with RHS Publishing – my thanks to Chris Young and Rae Spencer Jones in the Editorial Team for making this possible.

Finally, my thanks and love to Patrick, Liam and Joel for their patience on the many occasions that my attention was distracted by 105 long-dead young men.

PROLOGUE

'The Handwriting of Under-Gardeners and Labourers'

Thomas McCann admitted 22 June 1822 upon the recommendation of Sir Aubrey de Vere Hunt.

My father at the time I was admitted to the garden of the Society, was a gardener to Sir Aubrey de Vere Hunt of Currah in the County of Limerick. I was born at Galls town in the County of Dublin and was employed in Sir Aubrey de Vere Hunt's gardens and Nurseries from the age of 14 til I was 18, I then worked in London Nurseries for 8 months after which I came to the garden of the Society then 19 years of age and unmarried.

> *First entry in 'The Handwriting of Under-Gardeners and Labourers' book*

IN 2012 I STARTED WORK AT THE LINDLEY LIBRARY in London, which is the main library and archive of the Royal Horticultural Society and the largest and finest horticultural library in the world. In my first weeks I wandered through the stores, trying to understand what I had let myself in for. I saw a dizzying array of garden-related treasures, the fruits of the Society's 200-year-old obsession with plants and gardens.

Sumptuous botanical illustrations, imposing leather-bound herbals and garden designs were piled high on the shelves in the library storerooms. However, the item that intrigued me most in those first weeks sat in a rather unprepossessing cardboard box on a shelf in my new basement office, labelled in pencil 'Handwriting Book'. Inside was a slim cardboard-backed exercise book with a marbled cover and a maroon leather spine. A bit dog-eared at the corners, it looked like a standard piece of Victorian office stationery, apart from the title, which was embossed rather grandly in gold letters on a leather label on the front of the book: 'The Handwriting of Under-Gardeners and Labourers'. Inside was exactly that – 105 hand-written notes signed by young gardeners, spanning the years 1823–9 and recounting their working experience from the age of around fourteen until they were 'received into the Society's Garden'.

Each entry covered the young gardeners' careers from leaving school to the point where they had completed their early apprenticeship. Starting with their place and date of birth and their father's occupation, the short handwritten paragraphs outlined how the young men worked their way up through the different departments of a series of large gardens and commercial nurseries, gaining experience of ornamental flower gardens, kitchen gardens, hothouses and nurseries. Each entrant had to be recommended by a Fellow (a member of the Horticultural Society; the list of recommenders reads like a roll call of the aristocracy and the gardening elite). The entries in the Handwriting Book give a fascinating insight into the career structure of early nineteenth-century horticulture, revealing professional hierarchies and patterns of patronage, and interconnections between different gardens and nurseries across the country.

Even though the book was clearly written to a formula, the men's voices and stories shone through, a rarity from a time when most ordinary working people were voiceless and anonymous. From the first flick through, I was smitten and became determined to know more. What was this garden, and why did the Society take on so many gardeners to work in it? Why did it make them write down their CV by hand in this book when they started work? And what happened to the gardeners after they had thrown in their lot with the Horticultural Society and been 'received into the Society's Garden'?

The answers were sometimes hard to find. After the brief glimpse into their lives offered by the Handwriting Book, many of the men became elusive once more. By and large, they were not the type of men to write autobiographies, diaries or even long letters. Fleeting glimpses of them appear in newspaper articles, plant and garden descriptions and of course in the national census – that frustratingly slow stop–go animation, where the shutter clicks on a new frame every ten years, leaving the viewer desperately trying to fill in the gaps between the changed scenes: a shift in location, new occupation, new wives, tragic missing children. However, little by little the men began to reveal themselves, and the legacy that they left on our landscape and our gardens came into focus. Little did I know it, but following their trail was to take up most of my spare time over the next three years, and the trail was to stretch from west London to Bolivia and all points in between, taking in fraud, scandal, madness and, of course, a large number of fabulous plants and gardens.

These young men were fortunate enough to begin their careers in a remarkable garden at a time of enormous optimism and ambition. Britain's position as an imperial power – and her command of the trade routes – facilitated the discovery and importation of an enormous number of new and exotic plants. The discovery of new plants would have been of purely academic interest, if gardeners had not worked out how to grow them back home. However, scientific progress gave them the confidence that they could gain the upper hand over nature, particularly as new manufacturing technologies enabled the building of effective glasshouses to overcome the limitations of the English climate. Although the elaborate and mannered style of Victorian garden design and the highly labour-intensive practices that Victorian gardeners followed are both now long out of fashion, the evidence of the period's innovations still flourishes in our gardens. From tender bedding plants to repeat flowering roses, we take for granted plants that the men from Chiswick helped to develop and promote. Although they are now by and large forgotten, unearthing their stories has revealed that these men helped to shape our idea of the domestic garden.

NOTE

The process of translating historic monetary values into modern terms is a complex one, and since it happens several times in this book, I thought it worth explaining how I have approached it. Context is everything – to really understand what any given sum of money is worth to someone in the past, we need to comprehend its purchasing power at the time. A simple method, often used, is to multiply the sum by the percentage increase in inflation over the period, but this may be misleading. Inflation (the Retail Price Index) is based on the price of a notional 'basket' of goods. Our consumption patterns have changed so much that by the time you get back to the 1820s, this can be an unreliable measure. I have tended to use the 'labour value' as the multiplier – that is, measuring the amount relative to the earnings of an average worker, based on data from a wide range of studies, supplied by MeasuringWorth (a not-for-profit organization aiming to assist researchers in making value comparisons). If you are at all interested in the topic, I can heartily recommend the essays on their website, measuringworth.com.

INTRODUCTION

A Garden to Grow Gardeners

THE STORY OF THE HANDWRITING BOOK BEGINS IN
a vegetable field near Chiswick on a June day in 1821. The field
was located on a flat piece of ground of around thirty acres
(twelve hectares) close to the banks of the Thames, between the
hamlet of Turnham Green and the northern wall of the Duke
of Devonshire's house, Chiswick Park. Treading their way
through the rows of vegetables, a small party of four middle-
aged men were making a tour of inspection. At this time
Chiswick was a sleepy village on the western edge of a ring of
market gardens that ran almost uninterrupted from Tothill
Fields in the City on the north bank of the Thames, through
Pimlico, Chelsea, Kensington, Fulham, Parsons Green and
Hammersmith. Unlike the workmen bending to weed between
the rows of early cauliflowers, the four men in view were clearly
gentlemen. The party's leader was a distinguished-looking bald-
ing man in his early sixties. This was Thomas Andrew Knight,
president of the Horticultural Society of London and an
acknowledged authority on fruit trees. This unassuming market garden was an unlikely place to draw such an esteemed figure to make the long journey from his estate in Herefordshire.

Knight had an unusual upbringing. His father, a Hereford-shire clergyman, had died when he was only five, and his early education was neglected to the point that he was still virtually illiterate at the age of nine. However, he was intelligent, observant and fascinated by plants from an early age. Even though he led a retired life on his estate, he developed such a reputation as an expert plant physiologist and horticultural innovator that the great botanist Sir Joseph Banks sought him out and encouraged Knight to take a hand in the establishment of the new Horticultural Society of London. Having set out the objectives of the new Society, Thomas Knight was elected president in 1808. Although he was described by those who knew him as reserved and painfully shy, a careful observer on that summer day in Chiswick might have detected subtle signs of mounting enthusiasm. Knight's knowledgeable eye will have taken note of the fertile alluvial soil, which had been exploited by market gardeners for decades to grow fruit and vegetables for the London capital.

It is likely that the party also included an angular gentleman with a sharp, patrician profile. Joseph Sabine was cut from a very different cloth from the retiring Thomas Knight. An assertive and energetic man, he had been the driving force behind the day-to-day operation of the Society since he first became its honorary secretary in 1810. He was a member of a prominent Anglo-Irish family based in Hertfordshire and, in addition to holding the position of Inspector-General of Taxes, was a keen naturalist and horticulturalist and a founding member of the Linnean Society. He was one of the strongest advocates for the acquisition of a garden. As the party made its tour of inspection, the conviction grew that perhaps at long last the Horticultural Society of London could make the step from being a 'talking shop' – publishing theoretical papers and reviewing the fruits of other people's gardening endeavours at its regular meetings – to being a hands-on participant in the drive to experiment and develop modern horticulture.

The Horticultural Society had been operating for sixteen years by this point. It was founded in 1804 with the aim of 'the Improvement of Horticulture'.[1] The agricultural and industrial revolutions begun in the previous century were gathering pace and were being accompanied by social and scientific revolutions that were to be just as far-reaching. New wealth and prosperity, together with a widely held belief in rational, scientific progress, was fuelling a boom in interest in both botany and practical horticulture. In the eighteenth century, American plants were introduced to Britain in increasing numbers, and James Cook's three voyages of discovery across the Pacific between 1768 and 1779 had given a tantalizing peek at the botanical treasures to be found in far-flung lands. From 1815 onwards, with the burden of war with Napoleonic France removed, Britain was to find itself at the heart of an unprecedented period of exploration, trade and conquest, which was to create routes for new plants to arrive in the country at an almost unbelievable rate. It was in this heady atmosphere that the Horticultural Society of London was founded by Sir Joseph Banks (who had made his name as a botanist on Cook's voyage to Australia) and John Wedgwood (part of the entrepreneurial pottery dynasty). The Society aimed to develop horticulture as a science rather than a craft, and to base practice on empirical observation rather than folklore and tradition. In common with other learned societies set up at around this time, it had the culture and structure of a gentlemen's club.

In 1818 the Society had decided to set up a committee to look into the possibility of establishing a permanent garden. By this time the Society had accumulated a variety of plants donated by well-wishers and had been forced to rent a walled market garden, opposite Holland House at the south side of the Hammersmith Road, in which to keep them. However, the Horticultural Society was forced to admit that real success depended upon 'the establishment of an extensive Garden, in which plants may be placed, their peculiarities honestly remarked and the requisite experiments carried under the immediate superintendence of its officers'.[2] This trip to Chiswick was to inspect land owned by the Duke of Devonshire, which he had offered to rent to the Society for a period of sixty years at £300 a year. This was to become the Society's first proper garden. The Society later stated that the site had been preferred over other possibilities because of the suitability of 'the tenure, situation, the quality of the soil, the easy supply of water and every circumstance connected with the land'.[3] During the negotiations for the lease, the Duke of Devonshire insisted that a private door was installed in the wall separating the Garden from the grounds of Chiswick House, so that he could visit at his leisure. For one young gardener listed in the Handwriting Book, this doorway was to be the portal to a life of fame and fortune.

But that was several years away. In 1821 the flat fields near Turnham Green were far from being the showcase of horticultural excellence and innovation that the Council of the Horticultural Society aspired to. An appeal was issued to

Fellows to raise funds for the formation of a garden. His Majesty the King got the ball rolling with a pledge (never actually honoured) of £500. The initial response to the appeal was good, and by April 1823 contributions totalled £4,891. Plans were drawn up and approved by the Council. The Garden was to be split between a 'department' for fruit and vegetables and an 'ornamental department', the majority of which was given over to an arboretum of eight acres (3.2 hectares). Of course it was realized at the time that the establishment and stocking of the Garden would only be the beginning of the expense. In 1823 the Society estimated that the annual cost of running the Garden would be in the region of £1,200 (around £1 million in today's money).

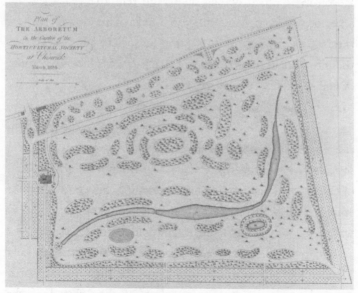

Plan of the arboretum at Chiswick – in a report on the
Garden of the Horticultural Society, 1826.

The key to the creation of the Handwriting Book was that this ambitious garden was always intended to be more than just a place to raise interesting plants. Even before the lease was signed, the Society proudly announced that it intended that its Garden should become 'a National School for the propagation of Horticultural knowledge'.[4] The young men listed in the book were its first students. Such a school was needed because there was a general feeling that standards of knowledge were too low. Writing thirty years later, the eminent head gardener Donald Beaton declared that in the mid-1820s 'some of the best gardeners in the country did not know or understand the principle of potting plants'.[5] In the previous generation, when Lancelot 'Capability' Brown's vision dominated the great estates, it was enough to have a head gardener who could keep the rolling lawns neat and manage the kitchen garden competently, in the tried and trusted manner of his forefathers. However, in keeping with the spirit of experimentation and improvement, the horticultural world now demanded a new type of gardener.

So the flat vegetable fields of Chiswick were to be the base for a garden that would 'grow' gardeners as well as the very latest garden plants. In February 1822, just seven months after agreeing to take on the Chiswick plot, the Society issued a 'Statement relative to the Establishment of a Garden for the Information of Members of the Society' to lay out the Society's aims and, presumably, drum up more donations to support the resulting work. It is in this document that we gain an early glimpse of the way the Council saw the 'National School of Horticulture' operating. It was declared that while the head gardeners would be 'permanent servants of the Society', the under-gardeners and labourers would be 'young men who having acquired some previous knowledge of the first rudiments of the art, will be received into the Establishment, and having been duly instructed in the various practices of each department, will become entitled to recommendations from the officers of the Society to fill situations of Gardeners in private or other establishments'.[6] The Society envisaged that, over time, the great gardens of the kingdom, and even the wider Empire, would be staffed with gardeners who had been trained at Chiswick. A powerful alumni would be created that would take the influence and reach of the Horticultural Society far and wide, in the process raising standards of horticulture across the globe.

From the very beginning, it is clear that there was a high demand for places. The reputation of the Horticultural Society of London as the nation's key authority on horticulture was already established, and the Chiswick Garden acted as a magnet to all the best and brightest young gardeners. The first Report of the Committee set up by the Society to oversee the running of the Garden, published in 1823, announced that 'applications for employment have been very numerous'. The very existence of the Handwriting Book shows that the Society was serious about selecting only the best candidates; it was intended to be a means of both demonstrating and recording that the men who were accepted met the Society's criteria for admission. The entries were written to a formula, dealing one by one with the different entry criteria, although the men clearly had freedom to use their own wording. Every man had to be recommended by a Fellow of the Society, though many seem to have come via Joseph Sabine, as his name is given as the recommender for thirty of the nominees.

The most fundamental way in which the Handwriting Book fulfilled its function as a record of the men's eligibility was by clearly demonstrating that they were literate, as each young man had to write his full CV in his own hand. Literacy was the bedrock for the improvement that many sought to see in the field of horticulture. This was a subject very close to the heart of one employee of the Society. At around the time the Horticultural Society took on the land at Chiswick, it appointed a young man to become assistant secretary in charge of the collection of plants in the new Garden. At just twenty-three, John Lindley was of a similar background and age to many of the men who were listed in the Handwriting Book. He was born in Catton, near Norwich, in 1799, the son of a nurseryman whose business struggled and left the young John saddled with debt. Whilst he learnt the basics of horticulture from his father, Lindley was hungry for knowledge and, in addition to the Latin and Greek he was taught at Norwich Grammar School, he also studied French and drawing skills from a French refugee. Despite the misfortune of blindness in his left eye, Lindley was a talented artist, but above all was a workaholic devoted to botany. Through diligence and hard work he became a leading authority on botany, and orchids in particular. His personal experience convinced him of the value of educating gardeners, whatever their background, and of the importance of a meritocratic approach to ensure progress. He was instrumental in encouraging the young gardeners to form a Mutual Improvement Society in 1828, and in creating a small library for the gardeners to consult in the Chiswick Garden.

The Council agreed to support this with a generous grant of £50 for books, and voted that the term 'Labourer' should be replaced by 'Student' when referring to the young men.

Pen and ink portrait of John Lindley,
Assistant Secretary of the Society, drawn
by his daughter Sarah in around 1850.

One of the most zealous campaigners for the education of gardeners and working men in general was John Claudius Loudon. Like Lindley, Loudon was possessed of an astonishing level of energy, for he was a garden designer, landscape architect and the leading horticultural journalist of his age. He took a close interest in the Chiswick trainees and monitored the operation of the Horticultural Society Garden closely in the pages of his *Gardener's Magazine*. He wrote that it was essential for a young gardener to 'cultivate his intellectual faculties'.

Reading widely and studying deeply were vital for professional progression, otherwise 'if he remains content with the elementary knowledge... as gardener lads acquire under ordinary circumstances, he will assuredly never advance beyond the condition of a working gardener, and may not improbably sink into that of a nurseryman's labourer of all work'. According to Loudon, a 'gentleman's gardener' would need 'not only be a good practical botanist, but possess some knowledge of chemistry, mechanics and even the principles of taste. Instead of being barely able to write and guess at the spelling of words, he will never be admitted, even as a candidate for a situation unless he writes a good hand, spells and points correctly, and can compose what is called a good letter.'[7] This gives a clear idea of the calibre of men the Horticultural Society was hoping to attract. The quality of handwriting, spelling and grammar throughout the Handwriting Book is generally very high.

The vast majority of the entries start with the writer describing the occupation of his father. In 1823 the Society had announced that 'In the selection the preference will be given to the sons of respectable gardeners'.[8] To twenty-first-century eyes, accustomed to initiatives to broaden access to professions, this focus on 'keeping it in the family' feels alien. However, for most of the nineteenth century, people saw nothing unusual or negative in professions being stocked from a limited range of families. Sons of gardeners were likely to have the basic grounding in gardening that the Society required, as they would have been surrounded by the processes and paraphernalia of horticulture from the earliest age. This was an initiative to raise the quality of horticulture, and not necessarily to broaden its base. However, despite the decision to prioritize recruiting the sons of gardeners, less than half (45 per cent) of the men in the Handwriting Book had a father or other close male relative working as a gardener. The majority of the intake to Chiswick were not simply following the family trade, but were entering the horticultural profession from scratch. This is all the more remarkable since, at the time when the Horticultural Society was recruiting, the profession of gardening had not reached the status it was to attain later in the nineteenth century. Although Capability Brown had demonstrated that it was possible for someone with relatively humble origins to use horticulture as a springboard to fame and wealth, he was very much the exception to the rule.

Portrait of John Claudius Loudon from his book
Self Instruction for Young Gardeners, published in 1845.

To see why a career in horticulture was such an attractive prospect to bright young men from working-class backgrounds it is worth looking at the state of the economy in the early 1820s. Ten of the young men described their father's occupation as 'farmer', and their decision to look to horticulture rather than agriculture for a living reflects the fact that this was a time of severe economic hardship in many rural areas, particularly for those with small farms. Returns from agriculture were depressed, as grain prices tumbled to less than half the levels they had attained during the years of scarcity caused by the Napoleonic Wars (1799–1815). At the same time, improved methods of agriculture had increased yields, leading to higher supply of produce, which in turn depressed prices. The process of Enclosure, whereby landowners used parliamentary legislation to consolidate small open fields into bigger 'enclosed' units, deprived many young men of the opportunity to follow their fathers as tenants of small farms. And it was not just farmers who suffered. In parts of the country there was severe unemployment as the British economy struggled to absorb the thousands of men who were discharged from the army, navy and militia at the end of the wars, and there was considerable worry about gangs of unemployed young men roaming the countryside looking for casual work. Average rural labourers' wages fell from around fifteen shillings a week to around nine shillings, and many families found themselves on the verge of starvation.

Additionally Parliament, dominated by the interests of the landowning elite, pushed through import duties on malt, butter and cheese – taxes that were most keenly felt by the poor. The Corn Laws that restricted grain imports further guaranteed the incomes of large landowners. Tensions rose steadily through the period when the men were writing their entries in the Handwriting Book. By 1830 landowners, parsons, overseers of the poor and better-off farmers were being terrorized by letters signed 'Captain Swing', threatening retribution for their perceived exploitation of the rural poor. Mobs were breaking threshing machines, burning barns and demanding higher wages and more employment. The growing industrial towns and cities of the North pulled a lot of young people from the countryside, although everyone was well aware that the streets of Manchester, Birmingham and other cities were far from being paved with gold. In this context, it is easy to see why entering a skilled trade such as horticulture had its attractions. Thanks to their privileged position and manipulation of the political system, landowners had the disposable income to maintain larger and more extravagant households, which meant that domestic service, indoors or outdoors, was a growing employment sector. Gardening offered the prospect of accommodation, relatively steady employment and, if you made it to the position of head gardener of a large country-house garden, status and a good income.

* * *

By the time the men were writing their entries, they had already committed a great deal of time and effort to advancing their horticultural training. The Society required that 'They will be young men who have been previously educated as gardeners, but who have not previously held situations as such.'[9] In practical terms, this meant they were looking for men who had been through their apprenticeship and were what was known as 'journeymen' gardeners. There was an accepted route for young men to become professional gardeners and it appears, from entries in the Handwriting Book, that most of the men accepted to work and study at the Chiswick Garden had followed a similar career path. At around fourteen a boy would be apprenticed to a gardener for around three years. Although the vast majority of the men in the book were at school until that age, some apprentices were as young as twelve, and it is likely that these boys would still be spending part of the day at school. In return for their labour whilst they were apprentices, they received instruction, food and very basic lodgings. This was a hard life, as an apprentice boy was expected to do the repetitive, basic jobs that needed doing in every large garden – washing pots, sweeping paths, weeding, lighting fires and stoking boilers. He would spend time in the different departments of the garden, learning by watching and doing.

At the end of the apprenticeship the young gardener would then expect to move on to spend time in a range of distinct situations, to get a fully rounded horticultural CV. This was a peripatetic life, something akin to a series of internships. A young gardener would be expected to spend around at least a year in a number of establishments, changing jobs to develop skills in the different branches of horticulture – propagation, fruit growing, hothouse operations, and so on. A very ambitious gardener would try to work in a broad range of different environments, which might include a public botanic garden, a nursery and a private garden. Some were known as good 'teaching gardens', meaning that the head gardener was well known and respected as knowledgeable and inclined to teach rather than exploit his young charges, and the garden itself was fitted out with the latest equipment and stocked with a good range of plants. Notable teaching gardens that reappear time and again in the Handwriting Book include Cassiobury in Hertfordshire, Valleyfield near Dunfermline and Haddo House in Aberdeenshire.

The Handwriting Book includes several entries where it is clear that the writer has made a distinct effort to extend his knowledge and experience in this way, sometimes travelling far and wide to do so. Loudon recommended that when a young journeyman needed to move on to his next garden, he should 'perform the journey leisurely and on foot; botanising and collecting insects and minerals and visiting every distinguished garden on his way'.[10] Such a leisurely road trip would have been hard to pull off, given the distances involved. William McCulloch, who joined the Garden in March 1826, travelled more than 1,000 miles as he moved from garden to garden. Having served an apprenticeship of four years on the same estate in Louth where his father was land steward, William, aged eighteen, travelled to work in a plant enthusiast's garden just outside Dublin for two years. From there he returned to Scotland to work under the famous curator of the Edinburgh Botanic Garden, Mr William McNab. After two years in Edinburgh, William McCulloch was promoted to foreman (so acquiring some management experience) under the head gardener, Mr Ross, at the Duke of Atholl's estate at Dunkeld. He then completed his CV with a stint at one of the great London commercial nurseries, Messrs James Gray and Sons of Brompton Park, before applying to work for the Horticultural Society.

The Handwriting Book captures a surprising amount of mobility, given that the entries span a period that pre-dated the railway age. Although the first passenger service (the Stockton–Darlington Railway) opened in 1825, George Stephenson's engine was still too feeble to manage the whole journey, and partway through wagons had to be hitched to horses to supplement the engine. It was not until 1830, when the Manchester–Liverpool line opened, that the first fully steam-powered service was in operation, and the initial boom in railway-building did not occur until 1836. The men whose notes appear in the Handwriting Book will most probably have relied on the network of public coaches. This network was extensive and services were frequent. For instance, in 1828 there were twelve coaches a day between Leicester and London alone. Nevertheless, distances of more than thirty miles involved overnight stays and were an expensive and (depending on the regions travelled through) fairly daunting undertaking. When William Craggs came to Chiswick in February 1825 from his father's garden at Weare House near Exeter, the journey of 175 miles would have taken approximately twenty-one hours by stagecoach. Progress on the poorest roads was slow, and coaching inns were busy, noisy places where uninterrupted sleep was almost impossible. Some of our gardeners must have arrived at the gates of the Chiswick Garden motion-sick, muddy and exhausted.

All the entries end with the phrase 'unmarried'. At this stage in their career, the gardeners could not afford to support a wife and family, and the Horticultural Society stipulated that all applicants should be single. Despite its aspirations to raise the standards of professional gardeners, the Society had no intention of tackling gardeners' wages. This would hardly have gone down well with its Fellows, who would have had to foot higher wage bills. An article on 'The Remuneration of Gardeners' by I. P. Bunyard of Holloway in the *Gardener's Magazine* refers to the Horticultural Society 'very humanely' giving its labourers fourteen shillings and its under-gardeners eighteen shillings a week.[11] This compares with an unskilled farm labourer, who would earn around nine shillings a week; and it compared favourably with the Royal Gardens at Kew, which in 1838 was still only paying its gardeners twelve shillings a week. Nevertheless, fourteen shillings was not a wage that could support a wife and family, and the young gardeners depended on being able to have free board and lodging, although of a very basic fashion, in the shared dormitory known as a 'bothy'. As Bunyard said in the same article, 'A woe may be pronounced against the gardener who marries so prematurely; and it would be well to have written upon the gates of the Horticultural Society's Garden at Chiswick, something like what Dante inscribes on the portal to hell "*Lasciate ogni amor voi che entrate*" (Abandon all love you who enter).'

However, many were prepared to make the sacrifice. Being knowledge- and skills-based, gardening undoubtedly offered opportunity for self-betterment for a bright, determined young man. Loudon believed that although young gardeners were paid much less than other skilled trades, people:

> should not overlook the difference between the prospect of a journeyman carpenter and those of a journeyman gardener... he is perhaps as well off at twenty five as an industrious journeyman carpenter at forty five, because it would probably

require that time before the latter could save sufficient money to enable him to become a master... The fact is that while other tradesmen require both skill and capital to assume the condition and reap the advantages of a master, the gardener requires skill only. Knowledge, therefore to the gardener, is money as well as knowledge.[12]

Chiswick offered unprecedented opportunities to add to that store of knowledge because it was the first place in the kingdom to see newly arrived plants from across the Empire. Even before Chiswick had been leased, the Society received plants from all over the world – including exotic fruits from Sir Stamford Raffles in Singapore, Chinese plants from John Reeves of the East India Company and seeds from Mexico via the foreign secretary George Canning. It was not long before the Horticultural Society decided to send its own representatives out to actively collect new plants.

The first was John Potts, a gardener who had worked for the Society at its small plot in Kensington. Beautiful paintings of Chinese garden plants sent to the Society by John Reeves were behind the decision to send Potts to China. His first shipment arrived in February 1822, including *Paeonia lactiflora*, *Hoya angustifolia*, several camellias and seeds of *Primula sinensis*. Unfortunately, poor Mr Potts returned in ill health and died shortly afterwards. The Society paid for his funeral and a gravestone in the churchyard at Chiswick. However, this unpromising start did not put off the Society or future plant collectors. Potts was followed by George Don (a distant relative of Monty Don), who joined Joseph Sabine's brother Edward on a trip to Africa and the West Indies in late 1821; John Forbes, who collected plants in South America, Madagascar and Mozambique in 1822 and 1823; and John Damper Parks, who travelled to China in 1823–4. So by the time the young gardeners were starting to arrive at Chiswick, the Garden's hothouses were already well stocked with exciting new plants.

In many ways the Society's star collector of the 1820s was the young Scot, David Douglas, who travelled across North America collecting a stunning variety of plants, particularly American conifers. No other plant hunter had added so many new species to English gardens. It was the job of the Chiswick gardeners to unpack the precious parcels that arrived, marry them up with the plant lists provided by the plant collector and then (if the plants had managed to survive the journey) work out how to germinate the seeds or keep the specimens alive and propagate from them. Plants could come from any climate, any habitat, and the gardeners at Chiswick had to do their best to discern and then meet the particular needs of these new plants, often on the basis of very limited information. As a later Chiswick gardener reminisced, 'Inhabitants of mountain, moor and fen, seaside and shady wood and plants from tropical and far lands, had all to be cared for, and the best soil, situation or treatments devised that would coax them to grow amidst the smoke and greasy fogs of an ever encroaching Greater London.'[13] This was no easy task, but the opportunity to be the first European gardeners to see and grow these fabulous new plants must have been tremendously exciting.

And it was not just the plants; the Society was also constantly seeking to test the latest technology and techniques, and it invested in a range of different glasshouses and heating systems. The Horticultural Society was at the heart of the debate as to which was the most efficient and effective design and construction, and invested in a number of glasshouses and glazed pits (a glass roof over a recess in the ground) heated by a variety of different means, from braziers to pits filled with dung or other rotting matter. By 1830 there were more than 450 feet (137 metres) of glazed pits in the Garden, and some 400 feet (122 metres) of hothouses. In every aspect, the Chiswick Garden was designed to allow the Society to conduct and report on experiments to advance horticulture as a science. The men who trained there were able to participate, observe and learn from these experiments, which included experiments on hardiness (leading plants through successively cooler sections of the greenhouse, and trying them outdoors in different situations) and experiments to force plants to flower or fruit out of season, using different heating apparatus.

In the six years covered by the entries in the Handwriting Book, 105 young men were given an opportunity to work and learn in a unique garden and to pick up valuable skills and insights. What they did with that opportunity is the subject of the rest of this book.

CHAPTER ONE

'The beau ideal':
The Horticultural Elite

*Joseph Paxton admitted 13 November 1823
upon recommendation of Jos. Sabine Esq.*

*John Collinson admitted 21 Mar 1825 upon the
recommendation of Mr Jos. Thompson*

*John Jennings admitted 1 February 1828 upon
the recommendation of Joseph Sabine Esq.*

*John Lamb admitted 1 February 1828 upon the
recommendation of Richard Arkwright Esq.*

*Donald McKay admitted 5 February 1828 upon
the recommendation of Sir G. S. McKenzie Bt*

*Thomas Lamb admitted 20 June 1828 upon the
recommendation of Richard Arkwright Esq.*

ONE MAN ABOVE ALL TOOK ADVANTAGE OF THE opportunities that the Garden offered. That man was Joseph Paxton, unquestionably the most significant figure in British horticulture in the nineteenth century. He spent just over two years at Chiswick, and those years were enormously important to his success. In Joseph Paxton's case, all the rags-to-riches clichés are true. He was born in Milton Bryant (now more commonly spelt Bryan), part of the Duke of Bedford's Woburn

estate. In his entry in the Handwriting Book, Joseph Paxton
described his father as a 'farmer'. However, there is no mention
of his father's name on any rent books for the Duke of Bedford's
estate and no mention of him in any of the land-tax records
for the area, so it seems unlikely he was a landowner or even a
tenant farmer. If his father was a simple agricultural labourer,
then Joseph Paxton will have had a very basic education, particularly as his father died when Joseph was just seven. It is
likely that Joseph's older brothers helped support the family,
and Joseph will have enjoyed basic schooling at a free school set
up at Woburn by the first Duke of Bedford. It is clear that the
ambitious young man felt it necessary to creatively enhance
the part of his CV covering his schooling, in order to get into
Chiswick. In his entry he gives his date of birth as 1801, when
in fact parish records show that he was born in 1803. By this
simple expedient he managed to suggest that he was at school
for two years longer than he actually could have been, saying
'at the age of fifteen my attention was turned to gardening',[1]
when in fact he was probably working as a garden boy from the
age of just thirteen.

There is another important anomaly in Paxton's entry.
The Handwriting Book says he was received into the garden
on 13 November 1823, upon the recommendation of Joseph
Sabine. Appointments were also recorded in the Garden Committee Minutes and when Paxton's appointment appears a full
five months later, the minutes record, 'It is ordered upon the
recommendation of the Secretary that Joseph Paxton, a person desirous of becoming a labourer upon the establishment
be permitted to be so employed, his having previously been
a Gardener notwithstanding.'[2] As we have seen, the scheme

to admit young men to train and develop at the Garden was designed for those who had not yet progressed too far in their careers. Yet in his entry in the Handwriting Book, Paxton admits that he had been employed as a head gardener to Sir Gregory Osborne Page Turner since late 1821. Why did Paxton leave a position of responsibility and status as a gentleman's gardener, to take up the lower-paid and lower-status position of 'labourer under the Ornamental Gardener' at Chiswick? And why did the Horticultural Society agree to this?

It appears to have been a mixture of push and pull factors. The push factor was that by early 1823 Paxton's employer, Sir Gregory Osborne Page Turner, was showing signs of insanity. Eventually his condition worsened and by 1824 he was declared bankrupt with liabilities of more than £100,000. Paxton may well have seen the signs and decided in 1823 that it was time to move on. Moreover, he was nothing if not ambitious. He must have understood that the opportunity to develop new skills and shine was much greater at Chiswick, the epicentre of cutting-edge horticulture, than it would have been in a relatively modest garden in Bedfordshire, with a mentally and financially unstable employer. We have no way of knowing exactly which strings Paxton pulled to get the Horticultural Society to overlook its own rules and let him in. Perhaps William Griffin, head gardener at Woodhall Park in Hertfordshire where Paxton trained for three years before coming to Chiswick, put in a word on Paxton's behalf. Griffin, an expert on cultivating pineapples, was one of a number of professional gardeners and nurserymen who, thanks to their knowledge and expertise, were admitted to the membership of the Horticultural Society.

Once in the Chiswick Garden, Paxton's prior experience appears to have allowed him to progress rapidly up the ladder. In November 1824, just under a year after he entered Chiswick, the Garden Committee Minutes record his promotion to Under-Gardener in the Arboretum.

Paxton's efforts to bend the rules to get into Chiswick paid off in a much bigger way than simply quick promotion. Everyone working in the Garden will have been aware of its landlord and next-door neighbour, the Duke of Devonshire. The Society's Chiswick Garden lay next door to the duke's impressive gardens of Chiswick Park. The story goes that in 1826 the thirty-six-year-old George Spencer Cavendish met Joseph Paxton (then aged twenty-three) as the duke let himself into the Society's Garden through the private door that he had insisted was constructed in the wall separating it from the grounds of Chiswick House. The unmarried duke was partially deaf and, despite his enormous wealth and social standing, was a shy and rather nervous man. In the young Joseph Paxton he met someone with a confidence and self-possession that he himself lacked. It seems that Paxton had the same knack possessed by an earlier giant of British horticulture, Capability Brown, of being able to speak affably and confidently with people from all stations of life, from garden labourers to dukes. Specifically, in the case of the Duke of Devonshire, Paxton also had the sensitivity to speak slowly and clearly, so that the deaf duke could hear him.

Over the past two years Paxton had worked his way through the different departments and had now been promoted to oversee the Arboretum, one of the most prestigious parts of the Garden. An arboretum was a collection of rare and beautiful trees and by the 1820s owning a fine arboretum was, for the landed aristocracy, a highly desirable status symbol. The Horticultural Society invested a lot of time and effort in ensuring that its tree collection was one of the finest in the country. The trees were arranged in 'clumps' surrounded by turf and ornamental plants, with a long canal running up the centre. Loudon heavily criticized the layout; it was too flat to be picturesque or aesthetically pleasing, and too erratically laid out to be systematic or scientifically informative. Whatever the arboretum's design faults, Paxton was nevertheless in charge of a collection of rare and valuable trees. He was able to answer the duke's questions with authoritative confidence and, in all probability, an enthusiasm that matched the duke's own growing fascination with the business of gardening on a grand scale. Since coming into his inheritance of estates in excess of 200,000 acres (81,000 hectares) in 1811, the duke had indulged in a spending spree on his collection of houses and gardens and now needed someone to take charge of the vast project to remodel Chatsworth in Derbyshire. The estate was already a building site, with the fashionable architect Jeffry Wyatt undertaking an ambitious remodelling of the house and pleasure grounds. The duke had already begun a massive tree-planting programme, covering an area of over 550 acres (223 hectares), more than sixty times the size of the Arboretum at Chiswick. Even if news of this redevelopment had not travelled, as it surely must have done in the horticultural world, Paxton needed only to poke his head into the duke's garden next door at Chiswick to see the resources to be enjoyed by a gardener lucky enough to work for him. In 1813 the duke had commissioned a 300-foot (91-metre) long conservatory to house the newly fashionable camellias from China.

In March 1826 the Duke of Devonshire offered Paxton the position of Superintendent of the Gardens at Chatsworth. This made him head gardener at one of the grandest estates in England, and an employee of one of the richest and most indulgent employers in the land. Indeed, the duke was so wealthy that he complained of having too many houses; when he went to his Irish property in Lismore in 1844, it was only his second visit in twenty-two years. As well as Chatsworth and Chiswick, he owned Burlington House and Devonshire House (two enormous mansions in Mayfair). He also owned large sections of the West End of London, as well as coal mines in Derbyshire. With the backing of such a rich patron, Paxton knew he would be able to take the things he had seen and learnt at Chiswick and try them on a much bigger scale.

After leaving Chiswick, he transformed Chatsworth at an amazing rate – improving the glasshouses, designing new buildings and waterworks and creating an enormous arboretum. With high-profile coups such as the Great Stove (then the largest greenhouse in Europe) and the colossal Emperor Fountain, it was not long before Joseph Paxton was in demand to work for other clients by contract. In the 1840s he began to lay out cemeteries and municipal parks. He branched out into publishing, becoming editor of *The Horticultural Register* in 1831 and *Paxton's Magazine of Botany* in 1834. He collaborated with John Lindley on the *Pocket Botanical Dictionary* (1840), *Paxton's Flower Garden* (1850) and *The Gardeners' Chronicle*, the weekly magazine that was to take on the mantle of the *Gardener's Magazine* as the essential newspaper of the horticultural world. Paxton reached the peak of his celebrity with his design for the world-famous Crystal Palace, the home of the Great

Exhibition of 1851, an achievement that resulted in a knight-hood. As if all this were not enough, he oversaw the provision of accommodation for troops during the Crimean War, was elected to the House of Commons as a Liberal MP and was heavily involved in a number of railway schemes. By the time of his death in 1865, Sir Joseph Paxton had transcended the world of gardening and was a national figure.

The problem was that Joseph Paxton's success was so extraordinary, so singular, it only served to overshadow all the other men who had also trained at Chiswick. However, he was far from the only success story to come out of this remark-able garden. During the 1820s the Horticultural Society's aim to recommend men to major positions across the country was realized to a considerable extent. Of the 105 men in the book, thirty-nine are recorded in the Garden Committee Minutes as leaving after being 'recommended to positions'. This is probably an underestimate of the number who went on to work in senior positions in significant gardens. The Garden Com-mittee Minutes cease in late 1829, so men recommended after that point are not recorded; and there were also several men who asked for 'permission to leave' because they themselves had obtained employment without waiting for a recommenda-tion. Today, with the exception of TV gardeners, horticultural careers do not have the status they deserve; whilst he was prime minister, David Cameron famously dismissed gardening as an occupation for those who did not excel academically. It is landscape architects and garden designers, rather than gar-deners, who take the plaudits and rewards. However, things were very different in the nineteenth century. Our gardeners were lucky enough to emerge from their training at Chiswick into a world that was much richer in opportunity for skilled professionals.

The first reason for this was that there were plenty of wealthy employers looking for skilled head gardeners. Whilst times were hard for the working classes in the first half of the nineteenth century, for those at the top of the social tree there was more disposable income available to spend on large-scale gardens, and these gardens required sophisticated professionals to manage them. The agricultural revolution had massively increased farming yields and this resulted in higher rents and higher incomes for landowners. The preceding generation's obsession with estate improvements à la Capability Brown, and others, had established that investing in the grounds of your country house was a socially acceptable way of flaunting your wealth and status.

Moreover, the style of gardening that developed in the first half of the nineteenth century was almost custom-made to both demand and showcase a new level of horticultural skill. Fashions in garden design had moved decisively away from the eighteenth-century landscaped park, which had aimed to turn the setting for country houses into an idealized image of nature. Humphry Repton and other designers and writers promoted the idea of returning the flower garden to the main view of the house, whilst Loudon and others emphasized the desirability of creating settings for 'star' specimen plants in island beds, designed to show off horticultural technique. The keenest garden owners would set aside areas to showcase specific types of plants – a rose garden, an American garden for acid-loving shrubs and trees, an alpine area, and so on. The net result was that during the career span of our gardeners there was more emphasis on the individual component parts of the garden, on artifice and temporary effect, meaning that the gardener could take centre-stage. If you were a rich landowner and you wanted a fashionable garden, you needed to employ a top-notch head gardener, backed by a large team of skilled under-gardeners, labourers and garden boys.

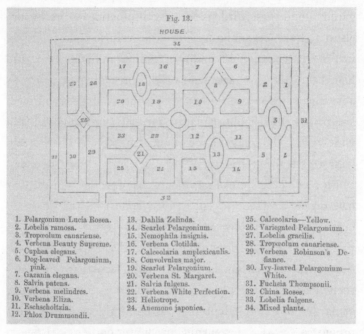

Fig. 13.

HOUSE.

1. Pelargonium Lucia Rosea.
2. Lobelia ramosa.
3. Tropæolum canariense.
4. Verbena Beauty Supreme.
5. Cuphea elegans.
6. Dog-leaved Pelargonium, pink.
7. Gazania elegans.
8. Salvia patens.
9. Verbena melindres.
10. Verbena Eliza.
11. Eschscholtzia.
12. Phlox Drummondii.
13. Dahlia Zelinda.
14. Scarlet Pelargonium.
15. Nemophila insignis.
16. Verbena Clotilda.
17. Calceolaria amplexicaulis.
18. Convolvulus major.
19. Scarlet Pelargonium.
20. Verbena St. Margaret.
21. Salvia fulgens.
22. Verbena White Perfection.
23. Heliotrope.
24. Anemone japonica.
25. Calceolaria—Yellow.
26. Variegated Pelargonium.
27. Lobelia gracilis.
28. Tropæolum canariense.
29. Verbena Robinson's Defiance.
30. Ivy-leaved Pelargonium—White.
31. Fuchsia Thompsonii.
32. China Roses.
33. Lobelia fulgens.
34. Mixed plants.

Plan for flower beds on a terrace featuring thirty-four different plants, published in 1865.

It was not just the traditional landed aristocracy who sought skilled gardeners. The Industrial Revolution was creating a new elite – industrialists and other entrepreneurs who became very rich, very rapidly. Many of the newly rich wanted to display their wealth in a way that would bring them

an air of respectability and acceptance into the upper ech-
elons of society. The purchase of a country house complete
with a well-manicured pleasure garden was an essential part of
the image of a gentleman. Moreover, an informed interest in
plants and gardens marked a man or woman as being cultured
and well educated, interested in both the arts and science.
By employing a top-notch gardener, the nouveau riche could
even hope to outstrip old money, by developing gardens in the
latest fashion, crammed with the most contemporary, rarest
and most expensive plants. The *Horticultural Directory*, published annually by the magazine the *Cottage Gardener*, provided
a listing of head gardeners for the country's largest and most
horticulturally significant private gardens. Its 1867 issue listed
more than a thousand head gardeners working at large establishments across the country. However, for a young gardener,
tying your career to these moneyed families was not without
its risks.

* * *

The career of one Chiswick gardener in particular demon-
strates the way in which the conspicuous consumption of
Victorian elites brought both opportunities and dangers for
gardeners. John Collinson left Chiswick around a month before
Joseph Paxton, having been in the Garden only one year. He
was a member of a Lincolnshire gardening family: his father
had been gardener to General Manners of Bloxham Hall,
before becoming a market gardener at Dorrington in Lincolnshire; one brother, George, was head gardener at Stubton Hall,
Grantham, whilst his other brother, Joseph, was also to join the
Horticultural Society's Garden at Chiswick. Prior to entering

Chiswick, John Collinson had served his apprenticeship at a nursery in Gainsborough and spent four years at the Duke of Portland's garden at Welbeck in Nottinghamshire. This background made him an experienced gardener and, taken together with the training and experience he gained during his year at Chiswick, it is not surprising that he obtained what, on the face of it, seemed a plum post.

In March 1826 he became head gardener to George Watson-Taylor, who had married a wealthy heiress, Anna Susanna Taylor, in 1819. This match enabled Mr Watson-Taylor, who was a Member of Parliament, an author and a playwright, to purchase Erlestoke Park near Devizes in Wiltshire. Watson-Taylor and his new wife used their 600-acre (272-hectare) park, with its extensive plantations of firs, beech and larch, as a backdrop for a series of lavish entertainments. In August 1827 they held a fete to which they invited 700 people to promenade through the flower gardens and then eat and dance in a specially constructed thatched building. As their head gardener, John Collinson had to deliver not only impressive ornamental gardens, but also a well-managed kitchen garden in order to cater on this scale. The culmination of any banquet was the dessert course, which was actually a fruit course with fashionable fruits such as grapes, melons and, above all, pineapples. To achieve a supply of perfect tropical fruits, Collinson needed to have a high degree of technical knowledge to create and maintain the perfect growing conditions in a wide range of specialist hothouses and stoves.

Hosting extravagant parties was not a purely self-indulgent and frivolous matter – events like this were essential for the political and social networking and marriage-brokering by which wealthy families like the Watson-Taylors managed and protected their wealth and power. As roads and (from the 1840s) railway networks developed, guests could travel much further and more frequently to attend lavish and sometimes lengthy house-parties. Entertaining required not only a beautiful garden and fine food, for visitors would expect that all the guest bedrooms and dining rooms were lavishly decorated with freshly cut flowers. There was fierce competition between hosts for the attention and patronage of the most wealthy and influential house-guests. The pinnacle, of course, was to host royalty, and in 1830 Erlestoke was visited by the young Princess Victoria and her mother, the Duchess of Kent. All this put significant demands on the head gardener; but, equally, the pivotal role he played in establishing and maintaining the social prestige of his employers meant that he could expect plenty of resources, such as the latest glasshouses and heating apparatus and a large team of under-gardeners and garden staff.

However, all this took money, and the head gardener's fortunes were tied to those of his employer. Even the wealthiest families depended on credit and often operated with enormous debts. For most of the nineteenth century, consumer credit was still informal and the decision to extend it was based on personal trust and an assessment of the buyer's ability to pay, when bills came due. It was simply not possible to run detailed credit checks, so buying on credit was essentially based on social position rather than on financial stability. It was therefore important for wealthy families to be seen to maintain a costly lifestyle. A high-maintenance garden was a very public way of showing that you had the resources to pay your bills, and gave suppliers confidence in providing goods and services 'on account'. However, any sign that this confidence was misplaced could bring a queue of suppliers to your door, demanding immediate settlement, and the whole edifice could come crashing down very quickly. Even the Duke of Devonshire, Paxton's fabulously wealthy employer, had debt problems – more than half of the duke's income of between £80,000 and £100,000 a year was spent on compound interest, on a debt of just under £1 million. One of Joseph Paxton's many achievements was to arrange the sale of land and properties in 1844 to settle the duke's debts sufficiently for him to be able to carry on spending so lavishly on his gardens.

Unfortunately for John Collinson, the show at Erlestoke was a façade that his employer could not maintain. George Watson-Taylor's wealth came via his wife's inheritance from her uncle, the wealthy Jamaican plantation owner, Simon Taylor. This meant that the wealth lavished on the gardens of Erlestoke derived from slavery, and Watson-Taylor became a Member of Parliament specifically to stand in the way of the growing campaign to abolish slavery in British territories. Thankfully, he and his ilk were on the wrong side of history. The 1807 Abolition of the Slave Trade Act had already outlawed the slave trade in the British colonies. It became illegal to carry slaves in British ships, though not illegal to own slaves who were already in the West Indies. The hope amongst reformers was that, with the removal of a fresh supply of slave labour, plantation owners would see that they would have to treat their workforce better and would gradually shift away from slavery of their own accord. Men like Watson-Taylor (whilst always claiming that they gave the utmost consideration to the 'welfare' of 'their' slaves) were determined that this should not be the case. However, the abolition of the trade in slaves did gradually begin to undermine their corrupt and cruel business model. By 1823 Watson-Taylor found his spending was outstripping his income and he had to sell books and paintings to cover his debt. His financial problems worsened over the next decade, until he finally became effectively bankrupt in the summer of 1832.

By the autumn of 1832 Watson-Taylor had fled to the continent to avoid his creditors, taking up residence in Holland. John Collinson needed to look for a new employer and, as it happened, an opportunity was just opening up. The previous year John Claudius Loudon had written a stinging review in the *Gardener's Magazine* of the Duke of Westminster's garden at Eaton Hall in Cheshire. The garden and park were poor in design and execution: 'A totally wrong character has been attempted in the lay out of the pleasure grounds about the house... the beds for the most part overgrown with large coarse shrubs', and the terraces were decorated with 'the most ordinary greenhouse plants'. Loudon wondered that a man of the Duke of Westminster's rank and wealth should not 'give orders to have it at all seasons in the highest style of keeping of which it is susceptible'.[3]

Loudon reassured his readers that Mr Duff, the head gardener at Eaton Hall, ranked 'too highly in his profession for anything we could say to do him the slightest injury'. However, the duke could not have enjoyed seeing his property and, by extension, his taste and social standing lambasted in print in this way, and Mr Duff's days were numbered. By 1835 John Collinson was head gardener at Eaton Hall. Whether Loudon's criticism stung the duke into making more funds available or Collinson was simply a superior gardener to the unfortunate Mr Duff, the fact is that from that point on one can only find flattering accounts of the Eaton Hall gardens.

In 1852 the most fashionable garden designer of the day, William Andrews Nesfield, was commissioned to design two terraces adjoining Eaton Hall. Nesfield's designs were part of a mid-nineteenth-century revival in interest in pre-eighteenth-century formal garden design. He was best known for creating *parterres de broderie*, elaborate patterns made up of trimmed box hedges and gravel. His work at Eaton Hall was not to everyone's taste. Thomas Appleby, writing in the *Cottage Gardener*, protested, 'The scrolls run to a great length and are, in many places, not six inches wide!! Nay even less than that. This struck us as rather bordering upon the ridiculous.'[4]

With designs like this, the job of the head gardener was simply to keep hedges trimmed and gravel swept, but there were plenty of other parts of Eaton Park where John Collinson could flex his horticultural muscles to greater effect. In 1857 Eaton Hall and Collinson received a very public accolade when the gardens were included in a lavishly illustrated book, *The Gardens of England* by the artist Edward Adveno Brooke, which showcased some of the country's most fashionable great gardens. The subtly coloured chromolithographs have a dream-like quality and give a strong impression of the elegance of the Eaton Hall gardens, with their elaborate bedding schemes of 'verbenas, calceorarias, geraniums and various other sorts of a gay flowering character'. The description to accompany the illustrations specifically praised Mr Collinson, 'who has ably and successfully superintended this department of the estate'.[5]

Producing impressive displays on this scale required real leadership and an ability to manage a large team of men and boys to deliver perfection all year round. This was gardening on an almost industrial scale. Taking the ornamental side of the garden alone, complicated and temperamental hothouses had to be tended around the clock to produce tender plants in their thousands to be transplanted at exactly the right time, en masse in summer bedding schemes. The technical, logistical and managerial challenges were enormous. The journalist George Glenny wrote, 'A master gardener with many men can do more good with his eyes than with his hands. Strict superintendence is more valuable than hard work.'[6] This was a seven-day-a-week responsibility, which was why it was common to place the head gardener's house within the garden, often within the walls of the kitchen garden, so that he could keep a close eye on every aspect of the operation of his team. *Gardener's Magazine* even carried a warning article 'On the evil effects of a Head Gardener being lodged anywhere else than in the garden'.[7]

* * *

A diligent head gardener was expected to maintain the garden in a state of perfect order and neatness throughout the year. Donald McKay was received as a labourer in the Kitchen Garden at Chiswick in February 1828 and, after leaving Chiswick, became the gardener at Whitmore Lodge, near Sunninghill, Berkshire. In a letter to the *Gardener's Magazine* he proudly itemized the flowers that were blooming in the open garden on Christmas Day 1834, and from which he made a nosegay.

McKay was charged with the care of a particularly interesting garden because his employer, Robert Mangles – described by contemporaries as 'a very large man with a very small voice'[8] – was a keen and well-connected horticulturalist. His brother James was a captain in the Royal Navy who sent back seeds from his travels in Australia. Many of these seeds were new introductions, grown for the first time in Britain at Whitmore Lodge. However, having a keen horticulturalist as an employer must have had its drawbacks, as Mangles was clearly a stickler for detail. In a review in the *Gardener's Magazine* of 1828 it was noticed that 'The pleasure ground at Whitmore Lodge comes up to the beau ideal of the highest order and keeping: the roses are gathered as they wither and the leaves as they drop every morning.'[9] Perhaps this regime took its toll. By the 1841 census the head gardener is listed as Charles Noble, and Donald McKay is nowhere to be found. The only reference to a Donald McKay is a death notice in Southwark dated January 1841. It is possible that the large but squeaky-voiced Captain Mangles drove poor Donald too hard. Unfortunately, the house and gardens were demolished in 1936, so no physical trace remains of this interesting and innovative garden.

Successful head gardeners were not just tasked with putting on a magnificent floral display and keeping the kitchens well stocked with exotic produce. The flood of new plants in the first half of the nineteenth century also opened up the possibility for diligent gardeners to play another important role, as developers and curators of plant collections. The Victorians seemed to have a particular talent and mania for amassing collections of everything from seashells to ferns. In horticultural circles, orchids were the prestige plant to collect, and several ex-Chiswick students had responsibility for looking

Head gardeners at large establishments would be expected to manage and maintain extensive and complex hothouses capable of growing impressive tropical species like this vanilla plant.

after extensive orchid collections on behalf of wealthy employers. Orchids make up around 10 per cent of all flowering plants and are native to every continent except Antarctica; more than 30,000 species have adapted to thrive in every environment from arid deserts to rainforests. The first tropical orchid flowered in Britain in 1732, and from that time onwards botanists and gardeners were fascinated with these exotic and mysterious plants. As Loudon's *Encyclopaedia of Plants* declared, 'Of all the tribes of plants, this is the most singular, the most fragrant and the most difficult of culture.'[10] The difficulty of keeping these rare plants alive only seemed to add to their allure.

Students at Chiswick were able to study the Horticultural Society's fine collection, held in its specially constructed orchid house under the watchful eye of the assistant secretary, John Lindley. Over the course of his career he was to become the leading botanical authority on orchids, describing and naming a vast number of new species. One Chiswick student, a Hertfordshire boy called John Jennings, worked particularly closely with John Lindley, having been employed for three months at Lindley's garden at his home in Turnham Green before joining the Chiswick Garden.

This may explain why the Earl of Derby selected Jennings to become his head gardener at Knowsley Hall near Liverpool. The gardens at Knowsley were extensive. The kitchen garden covered seven acres (2.8 hectares), with a very large and well-equipped 'forcing department', where grapes, peaches, cherries, figs, pineapples, melons and cucumbers were grown. However, horticultural pride of place went to the orchids. Like many members of the aristocracy, the thirteenth Earl of Derby

had been bitten by the orchid bug. Today he is best remembered as an avid collector and student of wild animals, and he
was an early supporter of the Zoological Society of London
and its president from 1831 until his death. As a result, John
Jennings had to share his garden at Knowsley with herds of
antelope and deer, ostriches and llamas. This will not have fazed
Jennings. As part of his pre-Chiswick apprenticeship, he spent
around eighteen months working in the Duke of Devonshire's
garden at Chiswick House, which was graced by a menagerie that included tigers, emus and a kangaroo. John Claudius
Loudon had seriously suggested that the new glasshouse technology could be used to create miniature exotic worlds where
plants, animals and even people should be exhibited together,
with natives in costume acting as guides and curators.[11]

On the plus side for Jennings, the earl's fascination with
animals led him to build up a worldwide network of natural-
history collectors and, as *The Gardeners' Chronicle* noted, he was
able to benefit from 'the exertions of his Lordships collectors,
who are in various parts of the world, and from time to time
keep transmitting to Knowsley what Orchidaceae they may
deem valuable'.[12] The Earl of Derby was part of an alliance of
collectors, natural historians and gardeners who wrote to each
other, shared plant specimens, seeds and drawings. Collectors
included Joseph Burke, who sent orchids from South Africa
for Jennings to care for in an extensive orchid house. Men like
Burke explored the tropical regions with the aim of finding
new or select orchids, and sent them back home in large numbers. In fact these collectors were so persistent in their mission
that desirable orchids became rare or virtually extinct in several areas in the tropics.

A high proportion of the orchids died while they were being transported and, as a result, prized orchid specimens were sold for huge sums, raising the stakes for the gardeners tasked with caring for them. Of course there were rivalries and petty jealousies, but as the gardeners grappled with keeping these precious collections alive, they shared their knowledge and experience. As was nearly always the case, Paxton outshone the rest of the gardening fraternity. The Duke of Devonshire had been an enthusiastic collector ever since he noticed *Oncidium papilio* on display at the Chiswick Garden in 1833. He spent heavily, buying up entire collections and even paying 100 guineas for a single plant, and as a result Paxton was responsible for caring for the largest private collection of orchids in the country. He experimented with temperature and humidity with increasing success, and discovered how important it was to understand and, where possible, imitate the native habitat of each orchid species. With the Duke of Devonshire's enthusiastic backing, Paxton had the resources to create an array of different glasshouses to create the perfect growing environments. He can justifiably lay claim to leading the way on orchid care and cultivation.

However, it is easy to get carried away with the idea of these head gardeners as supermen. At the end of the day, even a head gardener was still a servant, subservient and vulnerable to the whims and demands of his employer. In his *Handy Book of Gardening and Golden Rules for Gardeners*, George Glenny advised, 'Never interfere with household matters. Supply what is asked for in the best way you can, without troubling your head about what it is for or who has it afterwards.' The wise head gardener did not worry how his prize vegetables were used and abused in the kitchen, or whether his hothouse flowers wilted unnoticed in a cold bedroom. Even more important, like any servant, a head gardener should be discreet and should know his place: 'As regards the family matters "hear all, see all and say nothing". You cannot then be mixed up with any household squabbles and disagreements.'[13]

* * *

Employers could be capricious and demanding, but sometimes an employer's behaviour went beyond the bounds of simple eccentricity. Thomas Lamb worked at the Chiswick Garden from June 1828 until April 1829, when he was recommended to a position. By 1842 he was named as gardener at Hurstbourne Place in Hampshire, in the list of gardeners subscribing to the creation of a monument to the plant hunter David Douglas, who had died after falling into a buffalo trap whilst in Hawaii. Hurstbourne Place was the seat of the Earl of Portsmouth, but in the 1841 census Thomas Lamb answered the section on his occupation with the vague term 'Gentleman's Gardener'. It appears that he wanted to draw a veil over his employer's identity because his employer was John Charles Wallop, third Earl of Portsmouth, who had been the subject of one of the most notorious court cases in the country.

For years the family had managed to cover up the earl's increasingly strange behaviour, but they decided they had to act when he unexpectedly married the daughter of his scheming lawyer and there was a threat that the title and property might pass into their hands. In 1822 his family went to court to try to prove that the earl was a lunatic, and that his second marriage should be annulled and the heirs declared illegitimate.

More than a hundred people, including his gardeners, told sensational tales of his cruelty to servants and animals, his obsession with funerals and bloodletting and how he allowed his wife to commit adultery in his own bed. In 1823, after a court case that filled the newspapers with scandalous details for weeks, the Commission of Lunacy eventually ruled that he was insane and should be allowed to live his life quietly under supervision at Hurstbourne Place and, upon his death, should be succeeded by his brother.

By the time Thomas Lamb worked for him, the Earl of Portsmouth lived a secluded life, though still subject to delusions that he was the 'King of Hampshire' and planning imaginary military reviews in his park. In these circumstances Lamb cared for a park and gardens spread over 830 acres (336 hectares) that were seen by very few people. As a gardener, Thomas would have found it relatively easy to keep out of his master's way, unlike the house servants, who were paid extra to cope with their unpredictable employer. The Earl of Portsmouth died in 1853 and his younger brother lived only a year longer, never actually residing at Hurstbourne. Lamb's new employer was Isaac Newton Wallop, who became the fifth Earl of Portsmouth, and it is notable that in the 1861 census Lamb proudly stated that he was 'Gardener to the Earl of Portsmouth'.

His experience contrasts with that of his older brother, John. He joined the Chiswick Garden in February 1828 and went on to become head gardener at the less grand estate of Markeaton Gardens near Mackworth in Derbyshire. Although the garden was less prestigious than Hurstbourne Place, there were far more opportunities for John to shine as a gardener and to climb the social ladder. In 1843, along with his employer

William Mundy, MP, John Lamb was a subscriber to the private publication of a book of poems by Elizabeth Snow, an elderly lady and a family friend of the Mundys. The work, entitled *A Bouquet of Wild Flowers*, was full of very genteel and slightly maudlin poems, but John Lamb's inclusion on the subscriber list suggests that he saw himself as a cut above a mere servant.

At some point between 1844 and 1851 John followed a path that several gardeners trod, leaving domestic service to set up a more independent life – in his case, in farming. He moved just a few miles up the road (now the A52) to run Hazelhurst Farm at Brailsford, and upon his death in 1869 was able to leave his widow moderately wealthy.

Joseph Paxton was obviously the most successful at rising above the status of a servant; his achievements brought him wealth and social status and he became a genuine friend and trusted advisor to the Duke of Devonshire. However, even the great Paxton could not forget that he was at his employer's beck and call. On one occasion he was ordered to drop everything in order to arrange a supply of billiard balls to the duke's house in Brighton.[14] Moreover, even the most successful of our gardeners could never forget that they did not own the gardens on which they lavished such attention. Years of work could be overturned if the owners of the garden decided they no longer wanted to persist with a particular style or feature.

The most vulnerable time for any head gardener was upon the death of an employer, when the property was passed to an heir who might not share the horticultural enthusiasm or tastes of his forebear. In July 1851 John Jennings' employer, the Earl of Derby, died. His son Edward did not share his father's enthusiasm for zoology and botany, being far more concerned with politics (he was to become Prime Minister three times during Queen Victoria's reign). The collection of 1,293 birds and 345 mammals cost on average £15,000 a year to maintain, and the fourteenth earl decided to sell the animals. He also decided that the valuable orchid collection that Jennings had nurtured for more than ten years should be sold to pay off debts. On Friday 19 September 1851 *The Morning Post* carried an advertisement for the sale by auction of 'The rare and choice collection of ORCHIDS, including most of the East Indian, South American, Mexican and African varieties. The plants are well established and in fine health and may be viewed the day before the sale by applying to Mr Jennings at the gardens, Knowsley and catalogues had there and at Mr J C Stevens, 38 King Street Covent Garden.' Jennings continued to work at Knowsley until his death, but the garden must have been a duller affair without the exotic orchids, and with the park no longer graced by the chousingha antelope, the red-flanked duiker or the long-nosed potoroo.

Even the great Paxton was not immune to such vulnerability. When the Duke of Devonshire died in 1858, his heir, his cousin William Cavendish, second Earl of Burlington, found that the estate faced enormous debts. The new duke felt uncomfortable that he would have to ask Paxton to undo many of the features he had created at Chatsworth and the other Devonshire properties. Foreseeing the problem, Paxton tendered his resignation, citing his many 'other engagements', although admitting that 'my close and intimate relations with Chatsworth and the late Duke for a period of upwards of thirty years, cannot be severed without a pang'.[15] The new seventh Duke of Devonshire gave Paxton his house at Chatsworth for life and allowed him to make his own plan for financial cutbacks to the garden's operation, so as to minimize the damage. Paxton was lucky, because by this point his railway investments had made him a very wealthy man. However, many head gardeners, even when they were eminent figures in the horticultural world, lived in tied cottages on relatively modest wages, and faced considerable hardship after retirement. The lucky ones might be given a pension, but many were moved out of their homes with no more than a testimonial dinner and a parting gift.

CHAPTER TWO

'Much judgement and good taste':
The Gardeners Who Set Standards

*William Craggs admitted 21 Feb 1825 upon
the recommendation of Mr J. Miller*

*Henry Bailey admitted 1 May 1826 upon
the recommendation of Earl Spencer*

*James Duncan admitted 9 March 1827 upon
the recommendation of [left blank]*

WHILST ENORMOUS GARDENS LIKE THOSE AT EATON
Hall and Chatsworth were undeniably impressive horticultural feats, the impact of the Chiswick men would have been
limited, had it remained confined within the walls of the private gardens of the wealthiest families. However, a number of
factors combined to ensure that the work of head gardeners
could have a far wider impact on the way people gardened outside the rarefied atmosphere of a country estate.

Head gardeners in the nineteenth century were able to act
as trend-setters, influencing horticultural taste and practice
in far-reaching ways. With enormous resources at his disposal,
an ambitious head gardener could try out new plant combina-
tions, experiment with novel pruning techniques and hothouse
technologies or even select and breed entirely new varieties

of plants. Even in a garden that had been laid out by eminent landscape architects such as Nesfield, the head gardener had considerable leeway to make day-to-day decisions that could determine the appearance of the garden – from the way trees were pruned, to choices around seasonal plantings. The introduction of spectacularly colourful tender or half-hardy foreign plants, largely via the Horticultural Society's plant hunters and its Chiswick Garden, demanded a new style of gardening that offered plenty of scope for innovation.

The practice of planting tender plants outdoors during the warmer months, known as the bedding system, was developed during the 1830s. In 1838 Joseph Paxton went so far as to declare, 'We propose banishing entirely from the flower garden all such plants as are perfectly hardy, or, in other words, those which are generally termed hardy herbaceous plants, and supplying in their place the more showy and favourite kinds which require protection during the winter.'[1] Paxton was a vocal advocate for the impact of tender bedding plants, but he was far from alone. The bedding system gave the head gardener of a well-resourced garden the opportunity to transform the appearance of the garden each year. In the age of Capability Brown and the English landscape movement, remodelling gardens had involved massive earthworks and once-in-a-generation levels of expenditure. A Victorian gardener, on the other hand, could plant a dazzling new combination of bedding plants and attract a great deal of attention to himself. Several of the Chiswick gardeners were able to make names for themselves as creative and innovative designers.

One ex-Chiswick trainee who made his name as a creator of beautiful gardens was James Duncan. He was at Chiswick from

March 1827 until at least March 1829. The son of an innkeeper from Perth, he was one of several Chiswick gardeners who had served his apprenticeship under the eminent head gardener William Beattie in the Earl of Mansfield's gardens at Scone. After he left Chiswick, Duncan spent time as a gardener in central London for F. Bernasconi Esq., a plaster-cast manufacturer, and then at Walford House in Taunton, before becoming head gardener at Basing Park in Hampshire. He worked there for at least twenty years. Basing Park was owned by Sir Joseph Martineau, a Fellow of the Horticultural Society, member of the Royal Geographical Society and member of the Archaeological Institute of Great Britain and Ireland. He came from a wealthy family of industrialists – involved in dyeing, textiles, sugar, steel and steam-engine manufacture. With the backing of his employer, Duncan developed the garden gradually over time and his subtle plantings attracted attention in the press. As a result, there are many descriptions that give us a feel for the type of garden he created.

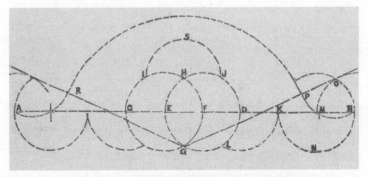

This illustration showing how to lay out a flower bed
indicates some of the technical skills required of a gardener.

For instance, his work at Basing Park received a lengthy review in *The Gardeners' Chronicle* in 1854. The author (probably another Chiswick employee, the garden clerk William Beattie Booth) wrote:

> On either side of the road the masses of plantations have been arranged with much judgement and good taste... they display an intricacy and variety of outline that is exceedingly pleasing and which is the great aim of the landscape gardener to produce. Indeed I question whether the late celebrated Gilpin, who was acknowledged to be a master of the profession and an accomplished artist, could have made a better use of the materials or created a series of more beautiful landscapes than has been done in this instance by Mr Duncan.[2]

In 1857 Robert Fish wrote an article in the *Cottage Gardener* and from this it is clear that James Duncan did not blindly follow fashion for massed bedding in bright colours. His key achievement was 'not so much a great blaze of level colour in summer as an interest and an elegance every day of the year'. He arranged his flower beds so that they were restricted to one or two colours and were 'surrounded with such plants as noble Araucarias, beautiful Schubertias, elegant Cypresses and massive Rhododendrons. The blaze of colour can hardly ever dazzle and pain the eye from the many tinted green shrubs in their vicinity.' He also avoided the 'monotonous sameness' that could be found in bedding schemes, by careful use of shrubs pruned as standards or pyramids within the flower beds, placed 'distinct and yet sufficiently near each other to combine and whilst each is beautiful contemplated separately they unitedly form an harmonious unity'.[3]

One of the most commented-upon areas of Basing Park was the evergreen garden, to the south and west of the mansion. The evergreen garden – or pinetum, as it was referred to – contained a fine collection of conifers, with the genera separated into specific areas. It included other evergreens such as *Ilex*, *Buxus*, *Cotoneaster* and *Mahonia*. Mown grassy pathways provided walks through the garden, where the trees were underplanted with laurel and *Mahonia repens*. Today these tough, evergreen plants are so heavily used by landscape architects and planners that they have become ubiquitous features of car parks and road verges, and it is hard to associate them with innovative garden design. But in the mid-1800s they were cutting-edge. Unfortunately, very little of the garden that James Duncan created survives today. The Basing Park estate was split up in the mid-1940s, the mansion demolished in 1964 and a new house built on the same site, with gardens and shrubberies redesigned. Some of the original conifers survive, but are now reaching the end of their lifespan and are very vulnerable to storm damage.

* * *

William Craggs was another Chiswick trainee who went on to look after an influential garden. He grew up in Devon and returned to that county after spending just eight months at Chiswick. He became head gardener to Sir Thomas Dyke Acland, tenth baronet, at his estate at Killerton, near Broadclyst in east Devon. William Craggs married the housekeeper, Anne Turvill, in June 1831 and settled down to spend the rest of his life tending this remarkable garden. Like many skilled gardeners, he entered prize specimens to Horticultural Society exhibitions and shows, winning medals and certificates – the most remarkable being for a bundle of 100 heads of asparagus, tipping the scales at nearly a stone in weight. Unfortunately, the distance from Killerton to London may have hampered his prize-winning capacity. In 1848, although he won a certificate of merit for *Laelia perrinii*, an orchid from the rainforests of Brazil, it was noted that it was 'a good plant but somewhat shaken by travelling'.[4]

However, it was to be in the field of plant introductions rather than prize exhibits that William Craggs was to make a significant contribution. By the time he moved to Killerton, the garden already had a strong association with the famous Veitch nursery business. The grandfather of William Craggs' employer (also confusingly called Thomas Dyke Acland) had employed John Veitch as a young man to lay out his garden. Veitch was such a success that Sir Thomas offered to provide capital for him to set up a nursery business using some land on the estate. Sir Thomas had land to spare; it was said that he could ride from the Bristol Channel to the English Channel without stepping off his own property. From this small beginning, the Veitch family nursery began to grow, a business dynasty that was to span several generations, with branches in Exeter and Chelsea, and which was to earn a reputation for the importation of exotic novelties for connoisseur gardeners. Inspired by the spectacular successes of the Horticultural Society's plant collectors, John Veitch's son James decided to employ his own plant collectors to make sure the Veitch nurseries were the first to market with new discoveries. This was a considerable investment and financial risk. Seeds and plants could be lost or could perish in transit, and even upon arrival there were many hurdles to jump before a plant could be grown in sufficient quantities to yield a profit. One of the biggest challenges was working out how to grow in a British climate new foreign plants of unknown hardiness.

Killerton was blessed with a remarkable microclimate, the sloping land being inclined to the sun, and was sheltered from cold north winds by a hill situated behind the park called, rather prosaically, 'The Clump'. This meant that the garden was protected from frost and was ideal for testing many of the less-hardy trees and shrubs that the Veitch collectors – the Lobb brothers, William and Thomas – were to send from North and South America, Indonesia and the Philippines. The Veitch and Dyke Acland association, married to Killerton's climate, led to an arrangement whereby Killerton was used as an experimental testing ground for new plants, in much the same way as Chiswick had been for the Horticultural Society's plant collections. The garden abounded in rare and exotic trees and shrubs, including sequoia seedlings and many other conifers. In these circumstances William Craggs' training at Chiswick must have proved invaluable.

Killerton also had rich, lime-free soil and this made it particularly suitable for establishing one family of plants that turned out to be perhaps a little too successful at making its home here. In May 1852 Killerton was one of a select group of gardens to which Kew sent rhododendrons that had been collected in the Himalayas by Joseph Hooker from 1848 to 1850. Species received included *Rhododendron dalhousiae*, *R. ciliatum* and *R. edgeworthii*. These were followed by a second consignment in 1853 and William Craggs planted them extensively through the woodlands at Killerton. The rhododendrons that Hooker sent back proved to be excellent garden plants, and many went on to become the basis for breeding an enormous number of rhododendron hybrids. Following the example of gardeners like William Craggs, many people seized on these showy plants to embellish and bring colour to native woodlands, using them as underplanting to their trees. Unfortunately, many of these new hybrids were grafted on *R. ponticum* rootstocks. *R. ponticum* originated in northern Turkey, the Black Sea region, Portugal and southern Spain and was first introduced into Britain in 1763. At the time no one realized what a very vigorous species it was, and in all too many cases the rootstocks overwhelmed the hybrid plants that were grafted onto them. As a result, there are clumps of *R. ponticum* in many old gardens, where originally more attractive hardy hybrids had been planted. To make matters worse, *R. ponticum* self-seeds prolifically and the resulting plants can grow into enormous bushes that crowd out other species. In fact the plant is now seen as an invasive pest and organizations like the National Trust have to spend a great deal of time and money trying to remove it. Those gardeners like William Craggs who embraced these showy new shrubs so enthusiastically had little idea of the legacy they were leaving behind.

In the thirty or so years that Craggs worked at Killerton he also left another, less problematic legacy, which can be found in the hedgerows that criss-crossed the estate. One of the many plants that the Horticultural Society distributed to its Fellows from its Garden at Chiswick was an Indian berberry. William Craggs knew it as 'the Kushmul Berberry' or *Berberis asiatica*.

Modern horticultural taxonomists have determined that the plant is actually a different species, called *Berberis glaucocarpa*. In 1850 Craggs was quoted by John Lindley in an article on evergreen berberries recounting how he had grown many of the plants from seeds sent to him by the Horticultural Society. He recounted how 'Finding the plants to be free growers, nearly evergreen and very strong and raising many thousands per year, I began by desire of my employer, to plant them out as hedges and they succeed particularly well... when strong, this Berberry is proof against cattle. Last spring I planted a stout bush in the deer park without protection. They have battled it with their horns but they have not killed it.'[5] Indeed, so hardy was this plant that more than 130 years later it was still to be found in hedgerows between Porlock and Minehead.

The achievements of innovatory gardeners like Craggs and Duncan were written up extensively in detailed reviews in the burgeoning horticultural press. Beyond the more academic papers published in the Horticultural Society's *Transactions*, new mass-market gardening publications gave respected gardeners an unprecedented opportunity to publicize their achievements and make their names known beyond their immediate neighbourhood. Gardening magazines that were issued monthly or even weekly had an insatiable demand for well-informed content. The more opinionated could aim to influence the gardening practices of thousands of people at every social level. Becoming a respected author was seen as part and parcel of an eminent head gardener's role; it was an essential part of their duty to the wider gardening world to share the benefit of their learning and experience. In his *Gardener's Magazine*, Loudon boldly declared:

Every gardener in short, who can now be considered worthy
of the name, must understand the principles of composition,
and be capable at the desire of his master, or of his own proper
motion, to write a paper on his art fit to be introduced in the
Horticultural Society's *Transactions*, or in the *Gardener's Magazine*. The gardener who has no desire to appear as a writer in
one or both of these works, must be a heartless mass of subsoil.[6]

As usual, Joseph Paxton went one better than his contemporaries. Rather than being content to pen a letter or have his
horticultural achievements written up in other people's publications, he set up his own. His first venture was a monthly
paper entitled *The Horticultural Register and General Magazine*,
which he established in 1831 with Joseph Harrison, the older
brother of a fellow Chiswick student, George Harrison. In
1834 this was followed by the *Magazine of Botany*, but his most
lasting contribution was to found *The Gardeners' Chronicle* in
1841, in partnership with John Lindley. This was to become the
century's pre-eminent gardening newspaper and was in print
for nearly 150 years. Subscribers could expect to see reviews
of the finest gardens, descriptions of new plants, accounts
of Horticultural Society shows and lively correspondence on
everything from colour theory to the best way to tackle moles.

* * *

In fact letters and articles in gardening publications like *The
Gardeners' Chronicle* are some of the best sources for tracking
the careers of the Chiswick students. Henry Bailey was one
of the most prolific and opinionated contributors. The son of
a Croydon gardener, he entered the Chiswick Garden in May

1826 at the age of twenty-three, following stints at Althorp, seat of the second Earl Spencer; the Earl of Plymouth's estate at Hewell Grange in Worcestershire; and Lee's Nursery in Hammersmith. According to the Garden Committee Minutes, Bailey had to leave his post in October 1827 on account of ill health.[7] It is not clear whether he returned, but he clearly recovered because by 1836 he was working as head gardener to Edward Venables-Vernon-Harcourt, Archbishop of York, at his property at Nuneham Courtenay just outside Oxford.

Nuneham Park was a famous garden, laid out by Capability Brown, with an impressive pinetum added by the fashionable landscape designer William Sawrey Gilpin. Taking on a garden with this pedigree was not for the faint-hearted, but Henry Bailey clearly did not lack confidence. He wrote articles on subjects from the correct way to lay a path – 'In the very humid and comparatively sunless climate of England, nothing conduces more to the enjoyment of a country residence than a good, firm and dry walk' – to the best distribution of male and female strawberry plants in a bed: 'Each gentleman is surrounded by four ladies.'[8] Nor did he restrict himself to practical matters, for he had the self-confidence to make sweeping comments on matters of taste. In 1849 he wrote a letter in *The Gardeners' Chronicle* lambasting an earlier contributor's advocacy of flower beds made up of mixtures of colours to create a 'picturesque' effect. Bailey was firmly on the side of the more 'modern' fashion for bedding schemes in blocks of single colour, and in his letter he declared:

He institutes a comparison between a garden of flowers and a picture, by which I presume he means a landscape painting.

While I admit that the colours of a carpet, the furniture of rooms, and the dresses of ladies, should be governed by the same principles of design as a well arranged flower garden, as to the distribution of colours, I am at a loss to trace the analogy between a landscape painting and a flower garden.[9]

Henry Bailey clearly did not think of himself as mere horticultural technician employed to do the bidding of garden designers or garden owners.

Like many other head gardeners, he had at least one other opportunity to become a public figure. Many large estate owners allowed the public to visit their gardens on selected days. 'Garden Tours' had been popular with the middle classes since the eighteenth century, and the arrival of the railways during the working lives of our gardeners made this pastime far more accessible. The head gardener was expected to take visitors round, explaining the various features of the garden. Bailey's garden at Nuneham Park was one of the most accessible and most-visited gardens. In 1845 the *Penny Magazine of the Society for the Diffusion of Useful Knowledge* contained the following description:

With Oxford holiday-seekers of all classes, Nuneham Courtenay is one of the most favourite resorts. It lies at an easy distance from the city, being about five miles by the road, and not more than seven by the river; and as the row to it is one of the pleasantest on the Thames, few make an aquatic excursion from Oxford without Nuneham serving as the goal: and it deserves the favour in which it is held. Few parts of the river are pleasanter, and fewer of the parks along its banks are so beautiful in themselves, or afford so rich a variety of views.[10]

This popularity was not without its drawbacks, and a plaintive notice in the *Oxford Journal* requested that 'those persons who have permission to land will not leave pieces of paper and broken bottles about'.[11] However, despite the litter, opening to the public offered Henry Bailey the opportunity to showcase his hard work to a much larger audience and, in the process, leave a surprising legacy. Amongst the crowds who took punts and small boats up the Thames from Oxford to Nuneham in the summer of 1862 was a party made up of a shy but brilliant maths professor and three young girls, the daughters of a friend and colleague. They were Charles Dodgson, now better known as Lewis Carroll, and Alice Liddell and her sisters. Alice said, 'Most of Mr Dodgson's stories were told to us on river expeditions to Nuneham and Godstow', and they were later written down as *Alice's Adventures in Wonderland* and *Through the Looking-Glass*. It is tempting to wonder how far the backdrop filtered its way through into the stories and whether, for instance, Henry Bailey's rose garden at Nuneham featured red or white roses.

It is clear that men like Henry Bailey, James Duncan and John Collinson were public figures, and their horticultural achievements and awards were often marked in the local press. Horticultural exhibitions and competitions offered an opportunity to shine and to test their plants and horticultural skill against their fellow professionals. Horticultural prizes could represent a significant source of income for a talented gardener. The big horticultural shows were also great places to network with fellow gardeners, to gossip and to compare notes. They were a high-profile testing ground: our head gardeners could be found pitting themselves in a very public way against their peers. It is easy to imagine them suited, booted, be-whiskered and bowler-hatted, prowling between green baize-covered tables nervously awaiting the judges' verdicts on their '25 varieties of carnation' or Muscat grapes. Shows were held at all levels from the local village hall to the national, and even international, level. The Horticultural Society's shows in London were the most prestigious, and ex-Chiswick gardeners crop up regularly in the awards lists. At local shows the head gardener of the local large estate might be co-opted as a judge, casting his expert eye over the amateur efforts of the local cottagers. All this would be reported exhaustively in the gardening press and in the local (and sometimes even national) newspapers, and this brought prestige to the gardener and reflected glory on his employer.

Those men in the Handwriting Book who made it to the top of their profession commanded large teams to produce immaculate gardens that, although they were designed for the enjoyment and comfort of a tiny elite, had a deep and long-lasting impact on our idea of a perfect English garden. This impact has been downplayed for more than a hundred years, as we have bought in to the vociferous Edwardian rejection of Victorian garden design. Writers and garden designers like Gertrude Jekyll dismissed the High Victorian gardens that our men created and cherished as being stiff, garish and contrived. The blowsy, romantic Arts and Crafts garden, with its hardy perennials, has triumphed completely over the bedding system. However, I would invite you to peruse the pages of Adveno Brooke's *Gardens of England* before you dismiss these gardens. Find the pages for Trentham, Eaton Hall and Nuneham and you will see controlled formality, but also grace. Or perhaps make a visit to one of the National Trust properties where Victorian gardens have been restored, such as Cragside in Northumberland or Scotney Castle in Kent, and marvel at the technical skill and attention to detail that are on display.

Today the style of gardening these head gardeners perfected also just about survives in some of our public parks, despite harsh spending cutbacks. The design language of traditional municipal parks features specimen trees, flower beds, terraces and sinuous walks that our head gardeners would have recognized, because they are adapted versions of Victorian country-house gardens. Joseph Paxton and John Claudius Loudon set a pattern that was followed from Birkenhead to Central Park in New York. And the technical skill and dedication to solving the problems of keeping tropical plants alive shown by Victorian head gardeners has undoubtedly given us a rich inheritance of plants to choose from, whether it is tender plants for our window boxes or reliable and robust orchids for our windowsills.

Paxton outshone everyone, of course, but this type of lasting impact requires more than just one superstar to embed and spread the change. The other head gardeners also played their part, showcasing and persuading through their gardens, their flower-show exhibits and their writings. But as we shall see, becoming a head gardener in a great country-house estate was far from the only way of making your mark or influencing future generations of gardeners.

CHAPTER THREE

'A great number of deserving men': Life Lower Down the Horticultural Ladder

Thomas McCann admitted 22 June 1822 upon the recommendation of Sir Aubrey de Vere Hunt

Joseph Collinson admitted in March 1827 upon the recommendation of Sir Robert Heron Bt

Cuthbert Embleton admitted 13 May 1827 upon the recommendation of Richard Bothell Esq.

John Gooud admitted 25 August 1828 upon the recommendation of Stephen Eaton Esq.

Robert Abbott admitted 25 May 1829 upon the recommendation of Roger Pettiward Esq.

ONLY A MINORITY OF THE MEN WHO LEFT CHISWICK were able to secure places as head gardeners in charge of large, well-resourced gardens, as the Horticultural Society had hoped. However, if that was the only criterion for success for the Chiswick Garden, a 100 per cent success rate was probably never achievable. The hierarchical structure of large garden establishments meant that, for every man who made it to head gardener, there were always more beneath him who could not. A letter signed 'One in the Chiswick Gardens', published in *The Gardener and Practical Florist* in 1843, eloquently explained the dilemma:

Sir,

I wish to bring the following to the notice of your readers. Every man who enters upon the profession of a gardener, does so with the ultimate view of acquiring a sufficient knowledge of his business to qualify him for a master gardener's place. It must however, be observed, that as the number of situations bears no proportion to the number of men qualified to fill them, it necessarily follows that a great number of deserving men must remain in a state of probation, perhaps to the end of their lives; and it is appalling to think of the miseries endured by these men from the time of their apprenticeship until they arrive at such a state of perfection as would warrant them in taking master places. And, after having arrived at such perfection, they see no prospect of an alleviation of their miseries: twelve shillings a-week, and the hope of a better place, is all they have to subsist on.[1]

Of course not everyone was capable of reaching a 'state of perfection' and some of the gardeners in the Handwriting Book must have fallen short in skill, knowledge or application. The Horticultural Society itself anticipated this in its rules and regulations. It specified that each October or November the head gardener, Donald Munro, should pass to the secretary a list of the gardeners who 'in his opinion are not likely to attain such proficiency in the business of gardeners as shall qualify them to be recommended to the situation of head gardener' and that these men should be simply dismissed from the Garden. When Loudon reported on this regulation, he cheekily inserted that these men were selected because they 'have not the proper bump on their heads', implying that the Society

could not be trusted to recognize a good gardener if it saw one
and might just as well rely on the new craze for phrenology
(the pseudoscience of determining a person's character from
the shape of their skull).[2]

John Reicks was admitted to the Garden on 19 May 1828
upon the recommendation of the Marquess of Ormond after
an apprenticeship at Castlecomor in the County of Kilkenny
in Ireland, but just four weeks later the committee noted that
he was discharged as 'not being likely to answer after a month's
trial'.[3] By the mid-1830s Reicks was working for a Miss Mary
Driver at Hawthorne Cottage, at Framfield in East Sussex.
He was a live-in gardener/general-purpose male servant and
was married to Anne, who was the cook. This does suggest
that in this case the Society was correct in its assessment of his
potential to become a head gardener. However, only seventeen
gardeners out of the 112 who trained at Chiswick between 1822
and 1829 were recorded as being dismissed for poor conduct or
inadequate progress. What happened to the competent, well-
behaved gardeners who left the gates of the Chiswick Garden,
and yet never made it to 'the head of their profession'?

Some chose to leave the horticultural profession altogether.
Despite early training on the prestigious Haddo House estate,
Alexander Davidson returned to the village of his birth, Old
Machar, just outside Aberdeen, to become a crofter and salmon
fisherman. On 1 September 1825, after twenty months working in the Chiswick Garden, William Cook, under-gardener
in the Kitchen Garden, 'was discharged at his own request,
he wishing to relinquish business as a Gardener'.[4] His Handwriting Book entry shows that his father was a brick-maker in
Suffolk, and the 1841 census shows William Cook, 'Occupation

Brick-maker', in Woodbridge, Suffolk. Francis Bridges, who entered the Chiswick Garden in June 1828, became a 'retailer of Beer and Porter and Grocer' in Abergivilly, just outside Carmarthen, before becoming a Collector of Quay Dues in Swansea. However, most of the men listed in the Handwriting Book appear to have remained within the horticultural profession, even if many of them never managed to become a head gardener.

There were plenty of other options for skilled horticulturists beyond managing large country-house gardens. The options available varied greatly in terms of income, prospects, status and workload. 'Roaldus' of Preston, writing in *The Gardeners' Chronicle*, divided gardeners into three classes: '1. Gardeners who have charge of first rate establishments and do not work. 2. Gardeners who have a man or several men under them, but are expected to take an active part in whatever is going on, and 3. Men who take single handed places and work hard.'[5] Head gardeners like John Collinson and Henry Bailey, managing thirty or forty men and facing the management challenge of keeping a large, complex estate garden running like a well-oiled machine, would probably take issue with the inference that head gardeners in first-rate establishments 'did not work'. However, Roaldus' point was that gardeners running smaller gardens had to be more hands-on, and this was undeniably true. The type of gardens employing 'working' head gardeners belonged to the minor gentry or the upper middle classes. Whilst big country houses could support a large garden staff with a clear hierarchy and specialisms, the vast majority of households were much more modest establishments. Even quite large residences had to make do with just one or two gardeners. One gardener complained in the letters pages of *The Gardeners' Chronicle* that he and one assistant had to work '4,848 sq yards of kitchen garden, 548 yards of wall trees, 38 yard long range of pines and 1200 pots of plants, 2 acres of lawn, shrubbery and a coach drive'.[6]

These smaller but still substantial gardens, often positioned on the edge of towns and cities, were becoming much more common. The period during which our men were training at Chiswick was one of rapid urban growth, and by 1851, for the first time in history, slightly more than half the British population was urban. Campaigners, writers and critics tended to focus on what was wrong with urbanization, and our image of Victorian cities is coloured by caricatures like 'Coketown' in Charles Dickens' *Hard Times*.

It is true that early Victorian towns and cities were still largely unpaved, ill lit and inadequately supplied with clean water or sewage systems. There was plenty to criticize, but not all large towns were smoky, squalid and overcrowded. Depending on your social class, even the largest and dirtiest had pleasant suburbs to live in. The rapid urbanization of the first half of the nineteenth century brought with it the construction of thousands of suburban villas, with gardens ranging in size from a quarter of an acre to up to ten acres (four hectares) in some cases. As the country put behind it the long, hard years of the Napoleonic Wars and the agricultural depression that followed, the economy gradually began to recover. With no wars to finance, the 1820s saw income tax drop, and this gave the new expanding middle class more disposable income. Having a garden tended by a professional gardener became an essential status symbol that more people could afford.

In the centre of cities, even quite wealthy families lived in terraces with little access to private garden space, beyond possibly a private square shared with their neighbours. However, as the century progressed, with the rise of a salaried middle class and the advent of first the horse-drawn omnibus and then the railways, those who could afford it wanted their home to be out in the fresher air of the suburbs. Smart new terraces were built on what were then the outskirts of town, and from the mid-century onwards especially, some were able to protect their privacy further by buying or renting semi-detached or detached houses, which tended to be described as 'villas'. A suburban villa would be endowed with a garden. In 1838 Loudon published a book aimed specifically at the owners of these gardens, entitled *The Suburban Gardener and Villa Companion*. He classified gardens and houses as first-, second-, third- or fourth-rate. A 'second rate' villa garden was considered to be between two and ten acres (four hectares) in size. However 'third rate' and 'fourth rate' gardens of an acre or less were by far the most common.

Loudon was the main champion of this type of garden and provided the template for the type of horticulture best suited to gardening on this scale. He was optimistic that gardens attached to middle-class homes could be just as horticulturally interesting as the traditional grand parks and gardens of the aristocracy. The style of gardening that he championed, known as the 'gardenesque', was tailor-made for smaller middle-class gardens, being 'more suitable for those persons who are botanists, rather than general admirers of scenery, because it is best calculated for displaying the individual beauty of trees and plants'.[7] In other words, gardens of more modest size could not rely on rolling acres and verdant views to make an effect, so the focus was in the foreground, on the individual plants. Victorians were just as inclined to fill every conceivable space in their garden with botanical and floral curiosities as they were to clutter their parlours with ornaments. Even relatively small plots could be crammed with an astonishing array of plants. Just because a gardener at a smaller establishment had to roll up his shirt sleeves and get involved with the actual gardening did not mean that his work was lacking in horticultural sophistication or ambition.

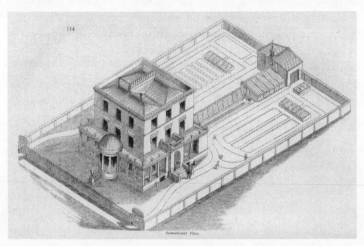

Loudon said that these 'fourth rate' suburban semi-detached houses could be managed by one jobbing gardener.

This type of property would probably not have space for a live-in gardener, and most gardeners working in towns and cities would 'live out'. For instance, before coming to Chiswick, Cuthbert Embleton trained at the enormous 13,000-acre (5,265-hectare) park at Rise Hall in Yorkshire. He had to become accustomed to a more confined environment when he became gardener to Mr Thomas Bernard, Esquire, of Park Terrace, North Brixton in Lambeth. Cuthbert lived with his wife and seven children at 30 Ingleton Street (just off the Brixton Road, close to where Stockwell Underground station is now). The quality of gardening that Embleton was able to undertake in this suburban garden can be seen by the Large Silver Medal he was awarded by the Horticultural Society in July 1844 for a display of twenty-four different varieties of carnation.

John Gooud was another Chiswick gardener who appears to have worked in suburban gardens. The 1841 census shows him living in Barrow Hill Road, St Marylebone, and the occupation given is 'gardener'. Barrow Hill Road is off St John's Wood High Street, close to Regent's Park. In the mid-nineteenth century it was a respectable area, catering for professional and commercial classes. St John's Wood was one of London's first suburbs to be developed with a large amount of low-density 'villa' housing, so it is probable that Gooud made his living looking after one of these villa gardens.

One of the challenges with those who were not live-in gardeners on a large estate is that it is often hard to untangle from the available records where they actually worked and what type of gardener they were. Very often their occupation in the census is described simply as 'gardener' and this could cover a multitude of roles. Sometimes it is possible, as in the case of John Gooud, to infer from the area they lived in where they probably worked, but sometimes it is much harder.

Thomas McCann, the first gardener to put his name in the Handwriting Book, is a case in point. Born in 1803, he grew up in Ireland, the son of 'a gardener to Sir Aubrey de Vere Hunt of Currah in the County of Limerick'. After serving a four-year apprenticeship under his father, he travelled to England at the age of eighteen to work in 'the London nurseries before joining the Horticultural Society's Garden at Chiswick'.[8] He was recommended to a place at the end of his training but, as was usual for the Society, the name of that place was not recorded. However, by the time of the 1841 census McCann has, on the face of it, a prestigious address: Eltham Palace in south-east London. But things are not what they seem.

Although Eltham Palace had been a royal residence, by 1841 it was in a state of some decline. The palace itself was used as a farm barn, and its buildings were rented to a variety of tenants. In the early nineteenth century a substantial villa was built on the grounds of the palace with its own ornamental and kitchen gardens, and it is possible that McCann was the gardener there, but lived in one of the small cottages formed out of the outbuildings around the courtyard. Alternatively, there were also market gardens close by, growing fruit and vegetables for sale in London, so he could have made his living working in one of those.

In fact running a market garden was an attractive alternative for a man of horticultural skill, providing he had the means to rent sufficient quality ground in a good location. At least six of the Chiswick gardeners worked in market gardens, which had for generations fringed the perimeters of every large town and city. It was reckoned, on average, that an acre put to growing a succession of crops such as early cabbage, cos lettuces and celery could bring in a profit of about £45 a year.[9] This looks like a healthy profit margin, but does not take into account the risk of losing crops from bad weather, pests or disease. As one contemporary put it: 'We have few instances on record of market gardeners becoming rich. By means of perseverance and great industry, however they manage to live comfortably and effect much good in the country by spending large sums of money in labour.'

The same author estimated that around London 12,000 acres (4,860 hectares) were occupied in growing vegetables and more than 5,000 acres (2,025 hectares) in growing fruit, together employing more than 35,000 people. Again, just because they were producing food for market rather than an aristocrat's dining table, this did not mean that the standards of horticultural skill involved were necessarily lower. Today it is fashionable to criticize supermarkets for promoting out-of-season fruit and vegetables, but London market gardeners were just as keen to satisfy the demand for asparagus in early spring or tender young peas in April, by 'forcing' crops under glass. It was even argued that when it came to food, commercial growers outshone the private head gardener, for 'whatever fruit, flower or vegetable a market gardener takes to grow, he never fails in producing a first rate thing. No doubt this is owing much to having his whole mind directed to it. He has none of those crosses of a private gardener, such as pleasing cooks, housekeepers, butlers and bailiffs.'[10]

* * *

Joseph Collinson – brother of John who was destined to work at the grand Eaton Hall after leaving Chiswick – joined the Horticultural Society in March 1827. He had exactly the same early training and upbringing as his older brother, learning his trade under their father at Bloxham Hall in Lincolnshire, before going to Worksop Manor and then working as under-gardener for another brother, George, at Stubton. However, after leaving Chiswick in January 1828, Joseph set himself up as a 'Cottager' at Scopwick in Lincolnshire on a smallholding of twelve acres (4.8 hectares). A cottager was someone who leased a small plot of land with a cottage on it. The land was usually worked like a family vegetable plot and may have had a pen for a pig or a couple of sheep. Some cottagers with enough land became essentially market gardeners, selling produce on market days. And, with twelve acres, it would seem that Joseph Collinson was in that category. He appears to have been reasonably successful, as the census shows the family employing a domestic servant. He died on 29 March 1873 at Scopwick, and probate records show that he left effects worth between £100 and £200 (£50,000–100,000 in modern terms).

As towns and cities grew, and as better transport links brought more competition from imported foreign food, many of these market gardens were swallowed up by housing developments. If the market gardener was wealthy enough to own the lease on the land he cultivated, he could turn property developer himself. William Mills entered the Chiswick Garden in February 1828, and by 1841 he was in the market-gardening line, just a stone's throw away from the Chiswick Garden, living with his wife and son in Burlington Cottage, Chiswick. The 1851 census describes him as a market gardener 'occupying 18 acres, employing 6 men' at the grander-sounding address of 132 Burlington Court, Chiswick. By 1861 he was living at Mills Cottage, Chiswick. This was one of a string of houses that became known as Mills Row, presumably named after William Mills. This row of two-up two-down cottages, each with a privy at the bottom of the garden, probably offered Mills a good supplementary source of income, although over time their status gradually declined until they were considered slums. This type of small-scale development built on suburban fringe land could be shoddily constructed, because leases were often comparatively short and the builder had no incentive to create anything more substantial. That said, Mills Row survived for around a hundred years, until they were compulsorily purchased and demolished by the council in 1958 to be replaced by a modern residential development.

However, some of our men did not manage the security or status of a market gardener or a steady position with a middle-class household. Despite the fact that they had already attained at least journeyman status by the time they arrived at Chiswick, some saw their progress up the horticultural ladder stall after they left the Garden. Some even appear to have slipped below this status and into the pool of unskilled labour, whose ability to earn a living depended more on their muscle power than on their skill or knowledge. These were men who had to scratch a living as a jobbing gardener: an itinerant self-employed tradesman who sought out his own customers, used his own tools and supplied his own seeds and plants, often from his own garden. At this time there was an army of tradesmen travelling from door to door looking for business: 'No sooner have the March winds licked up the moisture of February, than the travelling gardener comes round and pulls the bell-gate. His modest request that he may "do-up," as he terms it, your front plot for a few shillings.'[11]

Sometimes this class of gardener worked on a more or less casual basis for nurseries that would subcontract jobbers to work in their clients' gardens. Contract gardening was particularly attractive to wealthy city dwellers who spent most of the year in the country, but kept a town house for business or 'the season'. They wanted showy plant displays for relatively short periods, without the bother or expense of adding to their household establishment by employing a gardener. Large seasonal displays of potted flowers could be supplied, ready to be plunged into their flower beds, conservatories or window boxes on demand. Contracts involved regular visits from gardeners who pruned, syringed (washed plants with hand-operated spray pumps) and replaced wilted specimens. Temporary plant displays could be rented by the week, usually for between five to ten weeks at a time. The cost would vary according to the complexity of the planting. For example, window boxes to decorate the front of a large town house could be hired for a cost of around ten shillings a week. London nurseries would even hire out plants by the night to decorate halls and dining rooms for balls and parties. Nurseries often grew a small range of popular flowers in huge numbers, so that displays could easily be refreshed if they wilted or died from neglect. In this scenario, the role of the jobbing contract gardener in the spring and summer season was little more than that of delivery man, bringing plants in and out by wagon and tidying the garden.

When Loudon published his *Encyclopaedia of Gardening* in 1822, he laid out a hierarchy of gardening, which placed jobbing gardeners very low on the scale, just above an unskilled labourer. In general, they were sneered at and presented in the gardening press as a thing to be avoided at all costs. The popular garden writer Shirley Hibberd was positively scathing. In 1858 he wrote that a jobbing gardener 'fiddles away his employer's time and his own earnings in the low enjoyment of beer'.[12]

Thirteen years later his opinion had not softened. He declared to unwary garden owners: 'when you are tired of herbaceous plants, let the jobbing gardener keep the border tidy, and you will soon be rid of the obnoxious lilies, phloxes, ranunculuses [*sic*], anemones, hollyhocks, peonies and pansies without the painful labour of pulling them up and burning them'.[13]

The signs that our men were working at this level can be found in the addresses they lived at and in their marital status. A journeyman or jobbing gardener would struggle to keep a wife and family and would most probably have to live as a single lodger, either with a family or in a lodging house.

Generally, we do not know what combination of bad behaviour or ill luck caused a career to stall in this way, but in one gardener's case, the cause can be traced very precisely. Robert Poole Abbott was one of the last gardeners to be admitted as a student gardener, in May 1829. He was the son of a gardener from Suffolk and worked at Chiswick for five years, rising to under-gardener in the Ornamental Experimental Department. However, in December 1834 he was dismissed for negligence. It is difficult to imagine that he had much success obtaining a good position without a good reference from the Horticultural Society, but he appears to have remained in the horticultural trade and moved to Buckinghamshire, because in January 1846 he was tried and found guilty at the General Quarter Sessions at Aylesbury of 'unlawfully and by false pretences' obtaining on 12 October 1845 'twelve hyacinth roots and twelve tulip roots of the value of 10 shillings, the property of said William Cutter Brown with intend to cheat and defraud him of the same'.[14] Although the value of the fraud was relatively small, and Robert Poole Abbott had already been held on remand for two months by the time his case came to trial, he was sentenced to one month of hard labour in the Aylesbury House of Correction.

A sentence of hard labour at Aylesbury meant time on the treadmill, which was a man-powered wheel used to turn a heavy millstone to grind grain. Prisoners were put into closed compartments, within which they remained for up to fifteen minutes at a time, vigorously treading down on a wheel consisting of twenty-four steps, constructed as an ingenious system of vanes designed always to flap down under the prisoner's feet, making the wheel turn at an unrelenting pace. After a short break, whilst they were replaced by another prisoner, they would resume their position, continuing this exhausting and tedious process for six hours. Fifteen minutes does not sound long, but as a prison warder explained to the social campaigner and researcher Henry Mayhew in the 1850s, 'You see the men can get no firm tread like, from the steps always sinking away from under their feet and that makes it very tiring. Again the compartments are small and the air becomes very hot, so that the heat at the end of a quarter of an hour renders it difficult to breathe.'[15] The Aylesbury treadmill was heavily criticized for being unsafe, and injuries and even deaths were not uncommon. Robert Poole Abbott survived, but it was not unusual for prisoners to emerge from this experience as emaciated, broken men. The 1851 census finds Robert Poole Abbott described as a mere 'Journeyman Gardener' living in a cheap lodging house in Chelsea, probably working at one of the local nurseries or market gardens. By 1861 he had moved to the Ranelagh Tavern in Tottenham, where he worked as a servant and 'jobbing' gardener until his death of 'serious apoplexy' aged just forty-nine in August 1862.

Illustration from the *Gardener's Magazine* showing a nursery gardener
wearing typical working clothing, 1826.

Whatever the reason for their lack of progress, the conse-
quences for those Chiswick men who remained at these lower
levels of the horticultural career ladder were serious. Not only
were they on low pay, but working as a jobbing or journeyman
gardener for a nursery, market garden or private household

could be a precarious existence. The highest risk was not unemployment but under-employment. There were frequent periods of time when weather conditions meant they could not work and would have to get by on whatever savings they had managed to scrape together during the busy times.

In the fourth volume of Henry Mayhew's *London Labour and the London Poor*, entitled *London's Underworld*, there is a long list of the different types of beggar to be found on the streets of London, employing different scams and schemes to elicit money. One he lists is 'Unemployed Agriculturalists and Frozen-out Gardeners'. Mayhew describes this as a scam whereby 'Two gangs generally work together, that is, while one gang begs at one end of a street, a second gang begs at the other... Their "programme" is very simple. Upon the spades which they carry is chalked "frozen out!" or "starving!"' Mayhew notes that the gardeners are less strident than the agriculturalists or 'navvies':

> They affect aprons and old straw hats, their manner is less demonstrative, and their tones less rusty and unmelodious. The 'navvies' roar; the gardeners squeak. The navvies' petition is made loud and lustily, as by men used to work in clay and rock; the gardeners' voice is meek and mild, as of a gentle nature trained to tend on fruit and flowers. The young bulky, sinewy beggar plays the navvy; the shrivelled, gravelly, pottering, elderly cadger performs the gardener.

Mayhew says this can be a very successful act. 'The "profits" of the frozen-out gardener and agriculturalist are very large, and generally quadruples the sum earned by honest labour.'[16] Although what Mayhew described was clearly a scam, it would only have worked if it had a basis of truth – if people knew that gardeners really suffered unemployment and hardship during prolonged frosts.

Another hazard was illness – aches and pains, bronchitis and rheumatism were all common complaints for people who spent most of the working day outdoors. The wages of a jobbing or journeyman gardener did not allow for putting by much money for a rainy day. If he was the breadwinner for a family, sickness would immediately cut off the family's income and unless his wife and children could find employment and bring in money, the family would rapidly descend into such serious hardship that they had to resort to the workhouse. As one doctor from Leeds put it, 'Most operatives in this country prematurely sink from labour, if they be not destroyed by acute disease. "Worn out" is often applied to a workman as a coach-horse and frequently with equal propriety in reference to premature decay.'[17]

Whilst a treasured head gardener could hope for at least a parting gift or, if his employer was generous, a pension, for the jobbing or journeyman gardener old age did not promise a leisurely retirement. With no provision for an income, a man too elderly to garden could only hope that his children would provide him with a home. With no pension, and in all likelihood no savings, the workhouse or starvation were real possibilities for gardeners who struggled to find work. It was in order to provide aid to gardeners in this position that in 1838 a group of philanthropists led by George Glenny, a normally sharp-tongued and argumentative journalist, formed the Gardeners' Benevolent Institution. It took a couple of years before the Institution had gathered enough funds to provide its first pensions, but by 1852 it was distributing more than £500 each year. Its main fundraising event was an annual dinner attended by key horticulturists who wanted to do something to help fellow gardeners who had been less fortunate in their careers. The charity still exists today, although under the name Perennial, and is famous for its 'Naked Gardener' calendar.

* * *

Of the Chiswick gardeners whose later career it has been possible to track down, roughly a quarter were gardeners working either as self-employed 'jobbers' or journeymen for smaller households, commercial nurseries or market gardens. The actual figure is probably higher, as the more obscure gardeners, who did not win awards or work at a notable garden, tended to leave no mark on the historical record. They were gardening on a much more modest scale than the head gardeners in charge of enormous teams in 'first rate' gardens.

The Horticultural Society undoubtedly saw these men as having failed to take advantage of the opportunities that had been offered to them at Chiswick. On 1 May 1840 Fellows of the Society gathered at its offices on Regent Street to hear a paper given by George Bentham, who had replaced Joseph Sabine as secretary. The paper was a review of progress over the last ten years and covered how the Society was faring in achieving its objectives, one of which was 'The instruction of young men in the art of gardening'.

Whilst the review was very self-congratulatory when it came to other objectives, such as 'the introduction of new,

The front cover of the Handwriting Book, which is now part of the collections at the RHS Lindley Library.

A pensive looking Joseph Paxton in a photograph taken c.1853. By this time his fame overshadowed all his horticultural contemporaries.

Joseph Paxton   admitted   13 November 1823
upon the recommendation of Jos. Sabine Esq.

At the time of my entering in the Garden of the Horticultural Society my Father was dead – he was formely A Farmer at Milton Bryant in Bedfordshire where I was born in the Year 1801 at the age of 15 My attention was turned to Gardening. and I was 2 years employed in the Garden of Sir G. O.P. Turner Bart at Battlesden. from there I went to the Garden of Sam.l Smith Esq. at Woodhall. under Mr. Wm. Griffin where I continued 3 years. and then returned to be Gardener to Sir G. O P. Turner at Battlesden I remained there 2 years after which I came to the Garden of the Society being then 22 Years of Age and unmaried

Joseph Paxton

Page three of the Handwriting Book contains the entry written by Joseph Paxton in November 1823, where he lied about his age by claiming to be two years older than he actually was.

The Chiswick Garden trainees were the first to grow new plants sent back by the Horticultural Society's plant collecters, like this *Zephyranthes rosea*. This plant was collected in South America by George Don, an ancestor of TV gardener and author Monty Don.

菩 *Lou*
君 *Kiun*
眉 *mee*

紫 *Sidze*
龍 *Lung*
鬚 *Soo*

Chrysanthemum Indicum { *var. a Quilled pink*
{ *var. b White*

The 'Pink Quilled Chrysanthemum', one of the varieties of chrysanthemum sent from China to Chiswick by the Society's agent, John Reeves. As well as live plants, he also sent beautiful paintings like this one, painted by Chinese artists.

Eaton Hall in Cheshire, owned by the enormously wealthy Duke of Westminster, where John Collinson was appointed as head gardener. This view by Edward Adveno Brooke shows the elaborate terraces that John Collinson maintained in immaculate order.

The rose garden planted by Henry Bailey at Nuneham Park, as visited by Lewis Carroll. A colour lithograph by Adveno Brooke, published in 1857.

Oncidium papillio, published in Curtis's *Botanical Magazine* in 1828. This was
the first exotic orchid purchased by the Duke of Devonshire, the start of
an enormous collection to be cared for by Joseph Paxton.

A design for an elaborate flower bed which was published in the *Florist's Journal* in 1841.
This design shows the bright colour effects early Victorian gardeners aimed for
with their bedding plants.

William Craggs was one of the first gardeners in the country to be given the opportunity to grow rhododendrons brought back from the Himalayas by Joseph Dalton Hooker. This is *Rhododendron dalhousiae*, which was amongst the plants sent to Craggs' garden at Killerton in Devon in 1852.

(*Top left*) This book illustration published in 1862 shows some of the exotic fruits and flowers that head gardeners were expected to supply for elaborate table decorations.

(*Top right*) The Horticultural Society commissioned this painting of the *Victoria regia* in 1837 for the newly crowned Queen Victoria to sign. Excitement about the gigantic water lily mounted again when Thomas Bridges bought back seeds from Bolivia in 1846.

(*Left*) Photograph taken in the 1850s of William Jackson Hooker, Director of the Royal Botanic Gardens Kew. He was one of Thomas Bridges' main customers for seeds, plants and herbarium specimens.

useful or ornamental plants', the tone when it came to training was far more sombre. Bentham noted that on this particular aspect the Society's aims were 'but partially realised'. He put the blame for this firmly at the door of the young gardeners themselves, arguing that their early education before arriving at Chiswick had been too poor to allow them to take advantage of the opportunity they had been given:

> Some were found totally unacquainted with the commonest details of the gardener's art; others were illiterate in a lamentable degree; and notwithstanding the excellent example set by many who are now at the head of their profession, upon the whole it must be admitted that several of the men received in the garden were little improved in consequence.

It is hard to square this damning assessment of the men with the comprehensive list of prior experience, neatly written out in good English, in the entries in the Handwriting Book. The report laid a great deal of emphasis on how, from now on, the training of gardeners would involve a formal curriculum and examination overseen by John Lindley. However, it also reveals a very narrow definition of success – one which seemed to assume that the only horticulture of interest was that carried out by head gardeners at 'first rate' gardens.

Certainly the type of gardening these gardeners did, single-handed and often rushed for time and in an unpromising urban environment, was not the type of horticulture that won awards or was lauded in the gardening press. Indeed, contemporary writers, other than Loudon, were often dismissive of any urban gardens, seeing them as too beleaguered with pollution and other detritus of urban life to have any chance of becoming good gardens. Dickens' description of an urban garden in *Nicholas Nickleby* is not unusual; he depicted a typical town garden as being full of soil that was 'populated by a few hampers, half a dozen broken bottles and such like rubbish' scattered among 'scanty box and stunted ever-browns and broken flower pots'.[18] Another writer described the typical London garden as 'a square patch of dank clay mould... the hospital of a few roots of languishing flowers – the mausoleum of a small conclave of defunct shrubs and the privileged council ground of vagrant cats'.[19]

A genteel middle-class suburban garden in Hendon
from Loudon's *The Suburban Gardener*, 1838.

However, many determined owners and their gardeners found ways to overcome these difficulties, taking components of the fashionable garden designs of the day and adapting them to the narrow, house-width gardens that came attached to Victorian suburban dwellings. Whilst the gardeners who worked in them may have won no prizes, the work they did improved the quality of life and streetscape of towns and cities up and down the land. These gardens took components of the country-house garden and compressed them to fit the space available. If Paxton could create a massive rockwork imitating the Strid at Bolton Abbey for the Duke of Devonshire at Chatsworth, then a Croydon back garden could have a 'rockery' – a garden feature that was to become an essential fixture in the later years of the nineteenth century. If John Collinson could cultivate the Nesfield-designed terraces and parterres that swept outwards across the grand frontage of Eaton Hall, then gardeners in the suburbs of Manchester could tend terraces bordered by flower beds and shrubberies outside drawing rooms at the back of red-brick houses.

The plants selected for these suburban and urban gardens were the reliable workhorses of the garden, tough plants that earnt their keep and put on a show, even in partial shade and polluted, smoggy air. They are plants that remain familiar to us today, the staples of many front and back gardens, ranging from forsythia to *Viburnum tinus*. The components that evolved for this type of garden – the borders around the edge of a long thin lawn, a rockery, a small greenhouse, tender bedding in pots on the patio in summer – are a recipe that lots of people still stick to firmly to this day. These Victorian gardens saw the development of a type of domestic gardening adapted to smaller spaces and concentrated bursts of activity, rather than the seven-day-a-week attention that a live-in gardener could devote. The gardeners who tended them developed a style of gardening that, notwithstanding the absence of hover-mowers and other power-tools, many of us would recognize. The Horticultural Society and other members of the horticultural elite may have dismissed anyone who failed to make the grade as a head gardener in a large country-house garden, but in terms of setting the pattern of lasting and widespread relevance, these minor gardeners were every bit as influential.

CHAPTER FOUR

'The most splendid plant I ever beheld':
The Collector

Thomas Bridges admitted 12 March 1827 upon
the recommendation of the Revd G. R. Leathes

NOT EVERYONE WHO SIGNED UP AS A TRAINEE AT Chiswick aspired to be a head gardener. Thomas Bridges spent just under six months in the Horticultural Society's Garden before he left on 31 August 1827. This was nowhere near enough time to qualify him to manage a major garden, but his prior experience gives some clue to his real aspirations. Following stints with his father in the gardens of minor gentry in Norfolk, Bridges went to Suffolk to work both at the Bury and Suffolk Botanic Garden in Bury St Edmunds and at the garden of Robert Bevan.

The former was one of a number of subscription botanic gardens that sprang up around the country in the first half of the nineteenth century, designed to foster the spread of science and give their paying members access to the latest exotic plants, as well as a refined place to take the air, away from the lower orders. Bridges' other employer, Robert Bevan, was a banker, one of a network of Quaker families that intermarried and worked together to create the group of banks that eventually coalesced into Barclays Bank. As well as having an interest in finance, many of these families shared a strong interest in botany and horticulture. So from the age of sixteen or seventeen, Thomas Bridges worked with plant collections that were crammed with the newest and most exotic plants, arriving fresh from plant collectors in foreign lands.

It is highly likely that he joined Chiswick specifically to prepare to become a plant collector himself. His time spent with amateur botanists and plant enthusiasts will have made him well aware of the huge demand for natural-history objects amongst gentlemen collectors. Britain was a hotbed of botanical enthusiasm; microscopes and scientific journals were becoming more affordable; and collecting clubs were popping up around the country, where enthusiasts could pore over plant specimens and debate the latest taxonomical controversies.

Expanding commercial and imperial communication networks meant that it was now possible for botanists to have dried plant specimens sent from all over the world. There was an especially high demand for 'sets' of dried plants to illustrate the flora of a region or the diversity of a genus. Compiling and selling these sets offered a chance for a keen naturalist to make a living of sorts, even though the prices did not reflect the effort or the risks involved. It was undoubtedly a hazardous occupation. Three of the six collectors whom the Horticultural Society sent on expeditions in the 1820s and 1830s lost their lives. Even supposing the many tropical diseases that Victorian medicine had no answer for did not claim them, there were many other dangers for plant collectors to contend with. Robbery of instruments and possessions was an occupational hazard, and replacements had to be paid for from the plant hunter's meagre expense allowance. The drive to uncover plants new to science often took naturalists to dangerous parts of the world, in the vanguard of imperial expansion, where there was a high chance of conflict.

However, if Thomas Bridges was like most young men of twenty or so and was convinced of his own immortality, he will have paid scant regard to risk. For an ambitious young man, plant collecting promised adventure, fortune and the opportunity to make a name in science. For plant collecting was an earnest scientific endeavour, a drive to classify and understand the natural world that was undertaken with high seriousness. Some nurseries sent plant collectors to amass specimens that could become commercial assets, but most plant collecting was supported by patrons with scientific motivation, and most plant hunters were keen botanists themselves.

At Chiswick, Thomas Bridges had a unique opportunity to familiarize himself with the newest plants and spend time with the Society's assistant secretary, John Lindley, who in 1825 had written a helpful pamphlet entitled 'Instructions for Collecting and Packing Seeds in Foreign Countries'. Bridges was able to hear from the horse's mouth exactly how he could best ensure that the plants and seeds he hoped to collect could reach their destination alive. Lindley would have had professional and personal motivations for answering his questions. They shared a very similar background, both growing up in Norfolk, the sons of horticultural men of limited means, and sharing a passion for new and exciting plants. When he was a young man of similar age to Thomas Bridges, Lindley had also dreamt of being a plant collector and had taken to sleeping on the hard wooden floor of his bedroom to toughen himself up for future expeditions. Being blind in one eye and of delicate constitution, his talents were actually much better suited to life in the library and herbarium, and he was to serve botany handsomely without straying far from Britain. Bridges was to follow Lindley's packing instructions for the rest of his career, with, as we shall see, mixed results.

The aspiring plant collector may already have had a destination in mind and may have headed to Chiswick with a plan to study a specific consignment of plants – those that had arrived in 1826 from South America, sent by the Society's plant collector, James McRae. He had sailed on HMS *Blonde* under Captain Lord Byron, a relative of the famous poet. The main purpose of the voyage was to return to the Kingdom of Hawaii the bodies of King Kamehameha II and Queen Kamamalu, who had died of measles while visiting England. The ship stopped at Brazil, Chile, the Galapagos Islands and Hawaii, and McRae returned with collections of plants including hippeastrums, alstroemerias and, possibly most notable of all, *Araucaria araucana*, the monkey-puzzle tree. Thomas Bridges will have taken the opportunity to study all these plants whilst he was at Chiswick.

The Chiswick Garden also gave him an unexpected opportunity to encounter the wildlife of South America. In the corner of the Ornamental Experimental Department of the Garden was a wooden cage with a curved wire front. It housed a harpy eagle, brought back from Brazil by Edward Sabine. It was a male, which was fortunate as the female of the species is twice as large and fierce as the male. Nevertheless, the harpy eagle (*Harpia harpyja*) is the most powerful raptor to be found in the Americas and one of the largest eagles in the world. It inhabits tropical lowland rainforests in Central and South America, thriving on a diet of sloths and monkeys. Apparently the gardeners fed the Chiswick specimen on a diet of cats. By the time Thomas Bridges worked at the Garden, the poor bird had been through three cold and damp west-London winters, so may not have been the awe-inspiring sight it would be in the wild. Whether or not he already knew his intended plant-hunting destination when he arrived at Chiswick, or whether the sight of McRae's plants and the eagle convinced him, it is clear that at some point in 1827 Bridges made the decision to go to Chile.

Harpyia Destructor,

Illustration from the *Penny Cyclopaedia* of the harpy eagle that lived in the Chiswick Garden.

At the time Chile was a country newly independent after more than 250 years of Spanish colonial rule. Under Spanish control there had been very limited commercial opportunities for British subjects, but now the Foreign Office was keen to foster trade and investment in the new South American republics. In 1822 Britain extended the Navigation Acts to permit Latin American ships to call into British ports and, from the 1820s onwards, there was a steady stream of British traders and adventurers heading to Chile to seek their fortune.

Not so long before this time, British contact with South America was less peaceful and benign. One British visitor to Chile told a story of meeting an old lady at a dinner in Coquimbo who remarked, 'How wonderfully strange it was that she should live to dine in the same room with an Englishman. Twice as a girl, at the cry of "Los Ingleses", every soul carrying what valuables they could, had taken to the mountain.'[1] This was because since the 1500s British pirates had been raiding Spanish territories in the region. However, by the time Thomas Bridges was planning to go to Chile the British were held in higher esteem. This was partly thanks to the exploits of Thomas Cochrane, tenth Earl of Dundonald, who after being forced to give up a career as an MP in Britain, under accusations of stock-market fraud, had found a new career as commander of the Chilean navy. He is mainly remembered in this country as the model for the fictional naval hero Horatio Hornblower.

As the son of a relatively lowly gardener, Thomas would need to find sponsors to pay for his trip. In return for funding up front, sponsors could expect first pick of herbarium specimens, seeds and plants. In fact in order to fund his trip, Bridges also reached out to collectors of shells, birds, insects and animals and was described as 'a general collector and vendor of all the productions of nature'.[2] By mid-November 1827 he had managed to gather enough sponsors to pay for his passage to Valparaiso in Chile. These sponsors seem to have been gathered from contacts made in Norfolk and Suffolk, and included amateur botanists like the Reverend George Reading Leathes from Shropham in Norfolk, Robert Bevan of Rougham in Suffolk, and Robert Barclay, a wealthy brewer and nephew of the banker David Barclay, who owned a much-admired garden at Bury Hill in Surrey.

Bridges regularly supplied herbarium samples to John Lindley, and it is possible that Lindley also provided some funding up front. He possibly introduced to Bridges another Norfolk-born botanist who joined his early backers and was to become a major figure in his career. This was William Jackson Hooker, who by 1827 was already a key figure in Britain's scientific community. He was Regius Professor of Botany at the University of Glasgow and editor of *Curtis's Botanical Magazine*, the main publication describing and illustrating new plant discoveries. Unlike Bridges, Hooker was lucky enough to have been born to a wealthy Norwich family and had been able to use inherited wealth to indulge his interest in natural history with a self-funded expedition to Iceland in 1809 at the age of twenty-four. Hooker made it his business to know anyone and everyone who could help him add to his rapidly growing herbarium and store of knowledge on the world's flora. Thomas Bridges must have known that such a well-connected and influential man had the ability to put him in contact with a wide network of collectors and potential customers. He therefore made every effort to keep in regular contact, and it is thanks to these letters to William Hooker, kept at the archive of the Royal Botanic Gardens at Kew, that we have a vivid picture of Thomas Bridges' life and character.

Thomas arrived in Valparaiso in August 1828 after 'a long and painful voyage', which was not for the faint-hearted. In addition to the obvious physical discomforts, someone like Thomas Bridges, who was a mere gardener rather than a gentleman amateur, would also have to contend with the strictures of the rigid class system aboard a British ship. He might not have been deemed a desirable companion for a ship's officer, so would probably have to make do with inferior quarters. At the same time he needed to be seen as being above the status of a deckhand, if he was to have any hope of caring for his precious books, equipment and cargo. He was in an awkward social no-man's-land. Clearly relieved to sight land again after 138 days at sea, Bridges described his joy at seeing 'the prodigious mountains of Chile covered with perpetual snow with the Sun shining beautifully on their tops'.[3] Almost instantly on landing he was fascinated by the flora: 'I was struck with astonishment at the cacti growing in the almost perpendicular cliffs.' He was also struck by the 'strange appearance of the town'. Valparaiso was a thin, straggling settlement sandwiched between the sea and high mountains. It was a bustling port, with a small but lively community of British merchants and a colourful mixture of adventurers and other travellers.

These first impressions were included in a letter that he wrote to William Hooker within a couple of weeks of his arrival. Even in this first letter, he knew it was vital to pique Hooker's interest, so Thomas was at pains to point out the richness of the flora and his confidence that new plants could be discovered: 'Since my arrival I have made an excursion on foot almost every day and never returned without augmenting my collection of specimens. The variety of plants is truly astonishing.' It was important to maintain Hooker's interest, because Bridges' sponsors had only provided enough money for his passage and he urgently needed funds. He wrote: 'I feel most anxious to go south but long journeys here are very expensive and at present my means are very scanty.'[4] This was to be a recurrent refrain, and cashflow was to be a constant struggle. A well-resourced six-week expedition in South America, with bearers and supplies, could easily cost in excess of £100.[5] In contrast, the going rate for 100 dried herbarium specimens was only around £2 10 shillings.

On top of expedition costs, an independent plant collector like Thomas Bridges had to pay for botanical supplies and shipping costs. Each item had to be carefully preserved, catalogued and, ideally, named with full details of collection locality, habitat, cultivation requirements, local name and uses. This was a huge amount of difficult work, often undertaken in very demanding conditions. The other obstacles were lack of language and local knowledge. Astonishingly, Bridges did not seem to think it necessary to learn Spanish before he set out. For nearly a year he was unable to do much in the way of active plant collecting, beyond a few short excursions around Valparaiso. To make matters worse, he had to wait for nearly a year for a reply from Hooker, and the isolation clearly worried him. In his reply to Hooker's letter dated September 1829 he confessed, 'I can assure you it has completely revived my almost drooping spirits as I began to think that all my friends had forsaken or forgotten me.'[6] However, he was able to report that he had improved his Spanish sufficiently to be able to travel and request information from natives, and that he had recently sent to Hooker a shipment of more than two hundred species of dried specimens from around Valparaiso.

Cordilleras from Santiago de Chile.

This increased confidence probably derived from meeting a British collector who was to be another significant figure in Bridges' life. Hugh Cuming was born in 1791 in the village of Washbrook near Kingsbridge in Devon. His background was an even more humble one than Bridges' own, as he had had little formal education and as a young boy was apprenticed to a sail-maker. He emigrated to Chile in 1819 to set up a sail-making business in Valparaiso, which prospered, but at some point he caught the shell-collecting bug and began embarking on collecting expeditions in 1821. In 1826 Cuming decided to abandon sail-making entirely and created a new career for himself exploring the southern Pacific Ocean, collecting and selling natural-history specimens, with a particular focus on shells. He collected on an almost industrial scale, and his specimens were sold to a wide number of private collectors across Europe.

Well settled in Valparaiso, with a Spanish mistress and a young family, this stocky, red-faced and genial West Countryman would have been able to give Bridges a great deal of useful advice on how to make a living as a collector. This enabled Thomas to make more ambitious plans to travel to the Cordilleras, going by way of Quillota on to the Valley of Aconcagua and then returning by way of Santiago, 'a journey of nearly 100 leagues'. It was a major undertaking, traversing a mountainous region with many gorges and ravines, but very few roads. However, money was clearly still an issue, and Bridges was forced to ask his 'friends in the East of England' to send annual flower seeds and vegetables that he could sell in Chile.[7]

This was the state of affairs for Thomas Bridges for the next few years. He would write to William Hooker letting him know of his expeditions and promise to send 'interesting plants', all the time struggling to make ends meet. Occasionally, Bridges was forced to write a banker's draft against Hooker for cash, in the hope that he would agree to the payment in return for the expectation of further consignments of plants. To add to his difficulties, there was violent unrest in Chile, as royalists and other rebels fought for control. In December 1829 Bridges wrote, 'I should have collected much more had it not have been for the Revolutionary state of the country, so many murderers lurking in the mountains.'[8] Nevertheless, he managed to make a number of increasingly ambitious excursions into the interior of Chile and sent large consignments of seeds, bulbs and dried plants back to Britain.

Thomas Bridges' letters to William Hooker reveal a slightly tense relationship with his key patron and, on reading them, there is a clear impression that he felt slightly neglected by the great botanist, who sat comfortably at home, taking all the plaudits for the description of new plants in his own publications whilst Bridges languished, impoverished, in a far-away land. Plant collectors in the field and academic botanists were locked in an interdependent but sometimes fractious relationship. The botanists needed the collectors for specimens to analyse and the plant collectors needed the botanists, with their ready access to the latest literature and ample herbaria, for definitive identifications. Poor Thomas felt his isolation from the latest botanical knowledge keenly. So many new plants and places were constantly being discovered and, in the process, names and classifications called into question and corrected. The pace of discovery was so rapid that works could become outdated almost as soon as they were printed.

Bridges regularly wrote asking for books and journals to be sent out to him: 'If you could send me the *Edinburgh Journal of Science* for 1829 I should be much delighted as I want something to read.'[9] Time and again he also dropped heavy hints that he would like to have an account of his journeys published: 'Should you think a brief account of my excursions in this province among the independent and primitive people would be interesting and deserving of a place in any journal I would with pleasure remit you it.'[10] However, Hooker never seems to have responded. From his perspective, Bridges was just one of a plethora of collectors and correspondents sending him plants – and not a particularly reliable one at that. Several of the letters from Bridges contain apologies for not keeping notes of the location or habitat of the specimens he has sent back, information that would have been prized by a botanist like Hooker. Hooker's attitude to Thomas Bridges may also have been coloured by his association with Hugh Cuming, whom Hooker held in some disdain as a grubby commercial trader in specimens, and no friend to science. There are certainly stories of Cuming doing things that no modern naturalist would countenance, destroying habitats and clearing the seabed in his hunger to get as many specimens as he could.

However, Hugh Cuming was a valuable friend to Thomas Bridges. In 1831 Cuming returned to England to sell duplicates and enhance his own collection. From his new home in London, just behind the British Museum, he acted as an agent for Bridges, receiving shipments of plants, animal and bird skins, shells and insects and then forwarding them on to collectors and chasing them for money on Thomas' behalf. Amongst Bridges' best customers was the Earl of Derby, John Jennings' employer, who received shipments of live birds for his menagerie at Knowsley.

Despite sending several consignments home to collectors, by 1834 Thomas Bridges had decided to give up collecting and take up farming in order to make a reasonable living. He was employed as superintendent of an estate near Talca, south of Santiago. What he grew is not recorded, but Talca is renowned for its Mediterranean climate and has been a centre for vine-growing since the sixteenth century, so it is possible that he ran a vineyard. In July 1836 the British diplomat and

amateur naturalist Alexander Caldcleugh reported to William
Hooker that:

> Mr Bridges came up lately from the country and... he says col-
> lecting is quite out of the question at present, his employer
> will not consent to his dedicating any portion of his time to
> other pursuits. It seems he is in receipt of a good salary, is
> saving money and is fearful of risking his situation.[11]

However, whilst Thomas Bridges was quietly farming, two
developments occurred many thousands of miles apart that
were to bring him back to botany and change his life.

* * *

The first was a revolutionary discovery that transformed the
world of plant collecting. Back in England, Nathaniel Bagshaw
Ward, a London doctor with a passion for natural history, was
studying moths. He had placed a chrysalis on leaf mould in a
glass jar and sealed the lid. Although the moth never emerged,
a number of seedlings did, including several types of grass
and a fern. He noticed that the leaf mould remained moist,
and correctly assumed that the water originally in the mould
evaporated during the day, condensed on the sides of the glass
jar as the temperature dropped and dribbled back down into
the mould again. He had stumbled upon a means of creating
a self-contained environment and, as a keen botanist as well
as an entomologist, quickly realized the potential significance
of this discovery. Until this point, even with the expertise and
best efforts of men like Thomas Bridges, the survival rate for
living plant specimens on long sea journeys was appallingly

low. Dr Ward's miniature greenhouses could potentially provide a sealed world for plants on deck, where they could have access to light, but still be safe from the salt spray and wind that killed so many precious discoveries.

The glazed 'Wardian case' that revolutionized plant transportation,
luring Thomas Bridges back to the life of a plant collector.

In 1833 the enterprising Hackney nurseryman George Loddiges attended a meeting where Ward spoke about his experiments. Loddiges offered to arrange space for two cases filled with mosses, grasses and ferns on a ship bound to Australia. The captain and crew were told to leave the case entirely alone, with no attempt to water the plants inside. After a journey of four months, the plants arrived in Sydney in perfect health and, even more significantly, Australian plants survived the return journey. Whilst Thomas Bridges was quietly farming in remote Chile, Loddiges began to send hundreds of plants around the world, and news of the novel 'Wardian cases' created ripples of excitement within both horticultural and botanical circles.

The second momentous development was the discovery of a 'wonder plant' that was to capture the imagination not just of plant lovers, but of the whole world. This plant was to dominate the career not only of Thomas Bridges, but also of William Hooker, John Lindley and, most profoundly of all, fellow Chiswick alumni Joseph Paxton. It all began in July 1835, when a diminutive but keen German explorer called Robert Hermann Schomburgk was sent to South America by the Royal Geographical Society to survey the colony of British Guiana. All anyone in Britain knew about this new bit of Empire was that it was an area filled with rivers and swamps. John Lindley found Schomburgk twelve subscribers who would buy any collections of dried plants that he could supply. Like Thomas Bridges, Schomburgk was under-resourced and received little sympathy and support from home. On 1 January 1837, struggling up the River Berbice in a canoe, he saw a 'vegetable wonder' – a gigantic water lily with leaves more than six feet (1.8 metres) in diameter and beautiful white blooms the size of a man's head.

Schomburgk was a keen botanist and felt he had discovered an enormous new species of *Nymphaea*. He had months more surveying to do and could not abandon his mission to get a live specimen back to the coast. He tried to preserve a bud and a leaf in a barrel full of brine, but the leaf turned to slime and the flower lost its colour. Nevertheless, he sent the barrel back to Britain, along with a description and some sketches, which he hoped would give an impression of this amazing plant. Sure enough, when the consignment reached London, it inspired a frenzy of botanical interest. In June 1837 the nineteen-year-old Queen Victoria acceded to the throne and the Royal Geographical Society, spotting an ideal opportunity to curry favour, asked permission to name the flower for the new queen. The drawings and descriptions were sent to John Lindley to work on a full botanical account and naming. Opening the barrel and fishing around in the slimy, smelly liquid, Lindley pulled out and examined what remained of the specimens Schomburgk had collected. Even in its decayed state, he could see that the bloom had some very curious features, which did not correspond at all with those of a *Nymphaea*. The huge prickly leaves depicted in the drawings had more in common with another genus, *Euryale*, named after one of the sisters of the Gorgon Medusa. However, associating a plant to be named after the young queen with a Gorgon (*Euryale Victoria*) did not seem the flattering and courtly gesture the Royal Geographical Society had in mind.

Ordering a servant to bring him a specimen of *Euryale* from the Horticultural Society's herbarium, Lindley was relieved to find that there were small but critical differences (the number of cells in the ovary and ovules in each cell were much larger). He was therefore able to declare proudly that the plant was an entirely new genus, which he named *Victoria regia* (now called *Victoria amazonica*, although we will call it by the name John Lindley gave it, to avoid confusion). A copy of Schomburgk's painting was hung in one of the glasshouses at Chiswick for the gardeners and visitors to admire, and another was made for the queen to sign. But what was really needed was a living specimen. Loudon spoke for all when he wrote, 'We hope that this splendid plant will soon be introduced and that an aquarium worthy of Her Majesty and of the advanced state of horticultural science will be formed.'[12] Procuring a live plant and getting it to bloom on British soil became a national horticultural priority. Two men in particular vied for the honour of being the first to achieve this feat. It should come as no surprise that one of them was Joseph Paxton, the best-resourced and most ambitious gardener in the land.

When Schomburgk returned to England in 1839, Paxton lost no time in persuading the Duke of Devonshire to invite him to Chatsworth to discuss his discovery. Schomburgk was already well aware of Paxton's status as the nation's pre-eminent head gardener. For many months he had been sending orchids to the Duke of Devonshire, who by now was in full swing as an avid collector. The duke recorded his impression of the brave explorer rather curtly in his diary: 'Dwarf. Agreeable'.[13] Formalities over with, Paxton showed Schomburgk around the garden and hothouses, and the highlight of the tour must have been to see the orchid that had been named after him, *Epidendrum schomburgkii*. But for Paxton and the duke the main motivation for inviting Schomburgk was to interrogate him on *Victoria regia*: how big did it really get? At what rate did it grow and exactly what were its perfect growing conditions – what water temperature, air temperature, light levels? Schomburgk answered as fully as he could, but the only thing he could not supply was an actual plant or even a solitary seed. However, before departing from British Guiana, he had engaged a boat pilot to keep an eye out for *Victoria regia* and get a specimen back to the coast for shipping to England, if at all possible.

Meanwhile he was kept busy staging a public exhibition on British Guiana in order to raise money for his next trip.

Whilst Thomas Bridges had turned to farming to make ends meet, Schomburgk resorted to a more Barnum & Bailey approach. His exhibition at 'The Cosmorama' in Regent Street featured a painted mural with a life-size rendition of *Victoria regia*, many stuffed birds and animals and three disconsolate Guianan Indians whom he had brought with him specifically to 'exhibit' for the amusement and edification of Londoners. Dressed in skin-coloured clothes to spare the blushes of lady visitors, the three Indians huddled around a fire most of the time. Unfortunately they were judged to be no match for the more exciting exhibits at nearby Madame Tussaud's and the exhibit was a financial disaster. Thankfully for Schomburgk, the Colonial Office agreed to appoint him as boundary commissioner of British Guiana. And then in May 1840 he received more good news. A consignment of *Victoria regia* plants and seeds had arrived in good order at George Town and were ready for shipping to England. Paxton mobilized straight away to make sure that Chatsworth should be ready to win the race to make this remarkable plant grow and flower in Britain.

Unfortunately, the plants died before they reached England, but the seeds were more robust. However, when they arrived, Paxton was not to be the only recipient. By now William Hooker had left his position in Glasgow to take up the post he had aspired to for years – the directorship of the Royal Botanic Gardens at Kew, and he received seeds as well. Ironically, he had Paxton to thank for there being a botanic garden at Kew for him to run at all. After the death of Sir Joseph Banks in 1820, the gardens at Kew had gone to rack and ruin. The

royal head gardener, William Townsend Aiton, was not scientifically minded and had little time for Kew. Large areas of
the garden were given over to growing fruit and vegetables
for the royal kitchens, whilst rare and exotic plants, shrubs
and trees were allowed to die. When Treasury officials examined the royal accounts in 1837 after the death of William IV,
there was a feeling that it might be best to do away with this
drain on royal resources altogether. John Lindley was put
at the head of a committee to decide the fate of the garden,
alongside Joseph Paxton and another Chiswick alumni, John
Wilson, then gardener to the Earl of Surrey. The committee
recommended that Joseph Banks' original vision of the garden
as 'a great exchange house' of scientifically and economically
valuable plants should be revived as a matter of urgency. Lindley wanted Paxton to become director, but Paxton decided to
stay loyal to the Duke of Devonshire. The idea of taking on
a dilapidated garden in the face of constant penny-pinching
from the Treasury was no match for the facilities he enjoyed at
Chatsworth, backed by the ever-obliging duke.

In contrast, William Hooker was desperate for the chance
to run Kew and began a lobbying campaign, sending gifts of
plants and herbarium specimens that he had acquired from
Bridges and his other collectors to influential figures in the
political establishment. This worked and, by the time the
seeds arrived, he had begun a massive overhaul of the glasshouses at Kew and a tightening up of the entire operation of
the garden. Sadly, Schomburgk's seeds failed to germinate at
either Chatsworth or Kew, so the race between the two gardens was deferred for the time being, a fact that Hooker may
have secretly regarded as a good thing, as it gave him more

time to prepare the facilities at Kew for this mammoth horticultural challenge.

William Hooker also had another reason to be cheerful – he
had another potential source of *Victoria regia* seeds and plants.
For back in Chile, Thomas Bridges had tired of farming and
was giving plant collecting another try, partly because the new
Wardian cases enabled the opportunity to export living plants
as well as herbarium specimens. In April 1842 he wrote to
Hooker to let him know that 'I have rented a place in Valparaiso
from Mr Waddington $600 per annum which I intend to turn
into a nursery and Botanist's Garden and forward by every
opportunity plants to England' and that he would shortly
send '2 cases of living plants to Kew'.[14] At first his expeditions
were at altitude, 'rambles over the Andes', where the plants
he encountered were cacti rather than giant water lilies. However, by 1844 he had settled on branching out to Bolivia and
approached William Hooker to ask him to intercede with the
foreign secretary, the Earl of Aberdeen, to obtain a letter of
introduction to smooth his passage.

The Earl of Aberdeen was a keen gardener and had obtained
many exotic plants for his estate at Haddo House via Hooker,
and he was inclined to oblige when asked to support plant-
collecting expeditions. After some delay the letter was for-
warded, and Thomas Bridges headed for Cochabamba in
central Bolivia, where he presented himself to Charles Mas-
terton, Her Britannic Majesty's consul in Bolivia. With a letter
from the foreign secretary vouching for him, Bridges received a
'most cordial and gentlemanlike reception' and was introduced
to the president of Bolivia, General Jose Ballivián. He was
a modernizer and under his administration the guano riches

of Bolivia were exploited for the first time. Guano (the accumulated excrement of seabirds and bats) was a very effective
fertilizer, due to its exceptionally high content of nitrogen,
phosphate and potassium, and in the mid-1800s could sell for
as much as $55 a ton. So the president was interested to meet
a horticultural expert and explorer and treated Bridges with
'unexpected kindness', providing him with letters to all the
prefects or governors of the various departments of the repub-
lic, with the result that wherever he went in Bolivia, Bridges
'received every attention from the authorities'.[15] This attention was to prove extremely valuable.

The trip did not get off to a promising start, from a plant-
collecting point of view. In September 1844 Bridges set off
from Cobija on an expedition in the 'dry, lofty and arid mountains which run parallel with the coast', where 'scarcely a plant
exists'. He travelled by mule, accompanied by two Chilean
servants, and spent most of his time collecting insects and
shooting birds to collect their skins. He then set out eastwards
to 'fall into the tropical forests' of the River Mamore, which he
proposed to follow downstream to the town of Trinidad (the
capital of the province of Moxos). He wrote to William Hooker
that he knew the trip into the tropics would be arduous: 'It
is not possible for you to form any conception of the expense
and difficulty of conveying things after being collected in this
country without roads and the means of transportation.'[16] His
ingenuity in overcoming these difficulties was to be tested to
the limit.

In June 1845 he arrived at the Indian town of Santa Anna in
the province of Moxos and settled there, making excursions to
shoot birds rather than collect plants. On one excursion he rode

along the muddy banks of the Yacuma River and came suddenly onto 'a beautiful pond, or rather small lake, embosomed in the forest, where to my delight and astonishment, I discovered for the first time "the Queen of the Aquatics": the Victoria regia!' He was overwhelmed and later recalled that it was only the fact that his Indian guide reminded him the waters abounded in alligators that prevented him from diving into the lake to collect the plant there and then. As he later wrote, 'I now turned over in my thoughts how and in what way flowers and leaves might be obtained, and I clearly saw that a canoe was necessary.' Here his presidential connections paid off; when he hurried back to the town to get help, the local governor, Don Jose Maria Zarate, immediately arranged for a group of Indians with a yoke of oxen to draw a canoe upriver to the lake. Bridges wrote a detailed account of what happened next:

Being apprised that the canoe was in readiness, I returned in the afternoon with several Indians to assist in carrying home the expected prize of leaves and flowers. The canoe being very small, only three persons could embark; myself in the middle and an Indian in the bows and stern. In this tottering little bark we rowed amongst magnificent leaves and flowers, crushing unavoidably some, and selecting only such as pleased me. The leaves being so enormous I could find room in the canoe for but two, one before me and the other behind; owning to their being very fragile, even in the green state, care was necessary to transport them.

It was not just the size and fragility of the leaves that necessitated care, for the underside of the leaves and stems was covered in razor-sharp thorns. In the tropics even a scratch could become infected and rapidly prove deadly. After several trips backwards and forwards in the wobbly canoe, leaning out perilously over alligator-infested waters, he managed to take the leaves, flowers and ripe seed-vessels of two entire plants. There was no question of being able to transport a living aquatic plant; even getting the component parts back to town to preserve was going to be a challenge. After some thought, he 'determined at length upon suspending them on long poles with small cord, tied to the stalks of the leaves and flowers. Two Indians, each taking on his shoulder an end of the pole, carried them into the town.'

Plant collector climbing a tree to collect an orchid. Health and
safety was not a great concern for nineteenth-century
plant collectors like Thomas Bridges.

Returning to town like a big-game hunter, with the plant suspended like the carcass of a wild beast, Thomas Bridges must have caused quite a stir. He carefully dried segments of the leaves between sheets of paper and then tackled the seeds, which were held in seedpods about the size and shape of grapefruit, covered all over with tiny, needle-sharp spines. He carefully scooped out scores of green seeds, which were embedded in pith like the seeds of a pomegranate, and then carefully sandwiched them between damp clay to stop them being exposed to air that would cause them to rot, just as John Lindley instructed. He left the leaves and flower buds in his room, intent on preserving the buds in spirits later. When he returned to his room at nightfall, he found to his surprise that the flowers had opened and

> were exhaling a most delightful odour, which at first I compared to a rich Pine apple, afterwards to a Melon, and then to the Cherimoya; but, indeed, it resembled none of these fruits, and I at length came to the decision that it was a most delicious scent, unlike every other, and peculiar to the noble flower that produced it.[17]

He returned to Santa Cruz and promptly wrote to Hugh Cuming to let him know of the valuable find he had made. Bridges wrote excitedly, 'It is certainly the most splendid plant I ever beheld, to see its magnificent leaves four feet in diameter floating on the lakes, and its splendid white flowers which change to beautiful pink, fills the beholder with delight and astonishment.'

The specimens he collected survived the inland journey

much better than Schomburgk had managed: 'I have procured a fine specimen of the flowers preserved in spirits and leaves dried in paper. With these materials a drawing may be made of the plant,' he wrote. But the main prize was the seeds: 'I have also obtained fine, mature seeds preserved in bottles in a manner which I have no doubt will vegetate if treated as I direct on their arrival in England.' The letter to Hugh Cuming is an open and informal one between friends and Thomas Bridges makes clear that, aside from the *Victoria regia*, his plant-collecting efforts have been a disappointment to him:

> I have been much disappointed with the vegetable kingdom of this part of the world. I may say I have travelled 1000 miles without collecting 100 specimens. In fact I have quarrelled with Botany. The idea of 4s per 100 species has disgusted me, besides it is not sufficient to pay their carriage to the coast.[18]

There was clearly a lot riding on the *Victoria regia* for Bridges; this plant could make his name and at long last bring him fame and, if not fortune, then at least some financial reward to recompense for all his hardships and frustrations. Hugh Cuming's commercial expertise and contacts would be invaluable in spreading the word. Unfortunately for both of them, years of travel and collecting in the steamy jungles of the Philippines had taken their toll. In February 1846, shortly after he received the news of Bridges' discovery, Hugh Cuming suffered a stroke that left him partially paralysed. Thomas Bridges was going to have to oversee the sale of his specimens without much support from his friend and agent.

In July 1846 Bridges landed in Bristol. He had with him the precious seeds still wrapped in wet clay, a dried-leaf specimen and a jug holding a blossom submerged in botanical spirits. He quickly made contact with William Hooker to let him know he would sell him all the seeds at two shillings a seed, and he could have the flower in spirit for a guinea, but time was of the essence. Someone from Kew should come to his lodgings in Gower Street as soon as possible, since the specimens 'are certainly receiving injury in their present state'.[19] Hooker snapped up all the seeds and had them rushed back to Kew, where they were sown in a small tank in one of the glasshouses. Only two of the twenty-two seeds germinated, but this was more than anyone else had ever achieved. In August the shoots emerged and leaves unfurled, and growth continued well through September. Like an anxious parent, Thomas Bridges asked for regular bulletins and gave advice by letter:

> I am also pleased to hear that the two plants are still alive. If they have shown roots they ought to have plenty of mud to extend their growth. The water also in my opinion ought to be kept at 70 degrees at least. The information you required as locality, habit colour of flower and co I will willingly give.[20]

However, as the year progressed, the days began to get cooler and shorter and the light levels lower. In October, London's famous fog began to settle on Kew and the plants started to wilt. In November the yellow-brown smog caused by the mixture of mist and pollution was so bad that candles were lit after breakfast and gas lamps were illuminated across London by noon – actions that, of course, only served to make the fog thicker and more polluted. As he watched his precious plants waste away before his eyes, Hooker must have feared the worst. This was especially embarrassing as he was midway through composing a special account that was to be published in a full-colour New Year issue of the *Botanical Magazine*. As he wrote the article, the plants were barely clinging on to life and Hooker tried to manage expectations, writing, 'we have our fears that the plant being possibly annual and the season late (December) they may not survive the winter'.[21] Hooker pressed Bridges to give him an account of the discovery of the *Victoria* to include in the article, and it looked as if Thomas Bridges' long-held dream for immortality in print was about to be realized.

However, like the two precious seedlings, Bridges was also suffering in the English winter. Writing from 'Prospect Place St Michaels, Bristol', he apologized to Hooker for the delay in providing an account of finding the *Victoria*, because 'I have been expectorating blood from the lungs for nearly two months which has weakened me considerably… I have now the mortification to find myself with a broken and ruined constitution as a reward for endeavouring to promote Science.'[22] Doctors' advice and medicine did not work until he tried an infusion of one of the South American plants he had collected, which he called 'Matico Piperomia'. John Lindley identified this plant as probably being *Aranthe elongata* and in his book *The Vegetable Kingdom* described how it had first been discovered to staunch internal and external bleeding by a Peruvian soldier. Bridges reported that as a result of this medicine, his health had improved 'beyond the expectations of the Doctors and my Friends here'. His friends were probably relatives of Hugh Cuming. Cuming's brother-in-law, Matthias Benson, was a tobacconist in Bristol and it seems very likely that Thomas stayed with him and his family. In fact, whilst convalescing and waiting for news of the Victoria seedlings, Bridges made one very particular friend in Bristol, Matthias' daughter, Mary Cuming Benson. Despite his recovery, he reported to Hooker, 'I am ordered by my medical advisers to quit England without delay as they consider my life in danger from the climate.'[23]

Just four days after Thomas Bridges posted this letter, the plants at Kew were finally pronounced dead. Unfortunately, no correspondence recording his reaction to this news survives, but there can be little doubt that it was enormously disappointing. There was a distraction, however; on 2 January 1847, Thomas Bridges married Mary Cuming Benson in Bristol. Just twenty years old, she was clearly a tolerant and patient young woman, taking on an impoverished invalid who was going to have to leave the country for his health. Poor Mary did not even get to enjoy a honeymoon. Less than a fortnight after the wedding day, Bridges wrote to Hooker to let him know that he was working hard arranging his Bolivian herbarium collection. In February 1847 Thomas and Mary set off from Southampton to head to Chile via Panama. They settled in Valparaiso and Thomas resumed his attempts to make a living by raising plants at his nursery garden to send back to England. When Hooker's *Description of Victoria regia* was eventually published and a copy reached Chile, Bridges was to find that his detailed account of his discovery had arrived too late to be included in the main body of the article and had been relegated to a footnote in small print at the end.

* * *

To make matters worse, his achievements were shortly to be overshadowed even further. In February 1849 William Hooker received another package of *Victoria* seeds from the aptly named Mr Luckie of British Guiana. By the end of March six seeds had germinated and, with the earlier start, they prospered before the dangerous dark winter days loomed. By the beginning of summer they were outgrowing their tank. Hooker had learnt his lesson with Bridges' seeds and, rather than pruning them to fit the tank, he shared some seedlings with Joseph Paxton. On 3 August, his forty-sixth birthday, Paxton set off for Kew to pick up the seedling, returning to Chatsworth by express train from Euston. The plant had only four leaves and was a mere six inches (fifteen centimetres) in diameter.

In a special new water tank that had taken him only three weeks to construct, Paxton created the conditions that he understood *Victoria regia* enjoyed in its native habitat. He embedded heating pipes in the soil and added liquid sewage to the water, and installed small wheels in the tank to keep the water in motion. The lily began to grow... and grow. By October the leaves were four feet (1.2 metres) across and Paxton needed to build a larger tank. Meanwhile the plants at Kew had barely grown at all. At Chatsworth on the evening of 8 November a flower bud swelled and began to rise out of the water and slowly open. The flower was of the purest white. It lasted for three evenings, entrancing everyone who saw it, before it wilted and fell away. Other buds emerged and Paxton left for Windsor to enjoy the honour of delivering a blossom to the queen. There was a nervous moment when he cut the flower head and it immediately began to wilt, but the quick-thinking head gardener revived it by pouring warm water into the stalk and putting fine sand near its root. Shortly afterwards Paxton sent a forgivably smug note to Hooker: 'Victoria regia is now in full flower at Chatsworth... Most likely your plants are showing by this time, if not, the sight of our plants is worth a journey of a thousand miles.'[24] In fact once more the plant had failed to thrive at Kew, and Hooker had to suffer the indignity of begging spare plants from Paxton's supply.

The special heated water tank (complete with miniature waterwheel) which Paxton had built to house the *Victoria regia* at Chatsworth.

The news of Paxton's horticultural achievement spread rapidly, thanks in no small part to some canny public-relations work by Paxton himself. Artists from *The Illustrated London News* were invited to draw the flower. The leaves were so thick and broad that Paxton had the idea of putting his daughter Annie onto one of them. He prudently stood her on a tin tray to spread the load. *The Illustrated London News* printed a long report with a picture of Annie (missing out the tea tray), and *Punch* magazine was moved to poetry:

> *On unbent leaf, in fairy guise,*
> *Reflected in the water,*
> *Beloved, admired by hearts and eyes,*
> *Stands Annie, Paxton's daughter.*

Poor Annie was made to re-enact the feat of standing on the leaf again and again for the duke and his many friends and relatives. Soon Paxton the showman added fairy lights and dressed Annie up in fairy costume. He also created a special glasshouse especially for this star of the garden, situated in the kitchen garden, right next to his own house and the fruit of many years of structural experiments with glass at Chatsworth. Taking the form of a large glass box, it was just over sixty feet (eighteen metres) long, forty-seven feet (fourteen metres) wide and almost completely filled by an enormous circular tank. It had a flat ridge and furrow roof that was supported by just four, very thin wrought-iron columns, which doubled as drainpipes. Air and water temperature were maintained at between eighty and ninety degrees Fahrenheit.

Just as Paxton was perfecting his use of glass to house his star plant, a small group of men, led by Prince Albert, were vigorously promoting an ambitious idea – an extraordinary event that would showcase Britain's technological and commercial dominance to the world. 'The Great Exhibition of the Works of Industry of all Nations' was planned to take place in London from May to October 1851. All that was needed was a suitable building to house this Noah's Ark of human produce. The challenges were enormous; hundreds of thousands were expected to attend, and nothing on this scale had ever been attempted before. The building committee had just sixteen months to find and erect a solution on the chosen exhibition ground in Hyde Park. They needed a building that was temporary, safe and cheap to construct, but striking enough to demonstrate Britain's leadership in cutting-edge design and technology. Dissatisfied with all the submissions they received, the committee proposed their own plan: a long, low brick building surmounted by an iron dome designed by Brunel, twice the size of the dome of St Paul's. The press hated it – it was ugly, expensive and hardly temporary.

Paxton's attention was caught and he began to consider the idea of a structure similar to the lily house, but obviously much, much larger. During a meeting of the Midland Railway Board in Derby, he doodled a quick sketch on some blotting paper and over the next week prepared detailed plans at his office in Chatsworth. The building design was ingenious and fitted the brief perfectly; with no stone, brick or mortar, it could be prefabricated offsite and assembled at speed. With one of those strokes of luck that seem to characterize Paxton's life, he bumped into the engineer Robert Stephenson on the train to London and spent the journey extolling the benefits of his scheme. As a member of the Great Exhibition building committee, Stephenson was able to tell Paxton who to meet and how to launch a charm offensive. The committee was convinced and gave Paxton the go-ahead.

Contemporary newspaper accounts marvelled at the rapid progress onsite and crowds flocked to see the gleaming structure rise from the mud in Hyde Park. It was during construction that the term 'Crystal Palace' came into widespread use. Columns only eight inches (twenty centimetres) in diameter supported the enormous edifice, six times the size of St Paul's

Cathedral. Joseph Paxton gave a lecture on the design to the Society of the Arts in which he claimed that the structure was inspired by that of the *Victoria*'s leaf, which had ribs that radiated from the centre, acting as cantilevers to stop it buckling under its own weight. *Punch* magazine referred to the Crystal Palace as 'that pretty tasteful thing bent from the leaf of the *Victoria regia*'.[25]

The building was complete by February 1851 and passed all its structural tests with flying colours, including the rolling of 252 cannon balls along the wooden floor to replicate the effect of the footfall of thousands of people. On 1 May 1851 there was gridlock as carriages queued throughout the city to get to the opening ceremony. After weeks of rain, the sun shone and the sparkling Crystal Palace was filled with 30,000 season-ticket holders, crowding to see the queen officially open the Great Exhibition. More than 15,000 exhibits were installed, from more than forty nations. Paxton, decked out in full court dress complete with sword, led the procession to the centre of the building and was undoubtedly the hero of the hour.

No less an authority than Charles Dickens rammed home the connection between the Crystal Palace and *Victoria regia*. In his periodical, *Household Words*, he wrote an article entitled 'The Private History of the Palace of Glass'. This account completely skipped the role of Thomas Bridges and jumped straight from Schomburgk's discovery of the water lily in 1837 to Paxton's triumph in creating 'a tiny South America under a glass case' to coax the flower into bloom, before taking inspiration from the natural engineering of the plant to create the Crystal Palace.[26]

By September 1851 the news of Paxton's triumph had

reached Chile, and it does not seem that Thomas Bridges took it well. One of William Hooker's Chile-based correspondents, Alexander Caldcleugh, reported:

Mr Thomas Bridges is now in this place having formed a kind of nursery ground for the sale of every description of fruit and other Trees and Plants. He now collects little and is very sore upon the subject of the Victoria Regia which he asserts was introduced (at least the specimen with flower) by him and that he has received no medal and scarcely 'mention honorable' for having done so. I promised to mention the subject to you so that if you consider him entitled to some Reward he may have it.[27]

There is no record of William Hooker making any recommendation to the Horticultural Society, the Linnean Society or anywhere else for any formal reward or recognition for Thomas Bridges. However, Bridges could not afford to hold a grudge as he still needed Hooker's patronage. In 1856 he emigrated with his young family to California and took up natural-history collecting once more and naturally resumed contact with Hooker. In May 1858 he wrote to Hooker from San Francisco:

I can scarcely describe to you how pleasing and gratifying it has been to me to have found some new and rare plants – I was partially under the impression from the labours of Douglas, Hartweg, Jeffreys, Lobb and other travellers from Europe with the many United States Exploring Expeditions that little or nothing remained to be discovered and only gleaning were left to those of us of the present day... Although it is necessary to take into consideration that since the Gold discovery many new and extensive fields are open to the traveller where in former times no one could penetrate with safety from the Indians and other causes – I am now firmly persuaded that on the summit of Sierra Nevada there is a fine field for the Botanist.

Once more Bridges was on the plant collector's rollercoaster of hope and despondency, a lifestyle that, even with a family to support, he found hard to abandon. San Francisco was booming and the young city was still feeling the impact of the 1849 gold-rush. Although there was a strong element of frontier-town roughness to the new settlement, the gold-rush wealth did bring trappings of civilization. Bridges was able to consult books in the Library of the Academy of California and 'a friend here also possesses Hartweg's plants'.[28] He continued to send specimens of birds and plants to Hugh Cuming and was optimistic that in the summer he would be able to collect 200–300 species.

In about 1857 he went to British Columbia and stayed for nearly two years, collecting and exploring. It seems that his family, Mary and their four children, remained in Europe and did not join him in America until the winter of 1858, when they settled in San Francisco.[29] In 1861 his fifth child, Dora Bridges, was born in Valparaiso, so at some point the family appears to have moved back to Chile, at least temporarily. In April 1865 Thomas Bridges decided to visit Nicaragua to collect specimens, but on the way back to San Francisco he contracted malaria and died at sea on 9 September. He was buried in Laurel Hill Cemetery on the outskirts of San Francisco.

Mary and the children remained in the city and, in 1879, were able to come face-to-face with the plant that so nearly made their husband and father famous.

In the fourteen years since Thomas Bridges' death, San Francisco had expanded and begun investing in the trappings of a major city, including botanical gardens, complete with a glasshouse named 'The Conservatory of Flowers'. Whilst hardly a Crystal Palace, it stood at 12,000 square feet (1,116 square metres) and housed 1,700 species of tropical, rare and aquatic plants. On the opening day the prize exhibit was a *Victoria regia* grown from seeds donated by Joseph Hooker, son of William, who had succeeded his father as director of Kew in 1865. The sight of the plant and the crowds it attracted inspired Thomas' son, R. E. Bridges, to write to Joseph Hooker: 'I contemplate issuing a magnificent work on the subject' as 'a labour of love and a fitting tribute to the memory of my father – one who loved science and who met his death in its cause.'[30] He asked Hooker for permission to reproduce some of his father's article on the *Victoria regia* in his proposed book. In an eerie repeat of the relationship between their respective fathers, it seems that Hooker ignored Bridges' request and the volume was never published.

However, despite his near-miss with the *Victoria regia*, Thomas Bridges did achieve a level of immortality. His collecting work uncovered various species new to science and he had the honour of having several named after him, including *Octodon bridgesii* (a species of rodent found in southern Chile), *Copiapoa bridgesii* (a cactus that grows in the coastal areas of the Atacama Desert in northern Chile) and *Penstemon bridgesii* (common name 'Bridges penstemon', native to the south-western

United States and California). His herbarium specimens are now to be found in herbaria at Kew, the Museo de la Plata, the Natural History Museum, the Royal Botanic Garden Edinburgh and the Peabody Museum of Natural History at Yale University. However, his greatest claim to posterity is to be found at the Royal Botanic Gardens, Kew, site of the failure of his *Victoria* seeds.

When Thomas returned to England with his precious consignment of *Victoria* seeds, he also brought back others. He mentioned in passing to Cuming that 'the seeds of Palms have also called my attention'.[31] Amongst them were seeds of *Jubaea chilensis* – the Chilean wine palm – which, although described somewhat disdainfully by Charles Darwin as a 'very ugly tree', many people consider to be one of the most magnificent palms in the world. Its immense dark-grey trunk can reach up to eighty-two feet (twenty-five metres) tall. It is now endemic to a small area of central Chile and is considered an endangered species.

A plant grown from the seeds that Bridges gave to Kew was to set a world record as the largest individual specimen of an indoor plant in the world. From 1846 to 1860 it lived happily in the Palm House and was then transferred to the Temperate House when its fronds were six and a half feet (two metres) in length. It was then transplanted sideways in 1938, a major task as the leaves were already touching the roof and brushing the glass. The palm flowered and fruited for the first time in 1950. It continued in good health, despite the removal of the greenhouse roof in the 1970s during reconstruction of the Temperate House. Unfortunately, by 2014 this mighty plant was nearing the end of its natural life and was in poor condition. When the

Temperate House was closed for refurbishment, it was decided that the tree would not survive the move and it was chopped down. However, over the years Kew staff had propagated several new palms from seed produced by that original palm, and one of these took pride of place in the newly refurbished glasshouse when it reopened in May 2018 – a fitting tribute to a persistent plant collector.

CHAPTER FIVE

'Much attached to Egypt':
Travelling Gardeners

*James Traill admitted 19 April 1824 upon the
recommendation of Mr D. MacLeod*

*Wm McCulloch admitted 28 March 1826
upon recommendation of Jos. Sabine Esq.*

ON 10 JUNE 1854, JOSEPH PAXTON ONCE MORE WEL-
comed Queen Victoria to open his Crystal Palace, now greatly
enlarged and transplanted from Hyde Park to the suburb of
Sydenham. The building had been too much of a success to
simply demolish when the Great Exhibition ended. Paxton had
originally wanted to use it to house a Winter Garden – a giant
conservatory to give the public a taste of the indoor jungle
that he had created in the Great Stove at Chatsworth for the
Duke of Devonshire. The commercial syndicate behind the
new Crystal Palace Company had other ideas. Paxton was able
to demonstrate his horticultural ability in the grounds, with
elaborate massed plantings of brightly coloured bedding, but
the interior was to be filled with the same mix of 'improving'
and awe-inspiring spectacle as the Great Exhibition. However,
where the Great Exhibition aimed to showcase the best out-
put of current manufacturers, the new Crystal Palace displays

looked backwards for inspiration. They aimed to lay before visitors nothing less than the history of the civilization of the world. This was to be achieved through a series of galleries or 'courts', each illustrating the art and culture of the great civilizations.

Without doubt, the court that made the greatest impression was the first one: the Ancient Egyptian Court, which featured a reconstruction of the colossi of Abu Simbel. It had a stupendous impact on all who saw it. Row after row of monumental pharaohs and sphinxes, meticulously cast in plaster, stared blankly over the heads of the crowds that thronged to marvel at the achievements of this mysteriously seductive ancient world. As was often the case in the Victorian Empire, a strange process of transfer was taking place: whilst Joseph Paxton oversaw the creation of Ancient Egypt in south London, thousands of miles away two other ex-Chiswick trainees struggled against the heat and dust to create a convincing facsimile of an English country garden in Cairo.

Scotsman James Traill joined the Horticultural Society's Garden on 19 April 1824 and fellow Scot William McCulloch joined two years later in March 1826. They shared similar backgrounds and routes to Chiswick: both the sons of land stewards, working their way through the various departments of gardens on middle-sized country estates in Ireland. William McCulloch had the slightly stronger CV, in that he had also trained in major commercial nurseries and at the Botanic Garden in Edinburgh under the well-respected curator, William McNab – a man we will meet later, intervening decisively in the life of another Chiswick student. However, it was James Traill who made the more rapid progress within

the Chiswick Garden hierarchy. By July 1825 he was promoted
to under-gardener in the Ornamental Experimental Garden.
This was the section of the Garden where new plant introductions were kept and nurtured, in an effort to establish their
suitability for cultivation in the British climate, and where
experiments were carried out to establish the best methods
to propagate and grow ornamental plants newly arrived from
abroad. It was a high-profile, high-pressure part of the Garden. In 1827 Traill wrote a well-regarded paper, which was
published in the Horticultural Society's *Transactions*, on the
cultivation of *Hoya* and became an Associate of the Linnean
Society in 1827.

William McCulloch's career at Chiswick took a very different turn. In August 1826, just five months after he had joined
Chiswick, the Horticultural Society sent him to accompany
the Honourable Robert Gordon, one of its Fellows, to Brazil.
Gordon had been appointed Minister Plenipotentiary (a diplomatic agent ranking below an ambassador, but possessing full
power and authority) and wanted a gardener for his embassy
in Rio de Janeiro. The Council minutes record that Mr Gordon 'had offered to allow him to do whatever the Society might
require of him, not inconsistent with his engagements to
him'.[1] The Society gave McCulloch a £15 gratuity and agreed
to pay him £10 per annum to send back useful plants from
Brazil. Unfortunately, there is no record of the plants that he
sent back, in the Garden Committee Minutes. However, we do
know of one surprising consignment from him that reached
Chiswick in October 1828.

For some reason William McCulloch decided to send to
Chiswick a giant snail (*Megalobulimus oblongus* var. *haemastomus*)

– normally considered a gardener's worst nightmare. Not surprisingly, after a long sea voyage from Rio, 'at first it appeared rather sickly' but, after being protected from the cold London air in the warmth of the hothouse for a little while, it rallied and started to move about. Indeed, the snail recovered to the extent that it laid three eggs and:

> It fed upon lettuces and the tender leaves of cabbages, the former seemed to be its favourite food. Sometimes it would devour two large lettuces and then remain for days afterwards without touching food, or moving from its place, except when cold water was sprinkled on it. During the day it was usually in a dormant state in the shade, but towards the evening, when the house was moist and warm, it would spread itself out, and moved from one part to another.[2]

This luxurious life of daytime naps and binge-eating lasted for three years. William Beattie Booth, the garden clerk at Chiswick, reported sadly, 'On Saturday last it was at the end of the house where the fire comes in, and ventured too far upon the hot bricks after they had been watered. In the morning it was fixed to them, and quite dead.'[3] Once prised away from the bricks, the remains of the sorry snail and two of its eggs were donated to the Zoological Society. It is not clear whether McCulloch ever returned to work at Chiswick and saw the snail in the hothouse before its sad end. However, we do know that he reunited with his former colleague James Traill to start a new adventure.

On 31 March 1828 the Garden Committee noted that James Traill had informed the Society of his intention to quit, and he left the Garden on 9 April 'at his own request'.[4] Together with William McCulloch, he had been recruited to work for Ibrahim Pasha, son of the *wali* (or viceroy) of Egypt, Mohammed Ali. They may have been recommended to Ibrahim Pasha by the Horticultural Society, but the usual form of words in the minutes for this process was 'recommended to a place', rather than giving notice to quit. Mohammed Ali had agents operating on his behalf in horticultural circles in England, so it is possible that he used contacts based in England to scout out and recruit these two promising gardeners.

Today it is difficult to appreciate quite how poorly informed western Europeans were about North Africa and western Asia in the early years of the nineteenth century. Without telegraphic and rail communications, contact was slight and up-to-date intelligence was hard to come by. Information about Egyptian gardens was scarce, and the two gardeners would have had little idea of what to expect. Since April 1824 the Chiswick students had had access to a small library, made up of duplicate books from the Fellows' library in Regent Street. No record was kept of the contents, so we do not know whether it contained any relevant works. John Claudius Loudon's *Encyclopaedia of Gardening* was only able to give sketchy information about Turkish and Greek gardens, based on accounts dating from the previous century, but there was nothing about modern Egypt. What impressions the pair had of the country probably focused on the ancient world, and this interest was closely connected to Britain's defeat of France in the Napoleonic Wars.

Napoleon's expedition to Egypt had involved the acquisition of many significant artefacts, which were promptly

This cartoon from *Punch* magazine depicts a crowded horticultural fete at Chiswick. In the crowd you can just make out a man in an Egyptian-looking fez – one of the *Pasha's* representatives scouting for horticultural talent perhaps? (*London Borough of Hounslow, Chiswick & Feltham Libraries*)

confiscated when the British Army defeated the French in 1801 and were brought back for public display in the British Museum. From Nelson's victory at the Battle of the Nile in 1798 onwards, there had been a patriotic vogue for decorative obelisks, sphinxes and crocodiles in everything from interior design to painted panoramas. Traill and McCulloch may well have joined the crowds visiting the Egyptian Hall in Piccadilly, an exhibition venue built in the Ancient Egyptian style in 1812. Now a Starbucks, this striking building boasted columns decorated with bands of hieroglyphs, lotuses and Hathor heads and opened with a display of mummies.

Their decision to travel to Egypt was a particularly bold one because British public opinion of their new employer was far from universally positive; indeed, just a year earlier the British Navy had actually been at war with Egyptian forces. This was because Ibrahim Pasha and his father had been involved in a brutal suppression of Greek rebels fighting for independence from the Ottoman Empire. Egypt was part of this empire, and Mohammed Ali and his son were technically vassals of the sultan in Constantinople. Ibrahim Pasha launched a scorched-earth campaign on behalf of the sultan, which threatened the population with starvation and deported many civilians into slavery in Egypt. In response, Britain joined an international naval force with Russia and France, which defeated the Ottoman Empire's fleet in the Battle of Navarino in October 1827, the last naval battle to be fought entirely with sail-powered ships.

The Greeks, in the eyes of most British people, were gallant Christian fighters struggling to free themselves from a corrupt and oppressive Islamic tyranny. The atrocities committed by

Ibrahim Pasha's forces in the Peloponnese were loudly criticized in the popular press, sparking a furore throughout Europe. However, at the same time Mohammed Ali and Ibrahim Pasha were praised as ambitious modernizers in the territories they ruled, and there was a strong appreciation of the commercial advantages to be had for Britain in trading with Egypt. McCulloch and Traill were far from alone in seeing Egypt as a land of opportunity. Mohammed Ali's rule was marked by a drive to increase the prosperity and power of Egypt through the adoption of Western techniques and technologies. He reformed the army, established a navy, created Alexandria as a deep-sea port and initiated many massive irrigation projects. Importing foreign expertise was central to this drive, and Traill and McCulloch were part of an army of well-paid technocrats invited to bring their skills to bear. Horticultural skills were in particular demand because Mohammed Ali was interested in exploring new crops and growing techniques, which could be introduced and exploited to create new sources of revenue. Under Mohammed Ali, more than one million acres (405,000 hectares) were added to Egypt's farmland.

There is no record of exactly when the two men arrived in Egypt. Later reports suggest it was sometime towards the end 1828 or early 1829. Accounts from other travellers emphasize how overwhelming and chaotic the first impressions of Egypt were for new European arrivals: 'No description could convey a just idea of the fearful noise on landing. Hotel servants, screaming forth the comforts and advantages of their respective houses; boatmen, donkey drivers, baggage porters, quarrelling and vociferating in every living language.'[5] They probably sailed via Malta to Alexandria, and then up the Mahmoudieh

Canal by small boat to Cairo. The canal was built in 1819 and
it was said that more than 23,000 people died in its construction – a fact that, if brought to the attention of the two young
Scots, would have given them a chilling idea of the determination and ruthlessness of their new employers.[6]

They brought with them plants supplied by the Horticultural Society from its Chiswick Garden. In November 1829
James Traill wrote back to the Horticultural Society to let
them know that although he was well established in his situation, the plants had suffered on the voyage and he would like
a replacement of chrysanthemums, dahlias and strawberries.[7]
They found that they were not the only European gardeners
that Ibrahim Pasha had recruited. In 1828 Nicholas Bové, a
Belgian gardener, also arrived, sent by Oscar Leclerc-Thouin,
director of the Jardin des Plantes in Paris. As France was a rival
to Britain in the region, Ibrahim Pasha may well have thought
it diplomatic to ensure that a French-sponsored gardener was
'balanced' by two British appointments.

The two gardeners were given attractive, well-appointed
accommodation within Ibrahim Pasha's palace complex on
the island of Roda, on the Nile between old Cairo and Giza.
It was here that Ibrahim Pasha planned to have a new garden
constructed. Roda was home to many of the European consuls
and there was a small Arab village at the southern end of the
island, 'celebrated for its superior butter'.[8] Each gardener was
given his own house; McCulloch's was about three hundred
feet (ninety metres) from the Nile, with 'a large sitting room
on the second floor, opening on to a spacious verandah, the
front of which is closely latticed, the house having been fitted up for the harem of Ibrahim pasha.'[9] Settling down in this

strange new environment, without any knowledge of Arabic or local customs, must have been hard. It is highly likely they received support from a very remarkable source.

William Thomson was a Scottish soldier who had had the misfortune to be part of a British force sent out in 1807 to curb the growing power of Mohammed Ali, then thought to be a threat to British interests. Thomson was captured, along with many others. It was said that the prisoners were brought to Cairo and each man was required to carry the severed head of a slain comrade on a platter to present to Mohammed Ali.[10] After that ordeal, Thomson was then sold into slavery and given the choice of conversion to Islam or death. Choosing to convert, he was given a new name: Osman. He was lucky in his master, who left him an inheritance when he died. The British consul then persuaded Mohammed Ali to grant Osman his freedom, and he decided to stay in Cairo, integrating into the city's Turkish elite.

Osman Effendi, as he was known (Effendi being a form of address for men of high rank and stature), cut a remarkable figure: a tall red-haired man, dressed in impeccable Turkish costume, fluent in Arabic, but with a strong Scottish accent that he retained all his life. He purchased property that he rented out to travellers, and eventually became a bridge between the European and Egyptian worlds. He acted as an interpreter for the British consulate, and it seems that every British visitor relied on him to help them rent houses and boats, clear customs, fit out apartments and hire servants. As British newcomers to Cairo, it is highly likely that McCulloch and Traill would have relied on Osman in this way.

At first the situation for the gardeners was not a positive

one. Following the humiliating defeat in 1827, Mohammed
Ali's finances were in a poor state. That year John Barker,
the British consul-general in Cairo, wrote, 'Mohammed Ali
is ruined. He can no longer pay anyone.'[11] Even the weather
was unkind; following heavy rains in 1829, the Nile overflowed
its banks and ruined crops. However, it seems that the *pasha*'s
finances rapidly improved and by 1831 Barker reported to the
Foreign Office that Mohammed Ali had 'pecuniary resources
adequate to the execution of his designs'.[12] These designs were
certainly ambitious, and horticulture played a pivotal role
in them.

Books on the history of botany often present the nineteenth
century as a time when Britain practised 'economic botany',
moving cash crops around within its Empire to create new
sources of revenue. However, other countries practised this
too, and Mohammed Ali and his son were taking a page from Sir
Joseph Banks' book. Most significantly, he introduced the type
of cotton suitable for the European market and it soon came
to dominate the Egyptian export trade. The crop was mainly
sold to Britain, whose purchases of Egyptian-grown cotton
would rise in value from £50 million in 1800 to £300 million
by 1830. However, the *pasha* did not want to stop with cotton.
Egypt had no indigenous hardwood and was keen to develop
local supplies of timber. What was needed was an 'experimental garden' to trial new plant introductions, much as Chiswick
trialled plants. Up until Traill, McCulloch and Bové arrived,
the only significant garden belonged to Mohammed Ali, set
around his palace at Shruba, located south of Cairo on the east
bank of the Nile. This garden had been chiefly laid out under
Greek and Turkish gardeners in the early 1820s 'in the style of

a small Versailles with stretches of water surrounded by pavil-
ions and galleries'.[13]

In order to source new plants, William McCulloch was sent
off on his travels again. A British report to the Foreign Office
noted that Mohammed Ali 'has sent "travelling botanists"
to the East Indies and other parts in order to collect specimens of such vegetable productions as are likely to suit the
Egyptian soil'.[14] It seems that Bové travelled in Arabia, whilst
McCulloch was sent to India to collect plants in March 1837
and again in June 1838 and January 1840. There he made contact with the Agricultural-Horticultural Society of India and
eminent botanists such as Dr Nathaniel Wallich. This was not
just a simple matter of a polite plant exchange between fellow
horticultural enthusiasts; it was a matter of high diplomacy.
An arrangement was made between Mohammed Ali and the
governor-general of India, Lord Auckland, that English steam-
ships could continue to enjoy unhindered access to Egyptian
ports in return for plants from Bombay, Madras and Calcutta.[15]

James Traill also played his part in introducing new plants
to Egypt, although he was far more firmly rooted in Cairo. He
received plants from the Horticultural Society – for instance,
on 11 March 1831 the Council ordered that 'a collection of Pine
Apple plants be sent to His Highness the Pasha of Egypt'[16] –
and in 1832 was made a Corresponding Member of the Society.
This meant that he had the privileges of a Fellow, receiving plants and copies of the Society's *Transactions*, but was
expected to supply interesting plants to Chiswick in return.

Traill also corresponded with Nathaniel Bagshaw Ward and
was one of the very earliest recipients of plants shipped in
the new Wardian cases. In April 1835 he wrote to let William

Hooker know that a consignment of plants had arrived, and that 'the plants when removed from the cases did not appear to have suffered in the slightest degree, they were in perfectly fresh and vigorous state and in fact hardly a leaf had been lost during their passage'.[17] Traill encouraged William Hooker, then Regius Professor of Botany at Glasgow University, to promote the cases, as he could clearly see their potential: 'The plan I think decidedly a good one, and ought to be made generally known.'

To ensure a good supply of plant material, Traill entered into a number of reciprocal arrangements with botanists, horticulturists and societies whereby he provided Egyptian plant specimens in return for potential new introductions. As ever, William Hooker made sure he was part of the network. In a letter dated 17 March 1836, Ward told Hooker that 'like other residents in hot countries', Traill would not exert 'more effort than he can help', but that if Hooker would specify the plants he wanted, Ward would certainly write to Traill and seek his help.[18] By 1838 James Traill was able to supply a list of the plants that he had successfully acclimatized in Egyptian conditions, which included 'many highly interesting species as the mango, cocoa nut, black pepper, cinnamon, tea and c.'[19] Other highlights on the long list were 'Guava Psidium pomiferum', which Traill claimed was 'introduced by Mr Briggs many years ago but, having been neglected, no result was obtained till taken up by me in 1831, is now perfectly naturalised, producing fruit abundantly'; and 'Yam Dioscorea aculeata', introduced just a year earlier: 'from five tubers planted last year an average produce of fifteen fold was obtained, successful cultivation indubitable'.

One of the most economically and strategically important introductions was the teak tree, which promised to provide Egypt with a supply of hardwood for its navy and other construction projects. Starting with just 'six plants raised from Indian seeds', Traill was able to create a plantation of more than 300 trees and he proudly reported, 'one has now attained the height of 29 feet 4 inches, being an average growth of 4 feet annually'.[20]

Although the British government and British institutions such as the Horticultural Society applauded and supported Traill's efforts, there was still ambivalence regarding the ambitions of his employers and the implications these ambitions could have for wider British geopolitical interests. Even though the British government had felt compelled to defend the Greek rebels against the Ottoman sultan, during this period the overriding priority was actually to prop up the weak and corrupt Ottoman Empire. The concern was that if the Ottoman Empire broke up, other great powers would step in to assert their influence in the area and would interfere with British commercial interests and even threaten the precious land and sea routes to India.

Mohammed Ali, although supposedly a subject of the Ottoman Empire ruling Egypt on the sultan's behalf, was actually ambitious to create an independent dynasty that ruled not only Egypt, but also territory in Syria and other parts of the Middle East. In this context, his modernization programmes could be seen as a threat to British interests, making him strong enough to break away from the Ottoman Empire, triggering a 'free-for-all' in the Middle East. Britain needed to decide whether he was friend or foe. The information the British Foreign Office had at its disposal was so scanty that special investigators were sent out from time to time to supplement regular official sources of intelligence from ambassadors and consuls. They included Dr John Bowring, who was sent to Egypt by Palmerston in 1838 to investigate the commercial potential of that country. He was particularly interested in investigating an alternative sea route to India, via Egypt and the Red Sea, rather than the long sea voyage around the Cape. Bowring became a fan of Mohammed Ali, recommending that Britain should develop friendly relations with an independent Egypt under the *pasha*'s rule rather than suppress his ambitions. In his report, Bowring emphasized the Western 'civilizing' activities, such as horticultural and agricultural developments, and included extensive coverage of Traill and McCulloch's work. He praised Mohammed Ali and Ibrahim Pasha for their willingness to 'incur any expenses for the furtherance of botanical science and for making it instrumental to the general agricultural interests of the country'.[21]

* * *

From his perspective, Mohammed Ali was very keen to court British support. He even paid lip service to curtailing slavery, although there were slave markets in every major town. He lost no opportunity to stress to British travellers how he was a modernizing force, bringing Egypt into line with Western expectations, and a series of highly visible landscaping projects, including the Roda garden, formed a key part of this propaganda effort. To establish his Western-friendly credentials, the style of garden was as important as the content.

Bové was head gardener at Roda for three years and laid out a 'French-style' garden on the north side of the island. James Traill took charge from around 1830 and constructed an explicitly 'English-style' garden. He created an informal landscape complete with serpentine paths, ruined temples, grottoes, lawns, a winding waterway and a Chinese bridge.

Creating and maintaining an English idyll in Cairo was not without its challenges, and Traill must have faced a steep learning curve. His entire horticultural education had been focused on the challenge of growing exotic plants in Britain's temperate but unpredictable climate. In Egypt he faced an entirely different set of challenges to keep the impression of a well-managed 'English-style' garden in a landscape that, left to its own devices, would rapidly return to a desert state. Not least, he had to learn techniques of irrigation that there was no need for in rainy Ireland, or even Chiswick. Conversely, flooding was a danger when the Nile reached its peak. Traill built a wall around the garden to protect it, but occasional inundations were unavoidable.

He had to find imaginative alternative plants that could survive in these tough conditions and still give him the effect of a lush green English garden. This was particularly the case for that backbone of every English garden, the rolling green lawn, where Traill had to think laterally. 'As no green sward will grow here, all the spaces between the plantations are sown with clover and other fodder of a dazzling green.'[22] His success was noted back home. In 1840 the *Gardener's Magazine* reported on the 'great strides' made by Traill and noted: 'Letters between London and Alexandria arrive in from seventeen to nineteen days, and cost about 2s each. We mention these process because we have no doubt some young gardener will be disposed to offer his services to Mr Traill, who from our personal knowledge, we can state to be a most excellent man, much attached to Egypt.'[23]

However, there was one challenge that no amount of horticultural skill could overcome. In January 1835 bubonic plague broke out in Cairo. Most European residents resorted to household quarantine, staying indoors and avoiding contact with the local population as much as they could. Mohammed Ali withdrew to his palace at Shubra, guarded by a garrison of 400 soldiers, with orders to ensure that no one from Cairo or any other plague-ridden regions came close. By April the daily death toll in Cairo topped 700 and the city began to look like a ghost town, with no activity other than the ever more frequent funerals. This must have been a terrifying experience. James Traill wrote to Nathaniel Bagshaw Ward in April to apologize that 'I have not been able to do much for you in the way of plants... the plague which is here raging with frightful violence, having for the present totally put a stop to my excursions.'[24] By the end of the outbreak it was estimated that 75,000 people had died, approximately one third of the city's population.

Fortunately, both William McCulloch and James Traill survived and were able to return to their normal routine. The garden at Roda rapidly became part of the itinerary for all visitors to Cairo and, as a result, there are many detailed descriptions in travellers' journals, which give a good impression of its features. Military man Albert Hervey visited the garden in 1843 on his way back to England for leave, from his station in Madras. He recalled:

Our drive terminated at a quay, on the banks of the Nile; where we embarked in a ferry boat and were rowed across to a flight of steps leading to the entrances of the Pasha's botanical garden... It reflects great credit on his taste and, is in my opinion, a very fair specimen of horticultural skill. It is beautifully laid out, and abounds in numerous plants, and trees and vegetables from all parts of the world. It is managed by a Scotchman who, I suppose, is well paid for his trouble. Rhoda Garden is more like one of our own country than Shoobrah; the walks and beds, and box-wood hedges, nicely cut and trimmed, fruit nailed to the walls, the seats under the trees, all reminded us of England.

Hervey was particularly impressed by the grotto:

constructed by the head gardener himself. We visited it and were highly gratified by the tasteful way in which it was built and the manner the shells were arranged. The Pasha is very proud of his grotto; and moreover very jealous lest visitors should damage it by way of carrying away shells, or writing their names on the stones and co., extraordinary propensities, inherent, I believe, only in Englishmen![25]

Ibrahim Pasha had reason to be worried; English tourists frequently chipped away parts of the Pyramids and other ancient ruins to take home as souvenirs.

Not everyone approved of the 'Englishness' of the garden. The aristocratic landscape designer Prince Hermann von Pückler-Muskau wrote of his visit in 1837, 'This delightful wooded island has unfortunately been lately much spoiled by the unhappy idea of laying out what is called an English garden or park.' He laid the responsibility for this firmly at the door of James Traill, whom he described as 'an ignorant man, a true John Bull gardener, such as there are even now too many in England', who had 'accumulated the most tasteless absurdities at an enormous expense'. The meandering stream was dismissed as a 'small canal', which 'winds its tortuous course throughout the whole park, full of filthy mud, like a disgusting reptile, and terminates at length in a certain piece of furniture, which cleanly persons use at their morning and evening toilette'. As if referring to the Scottish James Traill as an Englishman were not hurtful enough, the prince called him an 'insular block-head' and was particularly disparaging about Traill's precious grotto: 'Among these absurdities I include a ridiculous building, in the style of genuine English nonsense architecture, where all kinds of styles are mingled together.'[26] The prince was a firm proponent of formal continental-style gardens and clearly had no time for the more informal and picturesque style of garden that James Traill had created.

Social reformer and novelist Harriet Martineau visited in 1846 and commented, 'It was painful to see the attempt at making an English garden of an arid plot, where it seemed as if all the plants had quarrelled and were trying how far apart they could keep.'[27] It seems, from this description, that Traill was simply working in accordance with the version of best horticultural practice expounded by John Claudius Loudon and virtually every other garden-design expert of the time. According to Loudon, the gardenesque style involved 'the distinctness in the separate parts when closely examined', so that individual specimen plants could 'arrive at perfection'.[28]

The critics were in a minority. Most visitors were delighted by the relaxing green shade and reminder of home that the garden provided in the midst of the noisy, crowded hustle and bustle of Cairo. Sir John Gardner Wilkinson reported that 'the inundations of 1840 and 1841 destroyed some thousand trees, mostly of India and other foreign countries'. However, by the time he was writing (in 1843) he could report that the garden at Roda was 'still in a very flourishing state'.[29]

It seems that by 1844 James Traill was also given charge of Mohammed Ali's garden at Shubra. This was already laid out in a formal 'Turkish' style, with straight pathways radiating from kiosks and arbours filled with jasmine. The grounds also featured an extensive orchard, which – in addition to growing traditional fruits like dates – housed 'exotic' apple and pear trees imported from England. By this time Traill was on his own. Bové left Egypt in December 1832; and in 1840, whilst in India on a plant-collecting trip for Ibrahim Pasha, William McCulloch was offered the post of Superintendent of the Government Botanic Gardens at Dapuri at a salary of 400 rupees a month. However, the local administrators who offered him the post seem to have overstepped the mark, because the London-based Court of Directors had ruled that there was to be no further expenditure on the garden and the decision was overruled. In September 1840 McCulloch seems to have landed an alternative post, at least for a time, taking charge of the Bombay Agri-Horticultural Society's garden. The only lead we have for this mobile gardener is a letter that Traill wrote to Dr Charles Lush in June 1840, explaining that 'McCulloch has left us some time ago' and 'was looking Cinnamonwards',[30] which probably meant that he had decided to try his luck on the

cinnamon plantations of Ceylon (now known as Sri Lanka).
McCulloch may have been tempted by the fact that, due to
the decline of the cinnamon trade, the government was offering plantations for sale at cheap prices. However, there are
no records of his arrival, and his fate after September 1840 is
unknown.

In contrast, James Traill was well settled in Cairo. By all
accounts he was very well paid and enjoyed a comfortable lifestyle. We have a picture of his accommodation from a Miss
Platt and her stepfather, Reverend Tatten, who stayed on Roda
in 1836, enjoying the song of the nightingale and the views:
'The scene is particularly attractive at sunset: standing on
the Western bank, on your right-hand are spread out beds of
blooming flowers, of rich and varied hue, emitting the most
delicious odour, from thousands of roses, myrtles, geraniums
and jessamines, blended with the fragrant scent of acacia and
orange trees.'[31] Commanding a view of the Nile, Old Cairo,
the Palace of Shubra and, in the distance, the Pyramids, it
does sound lovely. Visitors who admired James Traill's house
included a Scottish doctor who claimed that 'If anything could
tempt me to enter the service of a Turk, it would be such a
situation as that of Mr Trail [sic].'[32]

He was a figure of some standing in the European society of
Cairo, with a large staff at his command. Writer John Kinnear
described how 'upwards of two hundred are employed. They
are lodged, clothed and fed and taught to read and are allowed
a dollar a month; and their clean dress and healthy cheerful
occupation form a very agreeable contrast to the poverty and
squalor of the common labouring Arabs.'[33] Traill mixed with
a small but informal group of mostly British Egyptologists

who worked together, frequently exchanging information and material. Most adopted Eastern manners and dress, but it does not seem that Traill did likewise, as none of the European travellers who visited him in the garden make mention of native costume.

The most famous Egyptologist of all, Edward William Lane, identified Traill as a useful source of knowledge. In 1841 Lane planned to travel to Egypt to work on a massive research project to produce the definitive Arabic Lexicon. Where special technical knowledge and language was involved, he intended to split the work into 'departments' and employ relevant experts to assist him. Writing to the project sponsor, Lord Prudhoe, Lane explained, 'Mr Trail [*sic*] (to whom the plan has not been mentioned) will, I am told, be very glad to undertake the department of Botany, and with the assistance of a sheyk for the orthography of the words, will give (what is much wanted) a perfect Flora Arabica, as far as Egypt is concerned.'[34] This plan did not materialize, although when Lane arrived in Cairo in July 1842, James Traill became a regular visitor to Lane's lodgings, and Lane's sister and her children would visit the Roda garden to relax and play. Apparently, Traill's land-surveying skills (part of the essential toolkit of all head gardeners) were called into service by Lane to help him measure the pyramids. This will have been a physically taxing undertaking. When the famous French author Gustave Flaubert visited in 1849, he described the effort in scaling Pyramid blocks that were each chest-high, and the hardship in camping amongst the multitude of fleas, from which not even a sandstorm offered relief, surrounded by the human bones and bits of mummy cloth that littered the area.[35] Despite these hardships, Lane was quite satisfied with the results and reported, 'Traill is a very accurate man, and appears to have taken all desirable pains in this case.'[36]

James Traill was also well respected abroad. In 1838 he was accepted as a foreign member of the Horticultural Society of London, which was quite an honour, as Society by-laws limited the number of foreign members to twenty and the Society declared that 'great pains have been taken in the selection of those on whom this title is conferred'.[37] Traill was also made a Corresponding Member of the Botanical Society of Regensburg and an honorary member of the Agricultural and Horticultural Society of Bombay.

However, his good fortune wasn't to last, and in 1848 he endured a double disaster. There was another high flood, which inflicted an enormous amount of damage to the Roda garden, and Ibrahim Pasha died. His father, Mohammed Ali, was in very poor health and only survived his son for another year. He was succeeded by his grandson, Abbas Pasha, who turned his back on many of the modernizing drives of his grandfather and uncle. Faced with insurmountable debts and of a far less energetic nature than his forebears, the new ruler left the Roda garden to decline. Engravings made in 1849 by August Loffler show that it was left uncared for and overgrown. Today nothing remains of this remarkable garden – a little piece of England in the middle of the Nile.

Shubra fared little better. After Mohammed Ali's death the palace and gardens were given to his son, Abd El Halim Pasha. Some parts of the garden were destroyed in 1930 during construction of a road from Cairo to Alexandria; and in 1952, after the revolution, the grounds were given to the Ain Shams

University Faculty of Agriculture and were used as a farm and agricultural research station. Many original features were lost, but in 1978 a restoration project was launched and in 2007 it became a public park.

It seems that after Ibrahim Pasha's death in 1848, Traill went on to work for Soliman Pasha, alias Joseph Anthelme Sève, a French-born Egyptian commander who had been employed by Mohammed Ali to build a European-style army. However, by 1850, at the age of just forty-nine, Traill had retired from gardening, taking advantage of the generous pension built up under Mohammed Ali's scheme, whereby all employees were obliged to submit a day's pay each month to a central pension fund.

It does not seem that James Traill was ever tempted to return to Britain, and until his death in 1853 he remained 'much attached to Egypt', where he was a relatively wealthy man, enjoying a much higher social standing than he would have had in England. Perhaps he was of the same opinion as that other Scotsman-turned-Egyptian citizen, Osman Effendi, né William Thomson, who – when asked why he did not return home – always replied, 'In Scotland I shall be a poor man: and here, I am a gentleman.'[38]

CHAPTER SIX

'Young foreigners of respectability':
Trainees from Abroad

*Carl [sic] Rauch admitted 26 September 1825 upon
the recommendation of Joseph Sabine Esquire*

*James Arthur Floy admitted 31 January 1826
upon the recommendation of Joseph Sabine*

*Ludwig Sckell admitted 21 April 1826 upon the
recommendation of Joseph Sabine Esq.*

*Jens Peter Petersen admitted 13 June 1826 upon
the recommendation of William Atkinson Esq.*

*James George Watson admitted 23 July 1828
upon the recommendation of Dr N. Wallick*

THE MOVEMENT IN SKILLED GARDENERS BETWEEN
Britain and abroad was far from being one-way traffic. In its
report on the progress of the Chiswick Garden published
in March 1826, the Garden Committee proudly declared
that 'Several instances have occurred of young foreigners of
respectability being sent to the Garden for purpose of receiving an Horticultural education.'[1] In fact, within a few weeks
of the report's publication the committee decided it would be
best if no more than three foreigners were enrolled as labourers in the Garden at any one time, presumably to ensure that

the focus remained on improving the standard of horticultural training for British gardeners. As was its tendency, the committee pretty much immediately ignored its own rules, admitting a fourth foreign gardener in Jens Peter Petersen from Denmark in June 1826, even though there were already three foreign gardeners in place: James Arthur Floy from New York, Karl Rauch from Vienna and Ludwig Sckell from Bavaria.

Three of these four foreign trainees were what were known as 'court gardeners' – in other words, the employees of European royalty responsible for caring for the royal gardens associated with palaces or castles. Court gardeners had a tendency to form 'dynasties'; for instance, Ludwig Sckell was from a line that stretched back to his great-grandfather, Johan Georg Wilhelm Sckell, a court gardener in Brandenburg in the late 1600s. These royal gardeners were already a special class of horticulturist, with expectations of a higher quality of training. The court gardener combined, in an ideal case, all the skills of a gardener with those of a botanist and a landscape architect.

Travel and travel reports had played an important role in the education and training of court gardeners since the early eighteenth century, and the different parks and gardens they visited served as models across Europe. As part of their development, court gardeners were expected to visit, work in and observe practices at key gardens and then produce reports on their findings. These reports included precise accounts of the gardens they visited, covering everything from standards of care and horticultural techniques, to the quality of education and the discipline of the staff, and were one of the main ways that new styles and practices spread across borders. For instance, Ludwig Sckell's father was the famous Friedrich

Ludwig Sckell, who is often credited with being responsible for the introduction of the English landscape style to Germany. From 1773 to 1776 he worked in England and encountered the landscaped parks of Capability Brown, Sir William Chambers and William Kent. As superintendent of the Bavarian royal gardens, Friedrich Ludwig Sckell transformed the geometrical French gardens at Nymphenburg into a landscape garden in the English style and he was also an advisor for the creation and extension of the English Garden in Munich.

Chiswick appeared to slot into this international network of gardens remarkably quickly. Karl Rauch's superiors in Vienna thought he would benefit from working at the Horticultural Society's Garden in September 1825, even though serious work on the formation of the Garden had only begun less than two years earlier. Unfortunately, it has not been possible to track down any reports on Chiswick written by Karl Rauch, Ludwig Sckell or Jens Petersen. They were clearly men of high ability and considerable experience and it would be fascinating to read their impressions of the Chiswick Garden and the quality of training it offered. In Denmark it was customary for gardeners to have to sit a formal examination at the end of their apprenticeship (something the Horticultural Society did not consider until 1836). Jens Petersen wrote of the benefits of the scheme in the *Gardener's Magazine*, but concluded 'I do not think that such a plan would answer in a country like England, where the principle of liberty is the foundation of your institutions.'[2] It seems that on one level he was right, because the Horticultural Society struggled throughout the nineteenth century to arrive at a viable examination system that satisfactorily combined the practical and theoretical aspects of horticulture. The Horticultural Society also seemed to struggle with foreign names – the Garden Committee rechristened Ludwig Sckell 'Lewis Skell', and Karl Rauch became 'Charles Rauch'. However, it does seem that the three court gardeners found their experiences at Chiswick valuable, as they all made an effort to stay in touch with the Horticultural Society and British horticultural circles after they returned home.

After just under a year spent in the Chiswick Garden, Karl Rauch returned to Vienna in August 1826 and was given 'a collection of strawberries and seeds' from the Chiswick Garden to take back with him.[3] He established himself as court gardener to the Emperor of Austria at the royal gardens of Laxenburg, the court's summer residence just outside Vienna. From there he kept in touch with the British horticultural world, collecting contributions in 1835 for the memorial to the recently deceased plant collector David Douglas and sharing his knowledge of the benefits of double glazing via the pages of the *Gardener's Magazine*.[4] The influence of Chiswick's fruit collection was seen in Rauch's work in the imperial fruit gardens at Rennweg in Vienna. In 1836 Loudon reported:

All the best fruits of Britain have been introduced into the Imperial gardens about Vienna by M. Karl Rauch, who spent several years in England, chiefly in the garden at the Horticultural Society and at Kew; so that very few German gardeners know better what the gardens about London possessed, that was not to be found in the gardens of Vienna.[5]

If John Claudius Loudon is to be believed, the impact of Jens Petersen's stay in England was even more profound.

Petersen had first come to the journalist's attention in 1824 while he was at Lee's Nursery in London, where he worked for fifteen months immediately before starting at Chiswick. He wrote a long and articulate article for the *Gardener's Magazine* on the state of gardening in Denmark, which moved Loudon to write: 'the above paper, written in English by a foreign gardener lad, who has not been 18 months in England, is a proof of what may be done by a desire to excel and by persevering in the means'.[6] In 1837, ten years after Petersen returned to take up the post of gardener to the King of Denmark, Loudon noted the enormous strides that had been taken in progressing the state of horticulture in that country:

> When Mr Petersen returned to Denmark in the year 1827, gardening was in such a backward state, that an inhabitant of Britain now hardly credits the facts... tart rhubarb was not known there as a culinary vegetable... mushroom and sea kale were not at all cultivated; most of the New Holland plants were unknown, even in the botanic gardens and that the only new North American annual grown there at the time was the *Calliopsis tinctoria*. Such was the state of gardening in 1827.

Thankfully this shocking state of affairs had not persisted: 'In the course of 10 years, things have entirely changed. Every culinary vegetable grown in English gardens is now produced in the royal kitchen garden at Copenhagen' and 'almost all the herbaceous plants, annuals and perennials sent home by Douglas have been introduced'. Furthermore, progress was spreading beyond the royal gardens and new plants were being introduced into 'public nurseries' and 'the gardens of merchants'. Loudon attributed this improvement to just one man:

> All of this has been effected through the agency of M. Petersen, than whom we do not know a single individual in any country who (without the advantages of birth, rank, or fortune, and simply on account of his holding a public situation, and being a lover of his country and enthusiastically attached to gardening) has effected so very remarkable a change in so short a time.[7]

As impressed as Loudon was by the personal qualities of Petersen and Karl Rauch (whom he referred to as 'a young man of great talent and industry'[8]), he was under no doubt that the secret to their success was the opportunity they had to extend their horizons by travelling and working in gardens in different countries. In his *Encyclopaedia of Gardening* he wrote, 'It is only by travelling extensively in this manner that a gardener can know the precise state of his own garden, and become enabled to supply its deficiencies.'[9]

However, this was not something the Horticultural Society ever considered for its trainees; although Robert Thompson was offered the opportunity to travel to the continent to study foreign fruit collections, it was only after he was put in charge of the Society's own fruit collections. The only other Chiswick gardener to be given the opportunity to study gardens abroad was, of course, that exception to every rule, Joseph Paxton. The Duke of Devonshire brought Paxton along with him on several foreign journeys. In September 1839 he took Paxton on a nine-month-long tour of Europe and the Near

East, visiting France, Switzerland, Italy, Malta, Greece and Turkey. On this trip Paxton learnt Italian and soaked up an enormous amount of cultural and artistic knowledge, all of which cannot have failed to enrich his capabilities as a garden designer and architect. Although his patron was not a royal one, in many respects Paxton exemplified the court-gardener ideal.

* * *

New Yorker James Arthur Floy was the odd one out in the original intake of foreign gardeners. He was obviously not a court gardener, but he was the son of an eminent horticulturist. His father was Michael Floy, Corresponding Member of the Horticultural Society and owner of one of the most important nurseries in North America. Michael Floy owned a nursery on the corner of Broadway and 12th Street, New York, and another nursery ground in Harlem. He specialized in camellias; indeed, he was reputed to have been the first to have planted a camellia seed in North America in 1809. Over the course of his career, he bred and named forty-two varieties of camellia and provided the Horticultural Society with many interesting plants and seeds. He became a wealthy man and was elected vice-president of the New York Horticultural Society in 1829.

Upon his return to America in 1827, after just under a year at Chiswick, James Arthur Floy also made his mark, but not in horticulture. The whole family was gripped by religious fervour, being swept up in the 'Second Great Awakening'. This was a Protestant religious revival during the early nineteenth century in the United States. Revivalist preachers enrolled millions of new members in existing evangelical denominations such as the Wesleyan Methodists. Many converts believed that the Awakening heralded a new millennial age, which would remedy the evils of society before the anticipated Second Coming of Christ. James Arthur Floy's brother, Michael, recorded in his diary being 'born again' at a prayer meeting in New York in 1828. It is not certain whether James Floy was converted at the same time, but by 1835 he had gone one further, because he had abandoned the family nursery business to become a Methodist preacher. Later in life he recalled, 'I had an impression on my mind from my childhood that I should be a preacher.'[10]

His decision to become a preacher meant that his father's nursery business died with him in 1854 (James' brother Michael having already died at the young age of twenty-eight). However, horticulture's loss was society's gain. James was credited as being 'among the earliest and most able anti-slavery men of the Methodist Church'.[11] Incredibly, although Wesley himself had been an ardent anti-slavery campaigner, many Methodist preachers in the southern states of America had come to an accommodation with slavery, in order not to alienate the white farming and slave-owning communities they hoped to evangelize. James Arthur Floy condemned the failure of parts of the Methodist Church to speak out against slavery and declare the practice a sin. He was suspended from the New York Methodist Conference, and after his death it was recalled that 'He had to walk for a long time in the presence of social and Church ostracism on account of his identification with anti-slavery... and it was in conflict with such trials that he hardened his mental and moral muscle for his masterly ministry against oppression.'[12] He sounds a formidable man. The same article, presumably written by someone who knew him, recalled:

> In addition to all this power of leadership, there was a certain magic attractiveness in his personal friendships that held his friends with hooks of steel. There was a kind of hauteur about his bearing toward indifferent persons and a sharpness toward a troublesome opponent that changed to tenderness and even affection toward his friends.

By the time of James' death in 1863, his views had prevailed and mainstream Methodism was firmly on the side of abolition; in fact many Wesleyan churches were key staging posts on the 'underground railway', the clandestine network of anti-slavery campaigners that helped escaped slaves flee to safety in Canada.

* * *

The foreign-born gardener who is in many ways the most intriguing came from a very different background from that of the gardening aristocracy that nurtured James Arthur Floy and the court gardeners. In fact James George Watson's statement reveals an early life that was very different from that of all his contemporaries in the Chiswick Garden. In every way he was a product of the expansion and operation of British imperial and commercial interests in India.

His father came to India as a soldier in a very special army. In its early days the British East India Company was granted powers by the government to keep a private army and establish fortified bases under its own overseas governors in order to protect its trading activities. James Watson's father served as a quartermaster sergeant in the Ramgarh Battalion of this company army, named after the local rulers of the area in which it was stationed.

Appropriately enough for James Watson's future career, the name of the town he was born in, Harareebaugh (today spelled Hazaribagh) in the province of Jharkhand, derives from two Persian words: *Hazar* meaning 'one thousand' and *bagh* meaning 'garden', so the 'city of a thousand gardens'. Quartermasters were in charge of provisioning troops, and this was a position of responsibility. However, a quartermaster sergeant was a non-commissioned officer – in other words, Watson's father had worked his way up through the ranks. During this period he would probably not have had the status or income to bring a wife and family out to India with him. James George Watson's mother was most probably a local Indian woman, and later in his career James was described as Anglo-Indian, the usual description for people of mixed European and South Asian parentage. At around the time James George Watson was born, around one in four of the wills written by British men based in India made provision for their possessions to be left to Indian wives and Eurasian children. There is no record of his mother's name and we can only guess at the nature of the relationship. It is possible she came from a local orphanage, as it was common practice for orphanages to offer their female inmates as brides to men who were willing to marry them and pay for their upkeep. There are many instances in the late eighteenth and early nineteenth centuries of British men forming long-standing, equitable and loving relationships with Asian women. However, in common with all the gardeners in the Handwriting Book, James George Watson makes no mention of his mother in his early life story, so we have no way of tracking her down to find out more.

It does appear, though, that James was fortunate in that his father was clearly involved in his upbringing, as James was with his father until the age of fourteen, when he entered into his apprenticeship. This was far from a universal experience. The East India Company encouraged soldiers who had children with Asian women to declare these children as 'orphans', to be brought up in Company or missionary-run orphanages. It was felt that it was not desirable for children of mixed race to be brought up in Asian households, but neither was an army barracks a respectable home for a child. It does appear, though, that James was fortunate enough in that his father was clearly involved in his upbringing, as they lived together until James left to take up an apprenticeship at the age of fourteen. Rather than getting his education at the orphan school, it is possible that James Watson was educated at one of the small schools run by chaplains who were attached to British regiments.

His father appears to have had some horticultural skills, because after leaving the army, he took a post on an indigo farm and was then overseer at the H.C. (Honourable Company's) garden at Pusa, in north-east India. This was an estate acquired by the East India Company for growing tobacco, and was later to become the headquarters of the Imperial Agricultural Department of the British Indian government. Indigo farming in India was an enormously important local industry, but one that was a byword for exploitation and misery. The industry was managed on a tiered system: a director in Calcutta would be in charge, and below him would be managers of regional divisions or 'concerns'; below each regional manager would be an assistant manager (and it is probable that James Watson's father was one of these) in charge of subdivisions called 'factories'. This conjures up an image of a large industrial building, but actually indigo factories were clusters of workshops processing indigo dye, and were spread across different villages. At every stage of the process there was hardship and exploitation. Small-scale subsistence farmers were at the mercy of landowners, tax collectors and indigo planters. The peasant farmers paid their taxes and rents by taking advances on indigo crops from European factory managers like James Watson's father. The farmers became embroiled in an endless cycle of debt, forced to accept low prices for their indigo crops and to devote more and more of their land to growing *Indigofera tinctoria* rather than growing food to feed their families. Conditions in these workshops were also unappealing, to say the least. Indigo leaves were fermented in large vats and workers had to stand waist-deep in the foul-smelling liquid for hours at a time, stirring and beating it until a precipitate formed, which could be extracted and dried. Travelling between these small workshops on tours of inspection with his father, James would have seen the huge gulf in experience and life opportunities that existed between one side of his heritage and the other.

At the age of just fourteen, James Watson was sent hundreds of miles away to begin an apprenticeship in the Calcutta Botanic Garden. Sir Joseph Banks had urged the East India Company to set up such gardens in order to investigate the potential of India's flora for improved crops and medicines. The Calcutta Botanic Garden was established in 1786, and by the time James served his apprenticeship there, it was the largest and most scientifically organized garden in Asia. Donations of plants and money poured in from the UK and East India Company stations. James joined a workforce of about one hundred, tasked with looking after four nurseries, a kitchen garden, an orchard, a farm and of course a botanic garden, laid out in Linnaean order. The labourers were native Indians, whilst the higher, more technical posts in the garden were filled by white Europeans or mixed-race Eurasians like James.

Again, as in the barracks at Hazaribagh, James will have been acutely aware of his status in the middle of a highly stratified and racist society. He was unlucky to grow up at a time when attitudes to people of mixed-race parentage were worsening in India. As transport links improved, British wives, tradesmen and missionaries began arriving in larger numbers. They rarely integrated into local life, but instead brought their social customs and mores with them, leading to a hardening of boundaries between British and Asian communities. These boundaries were reinforced by racist attitudes, and Anglo-Indians like James Watson were often seen as an unwelcome reminder of an earlier degree of fraternization and integration that was now regarded as totally unacceptable. However, Calcutta was a relatively open and relaxed society, certainly compared to Madras and Delhi. Captain Albert Hervey of the 40th Regiment of Madras Infantry wrote a book aimed at advising young officers about to be posted to India, based on his experiences in the 1830s, and noted of the Anglo-Indian community in Calcutta that 'they are admitted into society and officers very frequently marry their daughters'.[13]

However, James Watson was not destined to stay in Calcutta. Instead he was to travel thousands of miles to London, accompanying the superintendent of the Calcutta Botanic Garden, Nathaniel Wallich, who had an exciting back-story. Born Nathanial Wulff Wallich in 1786 in Copenhagen, he was the son of a Jewish merchant who qualified as a surgeon and trained as a botanist before he joined the Danish settlement at Serampore, near Calcutta. He became a British prisoner of war when the British annexed Serampore in 1808. However, he was released in 1809 when William Roxburgh, superintendent of the Royal Botanic Garden, Calcutta, requested that Wallich be allowed to enter the Company's service as his assistant. Wallich succeeded Roxburgh as superintendent in 1815. Like James Watson, Nathaniel Wallich, with his Danish origin and Jewish faith, was an outsider to the dominant culture of the British community in Calcutta. He made efforts to assimilate, converting to Christianity and marrying an Englishwoman, Sophia Collings, in 1815 and even going so far as to become a Freemason. He was a consummate field botanist, an enthusiastic collector and describer of plants, distributing specimens to the chief gardens and herbaria in Europe and North America. Although he was clearly talented, contemporary accounts describe him as a harsh and hot-tempered man. However, it is unlikely that James George Watson would have seen much of the eminent Mr Wallich in the garden whilst he learnt the nuts and bolts of horticulture as a humble apprentice.

Despite his prolific workload, Wallich appears to have been a sickly man and had to take extended periods of sick-leave away from the demanding climate of Calcutta. In between bouts of sick-leave, Wallich also undertook lengthy botanical expeditions to Singapore and Nepal. By 1827 a combination of the need to recuperate in a milder climate and the desire to write up and publicize his findings at the heart of the horticultural world drew Wallich to plan an extended trip to London. He asked permission from the Court of Governors of the East India Company to visit England 'for the joint purpose of establishing my health and of publishing... without any charge upon the Honourable Company'. He explained that in order to publish 'the manuscript accounts of several thousand plants, made principally during my several journeys' he needed access to 'the Literary advantages which abound in Europe'. He was also anxious to make contact again with the 'yearly accelerated march of science from which I have been distanced by an absence from Europe of 20 years'.[14]

Nathaniel Wallich asked the East India Company for permission to 'take an assistant and one of the apprentices attached to the institution' and the nineteen-year-old James Watson was the apprentice he chose. We do not know whether this was based on any particular merit demonstrated by James, or simply because Wallich needed a pair of hands to assist him on the voyage and an apprentice could be most easily spared from the garden. Wallich brought with him his entire herbarium packed up in thirty cases, together with chest after chest of living plants and packages of seeds. Altogether the ship's precious cargo encompassed more than 8,000 species that had been painstakingly collected by Wallich and an army of other plant collectors. There can be little doubt that James Watson was kept very busy on the six-month-long journey, carefully monitoring the condition of the herbarium specimens against water damage or the many pests that accompanied any voyage on a wooden ship. As a trained member of the garden staff, he will also have had responsibility for the arduous task of trying to keep the living plants healthy. This was before the adoption of the Wardian case, where, once sealed away, plants could be left to their own devices.

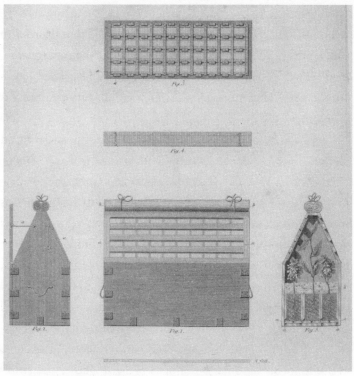

Plant-moving boxes of the type that Watson had to attend to on the long sea journey from Calcutta to London.

Wallich wrote a paper for the Horticultural Society that gives some idea of the regime Watson had to follow: 'In the treatment on board, too much attention cannot be given to the necessity of exposing the plants to the open air at all times

when the weather will admit of it.'[15] This involved going up
on deck and opening the lids of the chests that contained the
plants as the sun set, then getting up at dawn the next morning to close them. However, he also had to pay 'particular
attention to closing the roof if bad weather should come in',
so he was apt to be woken in the night to tend to the plants if a
storm came on. In addition, he had to keep the plants watered,
sprinkling half a pint of water on each plant before they were
shut up in the morning and another half-pint when they were
opened to the elements in the evening. The stakes were high.
This was Wallich's moment to establish his name in the annals
of science.

Upon arrival in London in 1828, Wallich set himself up in
a house provided by the East India Company on Frith Street.
Once they had settled, it is likely that he hardly gave James
Watson a second thought, as he was enormously busy. During
his stay Wallich was to distribute approximately 250,000 specimens to sixty-six individuals and institutions. This was a very
deliberate act of generosity. In return for these gifts, the botanical community collaborated in the enormous task of sorting
and labelling specimens. Herbarium specimens mounted up at
such a rate that whole teams of botanists frequently took years
to sort through a collection. By the following year Wallich was
able to publish the first instalment of his monumental book
Plantae Asiaticae Rariores.

Meanwhile, James Watson was dispatched straight to
Chiswick. The phrase he used in his entry in the Handwriting
Book – that 'Mr Wallick [*sic*] brought me for my improvement
in the different branches of Horticulture' – suggests that he
was taken to London not just to fetch and carry, but also as an

educational opportunity. It is hard to imagine what an overwhelming change this must have been. Despite its white stucco houses, opera house and cricket pitches, Calcutta was decidedly different from Chiswick. Everything from the climate and the food to the daily routine must have seemed strange.

After fifteen months at Chiswick, the Garden Committee noted that on 23 November 1829 'James George Watson left the Garden at the request of Dr Wallich with permission to return in the Spring.'[16] It seems likely that he was needed to help Wallich with the sorting and distribution of plant and herbarium specimens in the Frith Street house. This work must have added greatly to James' botanical knowledge and, taken together with the horticultural training he received in the Chiswick Garden, gave him a special skill-set that had the potential to improve his prospects in the face of widespread discrimination.

* * *

Coincidentally, at the same time that James Watson was working alongside Nathaniel Wallich in Frith Street, there was another Anglo-Indian visitor to London determined to reveal just how serious this discrimination was. John William Ricketts was sent from Calcutta to London in 1830 to give evidence on behalf of the community to a House of Lords inquiry into the affairs of the East India Company. He appeared before the committee on 31 March 1830, bearing a petition signed by more than 600 people. The petition complained that Anglo-Indians were not recognized as British subjects if residing in the Mofussil (the regions of India outside the three East India Company capitals of Bombay, Calcutta and Madras). This meant that they had to resort to Mofussil courts that were governed by Islamic law, which they felt was incompatible with their status as Christians. They could not hold commissions in the army, and from 1793 the Asian widows and children of British soldiers were denied the right to a military pension. As Ricketts declared in his evidence, 'We are sometimes recognised as Europeans, and sometimes as natives, as it serves the Purposes of the Government, there is no precise Character affixed to us in that respect.'

Another complaint related very directly to James Watson's situation, and it is hard not to wonder whether he followed the proceedings of the committee in the London press with special interest. Ricketts' complaint was that Anglo-Indians who had come to England for education and then applied for permission to return to their native country had been allowed to do so, but under a Penalty Bond, which meant that they should not enter into the service of any native state. They were effectively restricted to working for the East India Company. Ricketts complained:

> Many of my Countrymen have been educated in England, Scotland and Ireland but on going back to India they have been so much disappointed by the State of Things that they have in many instances returned to Europe to seek a Livelihood, finding that the Door was completely shut against them in their own Native Country.

Asked if they were excluded from British society, he responded: 'Not altogether excluded; but they have soon been able to feel the Public Pulse on the Subject and they could not brook anything of that kind and they would therefore much rather return to Europe than drag out an uncomfortable existence like that in India.' And he concluded his evidence: 'It is a Thing for which the Natives themselves cannot account, that the Government should reject, as it does, their own Christian Offspring, and threaten them with marked Neglect and Proscription.'[17]

There is no record to show if James Watson ever went back to Chiswick, as mentioned in the Garden Committee minute. In 1832 Wallich returned to India, sailing on HMS *Exmouth* to Calcutta. It is probable that Watson left with him, because we know that in 1832 he took up a new post in Sri Lanka (then known as Ceylon). He was appointed to the post of superintendent of the Peradeniya Botanic Gardens. According to John Lindley, Watson was appointed on 'the recommendation of those who had known him in Hindoostan',[18] which must mean Wallich.

Today, Peradeniya is acknowledged as one of the most beautiful and significant botanic gardens in the world. It was established in the heart of the island of Ceylon in the hill country of the Kandy Kingdom in 1821, following earlier false sites in two other locations. The site was 1,550 feet (470 metres) above sea level, on the horseshoe bend of a river just four miles from the town of Kandy. The availability of water and trees to provide shade made it a promising place to grow tender exotics. The garden was established by its first superintendent, Alexander Moon, who cleared the ground, established a cinnamon plantation and then gradually began to introduce plants from Calcutta. Moon botanized and started a herbarium and in 1824 wrote a bilingual catalogue of indigenous and exotic plants growing in Ceylon (a copy of which is in the Lindley

Library) and began to correspond with Kew. There were high hopes for the garden. As one European visitor wrote:

> Nothing about Columbo is more apt to excite admiration than the flourishing state of the vegetable world. So much beauty and variety are in few countries equalled and nowhere excelled. The thick shade of majestic trees, the open prospects, the lively verdure, the flowering shrubs and parasitic creepers, unite their charms to render the morning ride delightful.[19]

Peradeniya had the potential to be an invaluable addition to the extensive network of botanic gardens that was being established to serve imperial economic development and expansion. Sir Joseph Banks had been the main proponent of this system, proposing a worldwide network of gardens, with the Royal Gardens of Kew at the centre, undertaking scientific studies of local flora, acting as sources of seeds and plants and as testing grounds for acclimatizing and propagating useful plants, which could enhance the production of crops for the colonies and the mother country.

To be given charge of a botanic garden spreading over 140 acres (fifty-six hectares) at the age of just twenty-three was an enormous responsibility. However, there were distinct signs that life at Peradeniya would be far from an easy posting for James Watson. For one thing, his predecessors as superintendent had all died in post, succumbing to tropical illness. Moon had died in 1825 and was succeeded by another gardener with Chiswick associations, James McRae, who had acted as one of the Society's plant collectors, gathering plants in the Hawaiian islands and South America. He too died after just three years in post at Peradeniya in 1830. The garden had not had a permanent head for two years by the time Watson arrived.

He was met by a Singhalese employee of the garden named Harmanis de Alwis, who had been appointed as a 'native writer', or garden clerk, by Alexander Moon. To hold this post, he must have been fluent in English and was probably a Christian. Even though his original mentor had died, de Alwis was still at his post, patiently painting all the plants he came into contact with. At some point Moon discovered that he was a talented artist and paid for him to have lessons, so that he could make accurate scientific illustrations of plants. He also funded de Alwis' trips around the island to collect and paint plants. As a botanically interested and educated individual, with a similar mix of Asian and European influences, it is likely that the two men found they had a lot in common. However, de Alwis continued his plant-collecting forays, often staying for long periods in the remote rainforest, so it is not clear how close the men became. In the course of his career de Alwis painted more than two thousand plants. Most of the collection remained at Peradeniya until 1998, when it was transferred to the National Museum of Sri Lanka.

Unfortunately there is very little record of James Watson's activities at Peradeniya. He was to hold the post of superintendent for six years until his death in 1838, the causes of which are unknown. He sent a number of plants to Wallich and planted a grove of rubber trees, which survived until the early 1900s. However, the assessments that were made of his tenure by botanists shortly after his death were damning. Adjutant-General George Warren Walker was an amateur botanist and resident of Ceylon and sent specimens to William Hooker at Glasgow, sometimes accompanied by his wife's flower sketches. He castigated Watson as 'an ignoramus who could not read the language of botany'.[20] Even John Lindley, who presumably knew that Watson was an alumnus of his Chiswick Garden, cast him as one of a list of inadequate gardeners at Peradeniya who were at least partly to blame for what he saw as the chronic underperformance of the botanic gardens. He dismissed James George Watson as 'a half-caste Indian gardener, who proved entirely unworthy of the recommendation of those who knew him in Hindoostan'.[21]

Yet if we look at James Watson's work in context, these insulting assessments seem entirely unfair. Nathaniel Wallich would not have recommended Watson for the post at Peradeniya – a garden that he would expect, as curator of the Calcutta Botanic Garden, to have extensive dealings with – unless he was confident of Watson's capabilities. He had had far more opportunity to make an assessment of Watson than either John Lindley or George Warren Walker. It is true that the Peradeniya Gardens did not make any significant contribution to botanical science under James Watson. However, this was more likely to be due to the instructions and resources he was given by the officials in charge of the island, rather than to any shortcomings in skill or initiative on his part.

In the 1820s and 1830s there was no great enthusiasm in either the Foreign Office or the Colonial Office to take forward Sir Joseph Banks' vision for a network of botanic gardens. Kew was in the doldrums after the death of Sir Joseph Banks and, without Kew acting as the hub, most botanic gardens became isolated and sank into lethargy, becoming like the private estate gardens of the local governors, producing vegetables for the governor's tables and flowers for the governor's wife. Typical was the Governor of Cape Town, who was lambasted by the local press for being content to use the botanic garden to 'see their horses and cows supplied with green forage, their pigs with acorns, their fires with firewood and their pots and pans with cabbages, carrots, peas, leeks and garlic'.[22] The report that John Lindley and Joseph Paxton wrote, which led to the appointment of William Hooker as director and to the revival of Kew as a Royal Botanic Garden, came just too late for James Watson, being published two years after his death.

Furthermore, the economy of Ceylon was in trouble in the 1830s and there were limited funds to support the work of a serious botanic garden, even if anyone had wanted to. The ending of the government monopoly in cinnamon production in 1833 had hit government revenues hard, and as a result there was pressure to justify the expense of the upkeep of the garden by making it pay its own way. So James Watson was forced to operate the Peradeniya garden as little more than a government vegetable garden, serving the Kandy market. A later report recorded that Watson had had to devote one-third of the labour resources to market-garden activities. He was not equipped with even the most basic tools required to conduct serious botanical research: a herbarium and a library. Alexander Moon's herbarium of more than a thousand species had been removed to the botanic gardens at Madras (now Chennai) in India by its superintendent, Dr Wight, before Watson had taken up his post. When Watson's successor, George Gardner, arrived, he reported that 'It is with sorrow I make the remark that the room which serves as an office for the Clerk as

well as a place to keep specimens and seed is so damp naturally
and so pervious to rain, that nothing can be kept dry in it.' As
a result, the few books that had been collected for the gardens
had been completely ruined. As Gardner explained:

> The difficulty and labour in determining the name of a plant
> that no one has seen is much greater than is generally sup-
> posed. As about 100,000 species of plants are now described
> in books, it requires, beyond the labour a very expensive
> library; that which belongs to the garden is far too limited for
> such a purpose.[23]

In other parts of the Empire there were individuals within
the local administrations who were personally passionate
about horticultural and botanical science, and they ensured
that some semblance of scientific and taxonomic work was
maintained, but this does not appear to have been the case in
Ceylon in the 1830s. Only one plant appears to have been of
any interest to the local civil and military administration of
Ceylon – and that plant was *Coffea*, the coffee plant. The whole
island was gripped with 'coffee fever'. Whilst Watson was in
post, the government was keen to experiment with a variety
of plantation crops and move the island away from small-scale
subsistence agriculture, as practised by local peasant farmers,
and coffee was found to be by far the most successful crop. The
first coffee plantation in the Kandyan hill region was up and
running by the time Watson arrived. Governor Edward Barnes
soon introduced incentives, such as lifting coffee export duties
and exemption from land taxes for coffee growers.

When slavery in the West Indies was abolished in 1833,

coffee production there rapidly went into decline, creating an opening for coffee growers in Ceylon. The civil and military authorities became dominated by the interests of coffee growers, as many officials owned plantations themselves and often acted more in the guise of plantation owners than of government officials. The British government sold land that it had appropriated from the Kandyan kings to coffee growers, while local peasant farmers found it virtually impossible to prove that the land they farmed was not Crown land, and it was therefore subject to expropriation and resale to coffee planters. It was estimated that in the 1830s and 1840s more than 200,000 acres (80,000 hectares) of land was effectively stolen in this way. When new plantation owners faced serious labour shortages, because local farmers were reluctant to leave the smallholdings that their families had farmed for generations, the government encouraged the importation of thousands of Tamil workers from southern India. Despite the formal abolition of slavery across the Empire, the conditions these workers had to endure were little better than those experienced by slaves. But coffee was king, and estate owners were given free rein, with the government reduced to a mere appendage of the coffee estates. In this ruthless atmosphere, the job of the botanic gardens was confined to growing coffee seedlings for the plantations, and other economic crops that offered immediate financial rewards.

In this environment it would have been very difficult for James Watson to make a mark in the field of botanical science. Even John Lindley, as damning as he was of Watson, admitted that the garden had been chronically under-supported. In 1854 he wrote that 'the legislative council should double its staff and place more ample funds at the command of the super-intendent'.[24] Under subsequent directors – men with higher social status, who did not face the stigma that Watson undoubt-edly encountered – the funds were made available to develop Peradeniya as a more conventionally academic botanic garden. When a devastating disease hit the coffee crop in 1847, local administrators finally grasped the potential value of a botanic garden that could conduct research into a wide variety of local and non-native flora. We will never know how James Watson would have fared with a similar degree of backing.

One man who could have cast some light on James' worth as a gardener, having seen him at work at first hand, was Harmanis de Alwis. He lived to the age of 101 and remained employed at the garden as its official artist until 1861. The Lindley Library is lucky enough to have a beautiful collec-tion of drawings by de Alwis of plants from Peradeniya, and a splendid self-portrait. Unfortunately, no word has survived from him on the subject of the management of the garden that he served, so James Watson's reputation remains a clouded one.

CHAPTER SEVEN

*'A little order into chaos':
The Fruit Experts*

*James Barnet admitted 19 January 1824 upon
the recommendation of Patrick Neill Esq.*

*Robert Thompson admitted 21 October 1824 upon
the recommendation of Sir R. Fergusson [sic]*

IN 1824 TWO TWENTY-FIVE-YEAR-OLD GARDENERS
from Scotland joined the Chiswick Garden within nine months
of each other. The road to England was a well-trodden one for
Scottish gardeners. Altogether, thirty-two (just over one-
third) of the gardeners in the Handwriting Book hailed originally from Scotland. This was a very high proportion, given
that Scotland contained only around 14 per cent of the population of Great Britain during the 1820s. George Eliot famously
declared, 'A Gardener is Scotch as a French teacher is Parisian',
and various theories were posited both at the time and later as
to why that might be so. Loudon, a Scot himself, declared that
Scots made good gardeners because 'they are better educated
in their youth and more accustomed to frugality and labour'.[1]
Whether or not this was true, the structure of land ownership
in Scotland – where there were some spectacular large estates
and small householders, with very little in between – meant

that there were far fewer opportunities for employment in Scotland for gardeners than in England, so Scottish horticulturalists tended to travel to find work.

Having made the decision to try their luck at the Chiswick Garden, James Barnet and Robert Thompson were to find their lives taking remarkably similar paths, but to very different destinations. Both men did work that literally shaped the fruit we grow and eat today. However, whilst both were intelligent, talented and dedicated to their craft, one was shy and diffident, the other supremely confident and hot-tempered. Their fortunes were to be dramatically shaped by these differences in temperament.

Their Handwriting Book entries make clear that both James and Robert came to Chiswick with an extremely good horticultural pedigree. James Barnet's entry in particular reads like a *Who's Who* of early nineteenth-century Scottish gardening. His father, Peter Barnet, was a well-respected gardener who had been awarded medals by the newly established Caledonian Horticultural Society for his expertise in growing fruit and tomatoes. However, unlike many gardeners' sons, James was not sent straight into his father's garden at the age of thirteen or fourteen. Instead he remained at school until he was sixteen. After two years at the large estate of Lynedoch in Perthshire, James returned to work with his father at Kennet House, where he received a thorough grounding in the main duties of a gardener, particularly in the kitchen garden, growing fruit and vegetables for Lord Lynedoch's table. In order to broaden his knowledge of ornamental gardening, this was followed by a short stay at Valleyfield near Dunfermline.

At that time Valleyfield was one of the key gardens in

Scotland, being fashionable garden designer Humphry Repton's only work in the country, with ornate terraces between the house and its landscaped park. This was where the celebrated plant hunter David Douglas had learnt to garden. In 1821, now aged twenty-two, Barnet moved again, to the Edinburgh Botanic Garden, where he worked for two years under the esteemed curator and leading light of the Caledonian Horticultural Society, William McNab. McNab was one of the most respected gardeners in the country, and the Botanic Garden was the ideal place to develop a broader knowledge of botanical science. It was while he was at Edinburgh that James Barnet first met another man who was to have a major impact on his life. This was the curator's son, James McNab, another promising gardener who was also being nurtured through the ranks from garden boy to foreman. Whilst William kept his son close at hand, he sent James Barnet to the garden he had managed until 1810, the Royal Gardens at Kew. After a short stint at Kew, Barnet secured a recommendation for a place in the Chiswick Garden from no less a person than Patrick Neill, the secretary of the Caledonian Horticultural Society. This was clearly a bright and well-connected young man who had amassed a wide range of experience in influential gardens and, no less importantly, a network of eminent mentors.

Hailing from the tiny rural village of Echt in Aberdeenshire, Robert Thompson came to Chiswick with a slightly less impressive CV. Although he was at school until the age of eighteen, he appears to have been a part-time student, and school had to fit around working alongside his uncle, a head gardener in a relatively modest garden at Skene. Nevertheless, Thompson still worked at one of the great estates in Scotland,

Haddo House, home of George Hamilton-Gordon, fourth Earl of Aberdeen, the nobleman who gave James Traill his letter of introduction to the president of Bolivia. The Haddo estate was vast, and during the time Thompson worked there, woodland trees were being planted on an epic scale; the plantations at Haddo eventually totalled a mind-boggling eleven million trees. For three years before applying to study at Chiswick, Thompson was a gardener for the wealthy geologist Robert Ferguson, where gardeners had to work around long thermometers plunged into the ground to measure the temperature of the earth.

Once at Chiswick, both men were to focus their attentions on fruit growing – in many ways the most high-profile activity in the garden. When its president, Thomas Andrew Knight, drew up the first objectives of the new Horticultural Society, fruit was front and centre, an area ripe for improvement by the application of new scientific principles and approaches. The aim was to take fruit cultivation out of the dark ages of ignorance, folklore and chance. Knight confidently declared that fruit breeding and cultivation represented 'an ample and unexplored field for future discovery and improvement'.[2]

The formative years of the Horticultural Society also coincided with a period of fresh opportunity for fruit growers. The trade blockades of the Napoleonic Wars had been lifted and new varieties flooded in from France and Holland. The acquisition of the Chiswick Garden gave the Society the opportunity to compile a complete reference collection of living fruit trees. Grafting, pruning and other cultivation techniques could be tested, and trees could be studied to resolve any confusion of identities. At Chiswick they hoped to build nothing less than an international centre for pomological (fruit) research, so that commercial and private growers could be supported to seek out and grow new varieties from reliably named stock. Being employed at Chiswick gave these two bright young Scots the opportunity to work in a field that attracted a great deal of attention, being both scientifically interesting and economically significant.

Robert Thompson in later life, a portrait
printed in *The Gardeners' Chronicle* in 1918.

As the first to arrive, it was James who initially made the fastest progress. He started as an extra labourer in the fruit and kitchen garden, but in April 1824, just three months after arriving, he was promoted to under-gardener of the fruit department. When Robert Thompson joined the Garden in October, he was put to work as a labourer under James' direction. The walls that sheltered the orchard had just been completed, the bulk of the fruit trees had been planted and some of the apples were coming into fruit for the first time. Robert Thompson and James Barnet were to work together in this enclosed world for fourteen months. Whilst no record exists as to how they got on or what they thought of each other, it is reasonable to imagine that it may not have been the easiest of relationships between the two young men. Contemporary accounts describe Robert Thompson as a shy, quiet man, cautious of expressing an opinion even in areas where he had clear expertise. His move to Chiswick was his first trip away from Scotland, and although Chiswick was well outside the smoke and bustle of London, the Garden was still larger and more complex than any he had worked in before. This could not have been in greater contrast to his new master, the high-flyer James Barnet, who had already lived in a capital city and worked in a royal garden. His confidence in his own ability was to be tested when he took over one of the most ambitious projects undertaken by the Society in its early years at Chiswick.

It is hard to believe now, but strawberries as we know them are a relatively modern invention. Small woodland strawberries have been grown for centuries, transplanted from woodlands to our gardens from the Middle Ages onwards. However, though delicious, the fruits were small and it was not a commercially viable crop. This only began to change in the mid-eighteenth century when a French spy named Frézier was sent to Chile in 1712 to report back on fortifications near Concepción. In between noting the position of gun placements and moats, he spotted a large-fruited strawberry plant and, remarkably, had the presence of mind to collect specimens and bring them back to France. This was *Fragaria chiloensis*. The fruit was large but, unfortunately, tasteless. However, by the 1820s crosses had been made between the woodland strawberry (*Fragaria vesca*) and the Chilean strawberry.

English growers were the most enthusiastic breeders of strawberries, and the early years of the nineteenth century saw a proliferation of crosses. What was needed was a reliable system of classifying and comparing these new competing varieties, to identify the best ones to grow for different purposes and conditions. Two years before James Barnet started at Chiswick, the Society had sent out printed forms to 'all who are known to be attentive cultivators of strawberries', asking them to list all the varieties they grew. A total of seventy forms were received, and more than 400 parcels of plants were sent for and planted at Chiswick. James Barnet took over this collection and was tasked with the job of checking for synonyms (where two differently named plants were actually the same variety) and making considered judgements on their different qualities, as a guide for future cultivation and breeding programmes. His work was thorough and his judgements were crisply articulated and well ordered. Growers wishing to develop strawberry crops now had a reliable source of reference to guide them. Throughout the nineteenth century larger, more reliable and heavier-cropping strawberries were developed and it is the descendants of these varieties that we eat today.

As soon as Barnet's work was published, the horticultural world was aware that this was a significant piece of work. *Gardener's Magazine*, the most widely read horticultural publication of the time, wrote a gushing review: 'It would be little or no use to our readers to give the names of all the sorts described; but we shall give Mr Barnet's selection of them, as a guide to those who cultivate (and who does not?) this excellent fruit.' The article noted that James Barnet 'considers Grimstone Scarlet to have the sweetest fruit and The Bestock, whilst being the "greatest bearer" unfortunately is "destitute of flavour"'.[3]

The frequent name-checks in the most widely read horticultural magazine of its day must have been gratifying to Barnet. Normally garden staff were not referred to by name in this fashion, and the Society's achievements were generally attributed to secretary Joseph Sabine or assistant secretary John Lindley. The Horticultural Society's new rising star seemed to be living up to his early promise. The writer (probably the magazine's editor, John Claudius Loudon) was so impressed by Barnet's knowledge that he even tried a *Desert Island Discs*-style request, asking rhetorically, 'Mr Barnet is gone down to Scotland; supposing he had been going to Botany Bay, with permission to take only 3 sorts of strawberries with him, what sorts would he have chosen? We will thank Mr B. for his opinion on this subject for our next Number.'

Unfortunately, 'Mr B' did not reply, so we shall never know his choice. The reference to going to Scotland relates to the fact that by the time the *Gardener's Magazine* covered the strawberry trial, James Barnet had been appointed head gardener of the new Experimental Garden of the Caledonian Horticultural Society (CHS) based in Edinburgh. The CHS had been founded in 1809, just five years after the London Horticultural Society and with a very similar, though Scottish-focused remit and ambition. Things looked set fair for Barnet to make his mark on the horticultural world with control of his own version of the Chiswick Garden in his homeland. The CHS trumpeted the news of its appointment in its journal: 'The Council have engaged as Head Gardener Mr James Barnet, a young man of whose knowledge and zeal they entertain a high opinion.'[4] At the age of just twenty-six, James Barnet was to be in charge of ten acres (four hectares) of land in Inverleith, adjacent to the new site of the Edinburgh Botanic Garden, which was moving from its cramped quarters at Leith Walk. In 1825 plans for the new CHS Garden had been laid out by none other than William McNab, who had trained James. They included orchards, a kitchen garden, an area for growing stocks for grafting, a rose garden and compartments for annuals and perennials. The ambitions and focus were very reminiscent of Chiswick: the trialling, naming and distribution of new plants.

Back at Chiswick, it seemed as if the Society's plans for fruit had received a significant setback. One of the brightest gardeners in the country, working on the Society's most treasured project, had been poached. However, a letter in the archives at the Royal Botanic Garden Edinburgh (where the archives of the CHS are held) reveals an altogether different picture. The letter, dated 15 February 1826, is from Joseph Sabine to William McNab. Whilst Sabine writes that he consents to release Barnet, he adds, ominously:

> I am not without my apprehensions that he may defeat your good intentions towards him, for since he received your letter, and especially during the last three days, his conduct both regards his demeanour to every one of his superiors as well as those accounting for his charges has been such, that

if continued, I shall be obliged to dismiss him suddenly and in disgrace. This arises from his strange untoward temper and want of respect for anyone but himself and which if not reformed forthwith, must ruin him, I still hope however that he may retrieve himself and part from hence with some, though with diminished credit.[5]

It does not seem that James did 'retrieve himself', because the Garden Committee Minutes of 3 April 1826 record the secretary reporting that 'in consequence of the misconduct of James Barnet Under-Gardener in the Orchard, he had found it necessary to dismiss him from the service of the Society'.[6] Unfortunately, Sabine did not feel it necessary to put on record any further justification of his decision. As the Society's assertive secretary, with untrammelled executive control over the Chiswick Garden, Sabine was in the position to be judge, jury and executioner when it came to the discipline and dismissal of garden staff. This means that we will never know exactly what perceived or real offence James Barnet was guilty of, in order to provoke this reaction. In spite of this damning assessment, the Caledonian Horticultural Society confirmed Barnet's appointment. The CHS probably gave more credence to the views of its own member, William McNab, who had personally supervised Barnet for three years, rather than the views of Joseph Sabine. Indeed, a letter in the CHS archives from Barnet to McNab gives no hint of any 'untoward temper' or lack of respect. He writes, 'I cheerfully consent to take advice from you in all cases where difficulties may arise, and that I will always consider respectfully, from one who is superior in years, experience and general information.'[7] Joseph Sabine was known to be prickly and dictatorial, a man highly conscious of social hierarchies and the deference that he felt due to him. Reading the reasonable and respectful tone of James' letter to McNab, it is hard not to conclude that Sabine had simply decided that the attention given to Barnet's strawberry work had gone to his head and he needed taking down a peg.

The initial signs were that the CHS was right to have faith in its decision to choose James Barnet. He cultivated interesting and high-quality specimens that won accolades and prizes. In July 1830 the new garden was sufficiently well established for the CHS to throw its doors open to Edinburgh society with an afternoon promenade, featuring band music, an exhibition of plants submitted for judging and a special fruit-tasting event. A large tent was erected, with staging at each end for the display of exotics, proudly described as 'probably never surpassed in Britain'.[8] There was even a stage set up for an orchestra and dancers next to the pineapple stove, which must have caused Barnet some anxiety. Garden staff wearing smart new aprons were stationed around the garden to act as guides and stewards to more than 400 guests. Although rain cut the festivities short, the Society's secretary, Patrick Neill, was confident that the event had given 'general satisfaction'.

That test over, it was clear that Barnet's duties had built up to a point where he needed an assistant. The Caledonian Horticultural Society had just the man in mind – James McNab, still working in the Botanic Garden next door. He was appointed on a salary of £40 a year. His duties were to act as a clerk to Barnet, dealing with correspondence, attending to members, listing and labelling incoming and outgoing plants, keeping the garden books, taking minutes and, most importantly, chasing up subscription payments. Freed from these administrative burdens, perhaps James Barnet could now hope to have more freedom to return to the experimental work that had made his name? On the other hand, James McNab was suspiciously over-qualified to act as a garden clerk. He had been acting as a foreman in the Botanic Garden next door; from the age of nineteen his botanical drawings had been published in a wide range of respected journals and books. In the circumstances, Barnet could be forgiven for thinking that he had been landed with a rival as much as an assistant.

* * *

After Barnet left for Edinburgh, the Horticultural Society lost no time in promoting Robert Thompson to Barnet's position of under-gardener of the fruit and kitchen garden. His first task was to complete the catalogue of fruit growing in the garden. He began by classifying the cherries, apricots and gooseberries. By careful observation and comparison, he was able to reduce the number of named cultivars of apricots from more than seventy to just seventeen confirmed varieties. Loudon used the pages of the *Gardener's Magazine* to urge all nurserymen to apply only to Chiswick for correctly named grafts of fruit trees, so that they could be sure of what they were growing. He confidently asserted, 'In ten years, it will not be the fault of the Horticultural Society, if there is one bad sort of pear sold in the streets of any town on the island.'[9]

Over the course of four years the fruit collection under Robert Thompson's care grew richer, with additions from plant hunters like David Douglas, George Don and other foreign correspondents. Two years earlier the Horticultural Society had already boasted that 'The collection of Fruit Trees of all kinds has perhaps never been equalled.'[10] If you wanted to become an expert on fruit growing, there was simply no better place on the planet to be than this flat corner of ground by the Thames. However, whilst Stamford Raffles would send exotic tropical fruits from Singapore to Chiswick, it was the humble apple tree that was to be Robert's abiding passion.

Specific apple varieties cannot be propagated reliably from seeds. Cross-pollination between different varieties meant that the only way of reliably creating new trees with the same properties as a desirable tree is to make a clone of the original by taking a small piece, known as a scion, and grafting that onto a rootstock of another tree. The upside of the apple's natural promiscuity is that each apple seed offers the potential of a completely new variety. Each seedling is unique, and sometimes pips dropped by birds could give rise to new varieties that acquired local fame and, through networks of gardeners and nurserymen, grafts from these seedlings would be spread across the country. The problem facing the apple grower was that hundreds, if not thousands, of different apple varieties existed by the time the Garden at Chiswick was established, and very little was known about many of them. Buyers of a young sapling had to take the seller's word that they were buying a correctly named graft. Early apple books gave little more than a name, and illustrations were generally too poor to be relied upon for identification. As a result, a particular apple was often known by a different name, not only from one part of the country to another, but often from one village to another. Robert Thompson was to attempt to bring order to this confusion.

The stakes were high, for planting and maintaining an orchard was an expensive investment. It was also extremely fashionable to own a fine orchard – a sign that one was the owner of a serious establishment. Victorian apple enthusiasts discussed and debated the flavour of their apples with the discernment and passion of wine connoisseurs today. Savouring fine apples from vintage years and good regions, they had hundreds of varieties to choose from. It was not only dessert apples that were required. Britain was the only place in the world to develop special culinary varieties. Head gardeners needed to supply the cook with cooking apples that fulfilled a variety of needs. They had to know which apples could cook to a soft, juicy fluff that could be used in Apple Snow (a soufflé-like dish) and which apples to grow for an apple pie, which required a sharp, savoury apple that would not collapse into a mush under the pastry cover. In a large country-house orchard as many as one hundred varieties might be grown in order to provide continuity of supply and an amusing diversity of taste. At no other place and time in history has the status of apple cultivation risen to such heights.

Old and new varieties came into the Chiswick orchard from all over Europe, and Robert Thompson even taught himself French and German so that he could read up about these new apples. The traffic was not just one-way. Thompson's thorough assessment of the qualities of the apples he assembled meant that the Society was able to recommend and supply varieties to its Fellows and sister horticultural societies around the world. Scions of the hardy Russian varieties – Duchess of Oldenburg, Emperor Alexander, Red Astrachan and Tetofsky – were sent to America in 1832 for trial in the colder northern states, while

Blenheim, Ribston and Gravenstein apples were introduced to Nova Scotia, where they helped to found the Canadian apple industry. As a result of Thompson's work, apples like the Ribston Pippin, Golden Noble and Blenheim Orange were popularized and widely planted all over Britain in private and commercial orchards.

Thompson's apple descriptions were published by the Society and were the essential bedrock of a number of influential apple books by eminent authors such as Robert Hogg, John Lindley, Joseph Paxton and John Claudius Loudon. As the fruit expert Edward Bunyard wrote, nearly one hundred years later of Robert Thompson, 'He preferred to work behind the scenes, and so long as he could bring a little order into chaos, he seemed to care little who obtained the credit for such work.'[11] Contemporary accounts describe him as a man happiest pottering in his beloved apple store, a darkened room stacked from floor to ceiling with fragrant trays of carefully packed apples from that year's harvest. He tasted sample fruit from each variety, carefully noting its taste, texture and keeping qualities. Each year he gradually improved the garden's fruit catalogue, using patient scrutiny of the trees at every stage in their annual cycle of blossom, bud and fruiting to gradually whittle down the number of unidentified varieties. Quietly and unobtrusively he built up a reputation as an expert.

The collections at the Lindley Library include his apple books. In these leather-bound volumes, Robert Thompson would carefully record his reflections on each of the 3,000-plus fruit trees in his care. Not being much of an artist, he would record the appearance of each apple by cutting it in half, smearing it in ink and then carefully pressing it into the page,

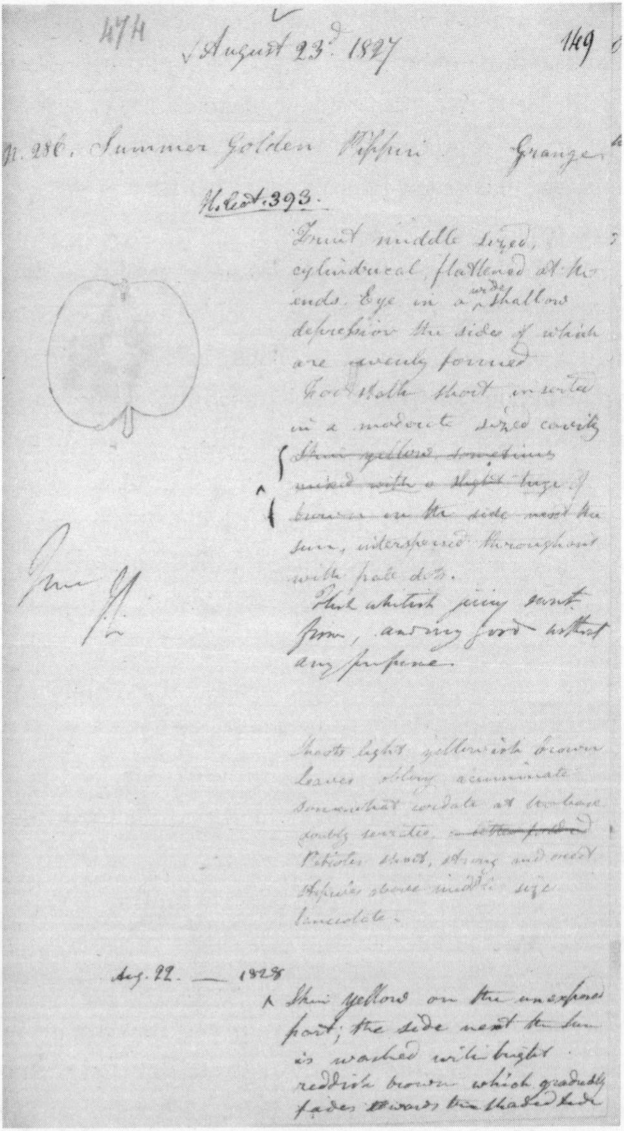
474 √August 23d 1827 149

N. 286. Summer Golden Pippin. Grange

H. Cat. 393.

Fruit middle sized, cylindrical, flattened at the ends. Eye in a wide shallow depression the sides of which are evenly formed. Footstalk short inserted in a moderate sized cavity ~~Skin yellow sometimes mixed with a slight tinge of brown on the side next the sun,~~ interspersed throughout with pale dots. Flesh whitish juicy sweet, firm, and very good without any perfume.

Shoots light yellowish brown. Leaves oblong acuminate somewhat cordate at the base doubly serrated, ~~rather folded~~ Petioles short, strong and erect. Stipules above middle size lanceolate.

Aug. 22. — 1828

^ Skin yellow on the unexposed part; the side next the sun is washed with bright reddish brown which gradually fades towards the shaded side.

Page from *Fruits Proved in the Garden* showing the Summer Pippen. Robert Thompson's careful description of apple varieties grown in the Chiswick Garden provided vital information for confirming identification and naming of trees.

like the potato prints so beloved of junior-school pupils. He would draw around the outline and then write short notes on the qualities of the apple, such as 'melting flesh, sweet with a hint of honey' or 'the size of a good swan's egg'.[12]

In 1828, now aged twenty-nine, Robert Thompson was given a pay rise to twenty shillings a week, and responsibility for both the Experimental Fruit and the fruit and kitchen gardens. A weekly wage of twenty shillings was not an over-generous one, considering how much the Horticultural Society relied upon Robert's skill and knowledge. However, it was enough for him to start saving and make plans for the future. Four years later, on 7 June 1832, he married Magdelene Norval at Chiswick parish church, St Nicholas. The banns show that Magdelene was from Abbotshall in Scotland. In fact she was the daughter of Charles Norval, head gardener at Sir Robert Ferguson's garden, where, as Robert Thompson had outlined in the Handwriting Book, he had worked immediately before coming to Chiswick.

Magdelene and Robert must have met during his stay there as a journeyman gardener from November 1821 to October 1824, learning the ropes under her father. As the daughter of the head gardener, Magdelene will have lived in the garden-er's house inside the estate and had plenty of opportunity to see Robert as he worked in the garden. The Raith Park estate was a romantic setting for a courtship, with picturesque follies dotted around a landscape of lakes, woodland and sea views. However, romance had to give way to practicality, as Robert needed to progress in his career sufficiently to earn an income that could support a family. Like many young couples of the time, Robert and Magdelene had endured a long engagement, waiting nearly eight years before they were in a position to marry. It was a long way from Chiswick to Kirkcaldy and the couple had had very few opportunities to visit one another. They had to keep in touch by letter and hope that each side of the partnership would stay loyal to their vows, despite the distance.

Robert and Magdelene set up home in a house on Devonshire Terrace (later known as Hogarth Place) just outside the Garden walls. This street was part of a new development called Chiswick New Town, a grid of terraced houses surrounded by fields and gardens. Later in the century the area was to go downhill and become a notorious slum, but when the newly married Thompsons moved in, there were houses for respectable tradesmen and shopkeepers, intermingled with cheaper terraced properties rented by labourers working in the surrounding market gardens. The outline of the properties on maps of the period suggests that their house probably had no more than three bedrooms, so the family's living arrangements must have become quite crowded. In 1834 they had their first of two children, and in the same year they were joined in the small cottage by Magdelene's two spinster sisters, who were to live with them for forty years.

* * *

Whilst Robert Thompson settled down to married life and quietly got on with his apple records, dark clouds were gathering for James Barnet in Edinburgh. The elaborate plans for the CHS Garden, its competitions and displays, were proving to be prohibitively expensive to run. The CHS found it as hard to raise regular subscription contributions and, as time went by, it was barely able to pay its wage bills. More worryingly for James Barnet, since the appointment of James McNab, the day-to-day running of the CHS Garden became increasingly entwined with the neighbouring Botanic Garden run by McNab's father, William. Planting displays on loan from the Botanic Garden became a prominent feature. Dr Graham of the Botanic Garden wrote complacently that 'the arrangements of the Experimental Garden have been made to harmonize with the Botanic Garden'.[13] Harmonizing the appearance and operation of the CHS Garden with the neighbouring Botanic Garden may well have been a pragmatic response to limited means, but it must have been a bitter disappointment to a man like James Barnet. However, he was not in a good position to fight what was increasingly looking like a slow merger of the two gardens, especially as his 'assistant' was so closely attached to the Botanic Garden.

In 1834 James McNab resigned in order to undertake a plant-collecting trip to America, but if Barnet felt any relief, it was not to last. McNab returned in April 1835 to work for his father at the Botanic Garden and, coincidentally or not, on 20 May 1836 the Council of the Caledonian Society decided to dismiss James Barnet from his post. The reason given in the meeting was his shortness of temper and 'stiffness of manner' with CHS members when they visited the garden.[14] This tallies with the remarks made ten years earlier by Joseph Sabine about Barnet's manner and character, but the timing of the dismissal suggests that the return of a favoured, alternative candidate was a factor. It is worth noting that when the CHS bade farewell to James McNab as he departed on his plant-hunting trip, several members of the committee made a point of complimenting him on his 'conciliating urbanity', a character assessment in stark contrast to the description of James Barnet.[15] Curiously, the secretary of the Society, Patrick Neill, was not present at the meeting that decided to dismiss Barnet, and many members of the Society later expressed themselves shocked by the decision. If the Council of the CHS thought Barnet would go quietly, they were in for a nasty surprise. What occurred next was so remarkable that it was written up in great detail in a special report for the Council to pass on to the sheriff's office.

At 5 a.m. the very next morning after the Council meeting that dismissed James Barnet, the foreman of the garden, George Henderson, noticed that several plants had been cut down and cauliflowers thrown over the garden wall into the neighbouring Botanic Garden. An investigation next door revealed even more shocking damage. William McNab's prized collection of Cape heaths (*Ericas*) had been uprooted and destroyed. Who could have done such a thing? Intriguingly, the footprints were discovered right by the porch of Barnet's cottage in the garden, and one of them was made by a stockinged foot. A report in the Council papers archly remarks, 'What a bold rascal to come under the windows of the house. Indeed Mr B said that he recollected hearing a noise as of dull footsteps when St Mary's clock stuck 2 or 3 but the noise was not sufficient to induce him to look out.'

If James was the phantom cauliflower-flinger, it seems he rapidly had misgivings and decided to take a more conciliatory line. On 17 June he wrote to the CHS Council apologizing for any failings in his manner and begging that he be given 'a chance of removing such a stain on my character which I will do all my power to prove before the month of November that I am not unworthy of further trial'.[16] It appears that the Council relented and agreed to keep him on until November. However, months passed and minds were not changed. In fact people started to notice that valuable plants were missing from the garden. It was at this point that events started to take an almost Gothic turn.

On a gloomy afternoon on 15 November 1836, secretary Patrick Neill went to the garden lodge to finally evict James Barnet and his thirty-five-year-old sister Mary, who had been living with him as his housekeeper. Barnet handed over the keys and had a short conversation with Neill, who:

> strongly urged on Mr Barnet the propriety and necessity of returning to the Council Room next day at 2 o'clock when a meeting of Council and committee was to be held on matters which deeply concerned him. He made various excuses for refusing to promise to come to the meeting on the morrow, which excuses appeared at the time as being evasive.

All the while during this conversation 'Mr Barnet's sister was waiting for him on the outside of the House'. Dr Neill was keen that Barnet should come and explain the missing plants, but it was clear that Barnet was reluctant, and was eager to get the interview over with as quickly as possible. As it was fast getting dark, Dr Neill and the garden foreman, George Henderson, locked up the house without further inspection and went home. As well as providing lodging for the garden superintendent, the garden lodge accommodated a seed room and the council room where the CHS held its meetings.

The next day Dr Neill ordered the lodge to be opened up, so that a fire could be lit in the council room, ready for the meeting that afternoon. The report recounts:

About 12 o'clock George Henderson... went to the Lodge and unlocked the door to let in Alison Napier (the woman who works in the Garden) in order that she might kindle the fire... After opening the door of the Council Room and whilst Alison Napier was employed in kindling the fire, then George Henderson went upstairs to the seed room to see in what state it was, and having never before having been upstairs, he looked also into the bedrooms and observed the written marks on the walls.

Henderson did not mention these marks to anyone and the meeting took place as planned. Ironically, it was Barnet's arch-rival James McNab who came on the scene next. After attending the Council meeting, 'Mr McNab went, for the first time, into the Parlour where he at once observed the written marks and defacements on the Doors, Windows, Shutters and Walls.' Unfortunately, the report does not describe any actual words or phrases included in these 'written marks and defacements'. However, the description of the damage suggests an angry, almost frenzied attack over the whole building. The report states:

The written marks on the walls appeared to have been made with some instrument which removed the coating of water colour and left exposed the white ground beneath. On the panels of the doors and window shutters the marks in some instances appeared like scratches made by some sharp instrument, in other instances they were more deeply engraven as with a knife and in others again they were burned in apparently by some heated iron instrument which has left black traces of its course.

The report tallied a total of twenty-seven marks across the house: two on the lobby wall, three on the kitchen walls, ten in the parlour, one in the Porter's Lodge and one on the desk where the weather reports were made, and ten in the different bedrooms of the garden lodge. It was also later noted that 'the musket belonging to the Society was left in the lodge in a loaded state' and that 'no caution of its being left in this dangerous state was given by the late superintendent'. The report scrupulously concluded:

> The facts and circumstances related above do not enable the Reporter to designate the particular individual by whom this wanton and malicious mischief has been done, but it is quite clear that it must have been done whilst the House was not only under the immediate charge but in the actual possession of the said James Barnet and whilst himself and his sister were its only inmates.[17]

Two weeks later a deputation of committee members met to discuss a letter from James Barnet, explaining how and why plants were removed from the garden. They reported back to the committee that they found his explanation that he had sent them to various nurserymen 'unsatisfactory' and that they had written to the recipients of the plants. Distributing plants to nurserymen was a perfectly normal part of the garden's operation and part of a regular exchange of plant material that benefited all parties. However, when the committee wrote to these nurserymen, their recollection of plants received did not tally with James Barnet's account.

The committee also noted that only a small quantity of seeds was found to be left in the seed room, and they were far from satisfied with Barnet's explanation 'that the season has been unsuitable' for seed collecting. They felt it was suspicious, at the very least, that a 'marked neglect has been shown towards saving seeds of the more rare and valuable plants'. Despite Barnet's claims that he had recently sold or given many plants to members, the committee noted that there were no entries in the Garden Sale Book or the Book of Plants and Cuttings to members since early September. To be fair to James Barnet, the keeping of accurate records of plant movements had been one of the administrative jobs that had been undertaken by James McNab, and Barnet had been without this help for more than a year. More incriminatingly, Barnet 'further stated that none of the Garden plants had been taken to his own nursery'. This opens up the intriguing possibility that Barnet, suspecting his days at the CHS Garden were numbered, had set up a personal business on the side. It also seemed that he was sending plants to his brother, as there were tales from garden staff of mysterious 'large packages' being dispatched to him from the garden. When a full inspection was made, there were missing plants, damaged plants, tender plants apparently deliberately left out in the frost, missing labels and everywhere 'signs of wilful neglect'.[18]

Reading this report back, even across a distance of nearly two hundred years, it is impossible to mistake the strength of feeling and sense of betrayal revealed in James Barnet's actions. He was driven to deliberately and violently damage plants that he had tended, day in, day out, for more than ten years. A garden is much more than just a workplace to a gardener; it is an expression of his care and his craft. Taking valuable plants may have been motivated by a desire for money, now that he was about to be made unemployed, but taken together with the vandalism and destruction across the garden, there was clearly more going on than simple theft. His actions do not suggest someone who felt that his dismissal was justified. Barnet felt that his garden was being stolen from him, specifically by the McNabs – hence the very personal attack on William McNab's favourite plants. And events proved James Barnet right. Within a couple of weeks of his departure, the CHS duly appointed James McNab as the new superintendent.

On 30 December the secretary of the Society, Dr Neill, reported to the committee that he had recently received an anonymous letter 'consisting of white paper containing nothing but a fragment of a newspaper, which fragment mentions the change in the superintendence of the Experimental Garden and has the word "Daft" written on the margin'. Neill concluded that the capital 'D' in the word 'Daft' was 'most evidently the work of the same hand which had scratched the word "Dollan" in the cottage walls and chimney piece'.[19]

The builder who quoted for repairs said that some message must have been intended, as the same words were repeated over and over again, but the words and marks seem to have baffled the investigators at the time. It is all suggestive of someone who was mentally unbalanced. There is no guarantee, of course, that it was James – his sister Mary, silently standing in the gloom of the garden, is an intriguing figure. She had as much to lose as he did. The Barnet family hailed from Forgandenny near Perth and it would be natural for her to return to the family home, and the anonymous letter had a Perth postmark. Perhaps her brother's sense of persecution spilled over to Mary, who was unmarried and was now jobless and homeless? However, earlier assessments of James' character, and the horticulturally-savvy attack on prize specimens in the McNab garden, do suggest him as the main culprit.

The final act recorded in the CHS archive is an exchange of letters in January 1837 between the Society and James Barnet, whose address by this time was given as Stanwell Nursery, Edinburgh. The Society demanded compensation for blinds and mounts taken by Barnet from the parlour in the garden lodge. Barnet refused to pay, claiming he was still owed money. The Society tried to send him a letter demanding payment for the blinds, but it was returned marked 'Dead Letter Office – Mr Barnet having refused to receive it'. *Gray's Annual Directory and Edinburgh Almanac* for 1837 lists James Barnet as 'nurseryman and garden designer', and the same details are in the Post Office Directories for 1838/9 and 1839/40.

A gardener's career depended on getting a positive character reference. His high-profile fallings-out with both the Caledonian Horticultural Society and the London Horticultural Society meant there was little hope of James finding employment in a garden. His only option was to leave horticulture altogether, or go it alone and set up his own business. Whilst he was carving out a new career as a nurseryman, he reached out once more to the Horticultural Society. In 1841 Barnet sent a young plum tree to Chiswick for Robert

Thompson to examine and grow. It was a Jefferson plum, an American variety that Barnet had obtained for his nursery from Mr Wilson, a nurseryman in New York. Thompson was impressed. When the tree fruited at Chiswick for the first time in 1845, he decided to write a description for the Society's *Journal*. In it he strongly recommended the Jefferson plum be grown more widely because 'the tree may be advantageously cultivated in situations where hitherto known varieties cannot acquire any tolerable degree of flavour'. In Thompson's opinion, by bringing the Jefferson plum to the attention of British growers, James Barnet had rendered a valuable service, for 'What fruit can be worse than bad plums? The most effectual means of driving such out of cultivation is the introduction of good and productive varieties.'[20]

It was fitting that the subject of the last known point of contact for these two very different men was fruit – the field of horticulture where they both started to make their mark at Chiswick. However, as we shall see with other ex-Chiswick gardeners, the nursery business was a very precarious one. Things do not seem to have gone well for James Barnet: there are no further references to his business in trade directories after 1840 and he does not appear to be living in Edinburgh in the 1841 census; and there the trail goes cold.

The 1851 English census does include a James Barnet, aged forty-nine, born in Perthshire, occupation 'gardener', living as a lodger at no. 32 Munster Square, Regent's Park, Marylebone. He is lodging with a young family, Henry Messender and his wife and their baby William, aged two. In 1851 this part of London was not a very well-to-do district. Set to the east of John Nash's Regent's Park, it was a neighbourhood of small houses

for tradesmen, set around squares intended to host markets to
sell hay, vegetables and meat. There was a commercial nursery
nearby. Could Barnet have been forced to descend to the role
of jobbing gardener in a minor nursery in London? Ominously,
this area was heavily hit by cholera in the 1850s. If James was
still alive by this time, he will have watched from a distance
as James McNab, now a fiercely bewhiskered horticultural
grandee, oversaw the final absorption of the CHS Garden into
the Edinburgh Botanic Garden, which he took over in January 1849, following his father's death the previous November.
McNab developed an elaborate rock garden, horticultural hall
and palm houses, and his name was to be lauded in the history
of Scottish horticulture, whereas James Barnet became a mere
footnote in the story of a lost garden.

* * *

To complete the contrast in fortunes, the 1850s saw Robert
Thompson promoted to share the oversight of the Chiswick
Garden with fellow ex-trainee George Gordon. In 1858 he was
made secretary of the newly formed Fruit Committee and
he was frequently asked to contribute to the main gardening
magazines of the day, although his articles were always anonymous and signed with a simple double dash.

Fame was to come even for this shyest of men when, in 1859,
he was approached to write a book on gardening. With typical
modesty, it is entitled *The Gardener's Assistant*, but was in fact
the most comprehensive guide to every operation expected
of a Victorian gardener. Published by Blackie, it could be purchased in twelve affordable instalments at two shillings and
sixpence each, and it became the gardener's 'bible' for decades.

With the exception of the almost unreadable chapter on botany contributed by John Lindley, the text is clear and still holds
up very well. As one later reviewer wrote, the book 'has the
true ring of the man who worked before he wrote'. Naturally,
Robert Thompson did not push himself or his credentials forward in the text, instead crediting all the practical gardeners
whose expertise he makes reference to: 'Mr Paul of Cheshunt
Nurseries for help with chapters on the rose and hollyhock',
'Mr Cock of Chiswick for his help on pelargoniums', 'Mr
Salter of Versailles Nursery, Hammersmith for help on Chrysanthemums' – this is a man with many friends in the world of
horticulture. *The Gardener's Assistant* stayed in print for fourteen editions and remains by far the best book to consult today
to get a true hands-on impression of the craft of a Victorian
head gardener.

In the long run, Thompson's work on fruit identification
– and apples in particular – was arguably even more influential, though in unexpected ways. By the 1870s the British
apple industry was being overwhelmed by cheap imports from
North America, where forty years beforehand Robert Thompson had helpfully sent suitable varieties to assist the growers
in developing their businesses. Whereas in Britain breeding
and selection had been driven by a desire for taste and beauty
for the private grower, in America commercial growers ruth-
lessly selected for crop yield and good handling in transit.
British growers felt that the answer was to be equally ruthless
and grow only apples that stood a chance of yielding a profit.
The enormous diversity celebrated in Robert Thompson's
notebooks and apple stores was only of interest if it could
bring forth these winning apples. This was the beginning of a

process of reduction in the range of apples grown, a trend that was exacerbated by the fact that smaller, more diverse local orchards were increasingly swallowed up by urban development. Many of the varieties so carefully listed by Thompson in his Chiswick notebooks ceased to be grown because their poor or irregular crops, tendency to disease or other shortcomings meant that they failed to meet the needs of the new, larger and more commercial orchards that were now concentrated in Kent and Norfolk.

Today the modern apple industry is characterized by intensive orchards with tightly packed rows of identical dwarf trees. The demands of supermarkets have directly influenced breeders, and relatively few varieties meet their demands in terms of storage and distribution. We have lost the Victorian notion of enjoying a succession of different apples throughout the year, each with their own qualities – ranging from fresh summer apples to richer autumnal and winter apples. Over the past century hundreds of varieties were lost, and for many of them the only records we have are in the yellowing pages of Robert Thompson's apple notebooks – a brown splodge and a few short words the only sign of their existence. However, there are teams of volunteers, with a keen eye and a love of apples that Robert Thompson would have identified with, who search tirelessly for lost varieties, and every year a couple are rediscovered and carefully saved.

A picture of Robert Thompson in the later years of his career survives in the memories of Brian Wynne, who came to Chiswick as a trainee in 1866. His train arrived too late for him to be given admittance to the Garden, so he went to an inn in Chiswick to find a room. The innkeeper pointed out:

an old gentleman sitting by the fire smoking the favourite 'churchwarden' of those days. He was very silent and reserved at first, but presently thawed and then I found myself in the presence of the great man – the author of The Gardener's Assistant – in his usual somewhat shy but most amicable mood.[21]

The two became friends, Wynne helping Thompson take his weather records when he became too frail to visit the Garden early in the morning and late at night. He recalled of Robert Thompson, 'His knowledge of gardening was encyclopaedic and when questioned on any subject, his answers were concise and to the point; but they were always given guardedly and seldom without the preliminary proviso, "I think"...'

Thompson eventually retired from the Horticultural Society in April 1868 after forty-six years working in the Chiswick Garden. He had stuck with the Society through thick and thin, even when financial cutbacks meant that this master of the fruit garden was reduced to growing potatoes and turnips in order to cover the costs of the Chiswick establishment. As a loyal and much-respected servant of the Society, he was treated well. He retired on full pay and towards the end of his life was presented with a purse of £400, raised by public subscription. He died at his home in Chiswick in September 1869, following Magdelene, who had died eight months earlier.

CHAPTER EIGHT

'For sale at moderate prices':
The Nurserymen

*James Barron admitted 31 January 1826 upon
the recommendation of Lord Aberdeen*

*Thomas Sibbald admitted 7 March 1826 upon the
recommendation of the Bishop of Durham*

*George Harrison admitted 19 March 1827 upon
the recommendation of Lord Wharncliffe*

*Neil Wilson admitted 27 May 1828 upon the
recommendation of Robert Ferguson Esq.*

IT WAS RARE TO MAKE MUCH MONEY AS A HEAD
gardener. Although Joseph Paxton was extremely well paid by
the Duke of Devonshire, in large part this was due to the wider
responsibilities he undertook managing the duke's very extensive estates. He was also able to make considerable amounts of
money buying stocks and shares and investing in railway projects. But for the majority of gardeners, the most likely path to
prosperity was to set up a nursery business. Nearly one-third
of the young men who entered the Chiswick Garden had spent
part of their early training in commercial nurseries, and several
headed into the commercial side of horticulture after they left.
Perhaps they harboured dreams of running their own business

and making a fortune; or perhaps the restrictions involved in being a servant – even such a high-status one as head gardener – did not appeal.

A career as a nurseryman was a well-respected path, particularly at the top end of the business, where a group of elite firms focused on the cultivation and sale of newly imported ornamental plants. The owners of these firms, whilst they would not describe themselves as botanists as such, had a good grasp of botany matched with excellent horticultural skills. They provided a link between botanists, plant collectors and learned societies such as the Horticultural Society and the wider gardening public. Things had come a long way since the days when nurseryman James Lee had hired a boy to collect the empty seed packets thrown into the Thames by Philip Miller, the curator of the Chelsea Physic Garden, so that he could monitor the new plants and possibly salvage some seeds for himself.

The Horticultural Society realized that commercial nurseries were essential partners in the drive to perfect and disseminate new plant stock into British horticulture. So as not to deprive these nurseries of potential custom, Chiswick avoided distributing plants and seeds to its members that could easily be purchased from nurseries, and instead distributed rare and new plants and seeds not yet on the market. During the 1830s Chiswick distributed 363,594 packets of seed, 95,325 plants and 54,571 parcels of cuttings, and many of these went to nurseries.[1] The nurserymen's role was to recognize the breeding potential of new plants distributed by the Society, so that within a few seasons of a promising plant's discovery and arrival in this country, gardeners would be given the chance to buy a large range of new varieties and hybrids bred by nurseries, from the small original stock that had been cosseted and nurtured at Chiswick. These new plants meant that nurserymen were frequent visitors to the Chiswick Garden, and even trainees who had not worked in a nursery themselves before coming to Chiswick gained a good knowledge of the trade and its key figures by the time they left.

Some of the men came from families that ran nurseries, and their stay at the Chiswick Garden was clearly designed to equip them with new skills and knowledge to bring back to the family business. Thomas Sibbald's father, also called Thomas, was head gardener to the Bishop of Durham, but also leased land around Bishop Auckland to run a nursery business as a sideline. As a young man, Thomas had worked alongside his brother Robert in the family nursery at Escomb, and in February 1828 he appears to have returned straight home to carry on working in the family business, after nearly two years spent at Chiswick.

Fellow Chiswick student George Harrison was also part of a gardening dynasty. His father, Charles, was head gardener to Lord Wharncliffe at Wortley Hall near Sheffield. George's older brother Joseph succeeded his father as head gardener at Wortley in 1828. However, George was not destined to follow in his father's and brother's footsteps to a head-gardener position. Instead, after just six weeks at Chiswick, he headed to Norfolk to set up as a nurseryman with another older brother, John. Together, the brothers ran nursery grounds at Downham Market and Stow Bardolph, growing tender hothouse plants and fashionable ornamentals such as lobelias, chrysanthemums and dahlias.

Others started off as head gardeners and then set themselves up in business after they had saved enough money to
rent land and buy stock. The path from head gardener to nursery owner was a well-trodden one. Indeed, many of the great
London nurseries set up in the eighteenth century were established by head gardeners. George London was head gardener
to the Earl of Arlington, before he set up in business with
Henry Wise to create the Brompton Park Nursery, which eventually extended over 100 acres (forty hectares) on the site that
now houses the Natural History Museum and the Victoria
and Albert Museum.

Perhaps James Barron had similar dreams. He was the son
of a tenant farmer from Newhills, just outside Aberdeen, and
his early training had taken place on two great estates, Haddo
House and Kenwood House; however, he also spent three years
at one of the most prestigious London nurseries, Messrs Malcolm and Co. of Kensington. When he left the Chiswick Garden
in March 1827 he was 'recommended to a place', the identity of
which was, unfortunately, never recorded. It may have been in
Yorkshire because, despite having no family connections with
the area, by the early 1830s Barron had purchased the Norton
Hammer Nursery just outside Sheffield as a going concern.

It is hardly surprising that so many ex-Chiswick students
chose to set up or work at nurseries. The early nineteenth century offered more opportunities than ever before to make a
living by raising and selling plants. Up until the eighteenth
century professional gardeners, herbalists and apothecaries
would swap or sell their excess plants as a sideline. The professional plant sellers that existed tended to operate on a small
scale and to focus on raising trees. However, the fashion for

large-scale landscape improvements championed by landscape architects such as Bridgeman, Kent and Capability Brown created a demand for plants on a much greater scale than ever before. These schemes depended on the existence of suppliers dedicated to providing trees and shrubs in vast numbers, and larger nurseries began to thrive, particularly in and around London. The growing industry also took advantage of the interest in new species being introduced, first from British colonies in America and other temperate places, and later from tropical and subtropical regions. These elite nurseries were renowned for their horticultural expertise and some, like the Veitch family nursery, were even to employ their own plant collectors to make sure they had the best range of new plants to appeal to the wealthy connoisseur and stay one step ahead of the competition.

However, the real business opportunities for our gardeners lay with a new class of clientele that was beginning to emerge. The rapid expansion of towns and cities populated by an increasingly large and prosperous middle class offered opportunities for new, smaller nurseries based outside London. Though they could not afford great landed estates, newly prosperous middle-class families could afford new houses in the suburbs with space for front and back gardens. Gardening was celebrated in contemporary books and magazines as a refined and rational amusement, which combined aesthetic expertise with knowledge of plants and the natural world. It was also a pastime directly connected to the cultivation and demonstration of taste, with a long association with the landed classes. As a result, gardening had a social cachet that was irresistible to the aspiring middle classes. Moreover, the new style of gardening championed by people like Loudon and Paxton, with the support of the Horticultural Society, placed a great deal of emphasis on flowers presented in ways that worked in smaller spaces as well as in the pleasure grounds of the great estates.

Customers inspecting the displays at a large nursery
at Coombe Wood just outside London.

When the Chiswick Garden started, summer bedding – flowers that we now think of as quintessentially Victorian (pelargoniums, petunias, fuchsias, verbenas, salvias, and so on) – was just coming into use. Almost none of these flowers were available before 1820, and none could be raised by any other than the very rich, with access to expensive heated glasshouses. However, by the time our men were leaving the Garden and starting to make their way in the nursery business, these half-hardy plants were joined by a whole host of others that could be marketed as accessible and affordable to a much broader range of gardeners.

The plant names to be found in old nursery catalogues and plant lists are obscure to us now and, if grown at all, are known under different names, but alonsoas, alternantheras, bouvardias, hebenstreitias and perillas were once familiar garden stock. Some of these new plants were foliage plants, and the rich patterning and textures of the leaves were essential to creating the designs that became known as 'carpet bedding'. Victorian gardeners, egged on by the gardening press, strove to create new effects in their flower beds each growing season, and this ensured that each year there was a demand for new spring and summer bedding plants.

After 1845 and the abolition of the tax on glass, even small-scale nursery businesses were able to afford to build glass-houses to raise tender plants for sale. The brilliance of brightly hued bedding plants such as verbenas, calceolarias and pelargoniums could now bring colour to drab urban environments. They could also be propagated in huge numbers to a uniform size and appearance, so they were perfect for a mass market. Even though you would think he was fully occupied running Chatsworth, editing magazines, designing public parks and cemeteries and building the Crystal Palace, Joseph Paxton spotted the money-making potential of this new market of middle-class and provincial gardeners. He entered an agreement with Samuel Hereman for him to manufacture and sell Paxton's design for a 'portable hothouse... of unparalleled cheapness', which was marketed under the snappy catch-phrase 'Hothouses for the Million'.[2] He even branched out into licensing niche products such as a 'strawberry crinoline':

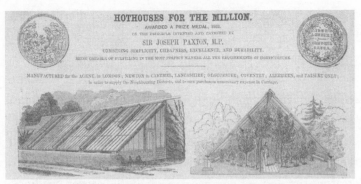

Advertisement for Joseph Paxton's 'Hothouses for the Million'.
Joseph Paxton was adept at exploiting the commercial opportunities
afforded by his reputation as the nation's most famous gardener.

a wire framework similar in appearance to a lady's crinoline
skirt, to lift strawberries away from wet soil and slugs.

* * *

Whilst Paxton was well positioned to make money from his
reputation as the nation's pre-eminent gardener, others without access to his fame or resources could also take advantage
of this horticultural boom. James Barron's nursery business
on the outskirts of Sheffield was established in the 1830s, at
a time when the town was growing rapidly. Situated amongst
fast-flowing rivers and surrounded by hills containing raw
materials such as coal, iron ore and millstone grit for grind-
stone, it was an ideal place for water-powered industries to
develop, particularly the production of cutlery, for which the
town gained a worldwide reputation. As workshops and factories expanded, the population boomed. In 1801, at the time of
the first census, Sheffield had a population of more than 31,000
and by the standards of the time was a large town. However,

by 1851 the population had grown to in excess of 135,000. The town had a reputation as a grimy and dirty place, and in 1832 there was an epidemic of cholera that killed 402 people.

This may seem an unpromising place for James Barron to choose to set up a nursery business, but not all the houses were slums. In the early nineteenth century a middle-class suburb was built west of the town around Glossop Road. As a result, Sheffield had a strong contingent of prosperous horticultural enthusiasts and it supported three well-illustrated monthly periodicals on botany and horticulture. In 1830 the Sheffield Horticultural Society was founded by Jonathan Salt, a local manufacturer and noted botanist, and by 1834 it had managed to raise enough money to purchase eighteen acres (seven hectares) of farmland to the south-west of the town to create a garden. It was laid out by the up-and-coming garden designer Robert Marnock in the gardenesque style and featured a handsome glasshouse. The garden was only open to the general public on four gala days a year; the rest of the time admission was limited to shareholders and annual subscribers, who paid 10s 6d annually. Nevertheless, as many as 12,000 people were estimated to have visited in the summer of 1836. A report on the Society's first flower show held in 1832 confidently asserted, 'All our townsmen who have a taste for cultivation of flowers, plants & c. and who love to behold the beauties of nature, as exhibited in the vegetable world, will come forward... The Society is now permanently established and is very likely to be one of the first of the kind in the kingdom.'[3]

Not only did the Sheffield Horticultural Society demonstrate that there was a strong local interest in horticulture, but it also provided a good route for James Barron to network with potential customers, and by August 1836 he was listed as one of its members. In March 1839 Barron advertised for an apprentice, 'a country youth preferred'. In the advert he was listed as owning a nursery grounds at New Haymarket, High House and Norton Hammer. He also rented a shop to sell 'Garden and Farm seeds of True and Genuine Quality' at 10 Haymarket in the centre of Sheffield, near the newly built Corn Exchange. By this time he was a married man living with wife Sarah near his nursery ground at Norton Hammer, in the Ecclesall Bierlow area. This was a rural area of villages and hamlets, south-west of the main Sheffield town centre. Tragically, their first child was born prematurely and did not survive, but in 1842 James and Sarah were to have a baby girl named Charlotte. In the meantime, business seemed to be going well. On 16 May 1837 he took out a large advert on the front page of the *Sheffield Iris*: 'James Barron Nursery and Seedsman, Haymarket and High House and Norton Hammer Nurseries begs leave respectfully to invite the attention of Noblemen, Gentry, Farmers and Gardeners of Sheffield and the Surrounding Country, to his Farming, Gardening and Nursery Stock'. The farming stock included turnips, swedes, mangel-wurzel and rye-grass seeds. He also invested in a stock of farming equipment to sell and:

> having just returned from an extensive tour in the agricultural districts of Scotland has purchased Subsoil Ploughs, Green Crop Harrows of different sorts, Turnip Sowing machines, Curd Breaking Machines, Potatoe [*sic*] Washers, Improved Oval Churns, Stable Lanterns, Potatoe Shovels & c., all of which may be seen at the Corn Exchange.

This must have involved a considerable capital outlay and demonstrated a deal of confidence in his business. The field of ornamental gardening was not ignored, either, and the advert proudly declared, 'In the Horticultural Department J.B.'s seeds are carefully selected from the best markets, he has also a superior collection of Dahlias, Auriculas, Calceolorias [sic], Greenhouse Plants & c.' Like many nurseries, James Barron also sought to provide gardening services, and the advert ended with the reminder: 'Gentlemen supplied with first rate, steady gardeners by the day or week'.[4]

His trip to Scotland in 1837 was followed in 1839 by a shopping trip to London. In another advert in the *Sheffield Iris*, Barron announced:

> J.B. having just returned for London, where he has purchased a large stock of the best Horticultural and Agricultural Productions, the superior excellence of which induces him to solicit the attention of his Friends and Neighbours, and hopes that they will honour him with an early call, so they may examine, judge and select for themselves. He has all the usual kinds of Forest Trees, Evergreen and Flowering Shrubs, Roses in great variety, Standard and Trained Fruit, Currant Bushes & c. with a selection of the most recent introduced plants from all parts of the country, in excellent condition, and for sale at moderate prices.

Not content with developing his stock for sale, Barron decided to spearhead the development of agricultural science in the Sheffield area. Apparently, when he had visited Scotland he had observed 'the great utility of Agricultural Museums which are now formed in many of the Principal towns', and was convinced 'much benefit would be derived from the formation of one in this neighbourhood'.[5] Agricultural Museums were set up in Scotland and organized displays of the latest agricultural innovations and stock, and gave out medals and cash prizes to inventors and producers. The most famous was the Highland and Agricultural Society of Scotland, founded in 1784, which created a museum of miniature agricultural machinery at a scale of three inches (7.6 centimetres) to one foot (thirty centimetres).

By February 1838 Barron was confident that he had enough local backing from 'various Farmers & others' and was ready to put his plans into action. In another front-page advert in the *Sheffield Iris* he announced that he had 'made arrangements for Opening an Agricultural Museum for the support of which he has been promised the valuable assistance of various Noblemen and Gentlemen in Yorkshire, Nottinghamshire and Derbyshire'. His confidence and level of ambition were admirable: 'J.B. feels assured he will have the co-operation of the Highland Society, as well as the principal Agriculturalists and Horticulturalists in every part of the British dominions and on the continent of Europe.'[6] Sheffield seemed to be a promising venue for a nursery business, and James Barron looked set fair to carve out a prominent place for himself in the local agricultural and horticultural community. Indeed, in 1840 the Horticultural Society listed him as one of the ex-Chiswick trainees it considered to be 'at the head of their profession'.[7]

* * *

Although Bishop Auckland was smaller than Sheffield, Thomas Sibbald's business venture also prospered in the 1830s. His father died in 1833 and probate records show that he left a considerable estate, valued at £1,000 (over £800,000 in today's terms). These assets were shared between Thomas and his brother Robert, who was also a nurseryman. By November 1833 Thomas Sibbald was well enough established to support a wife, and he married twenty-two-year-old Mary Tomlin from Gosforth at Auckland St Andrew Church. That same year he was one of the subscribers to 'An historical, topographical and descriptive view of the county palatine of Durham' by E. Mackenzie and M. Ross, suggesting that he had money in hand. By the time of the 1841 census, Thomas and Mary were living in Market Place in Bishop Auckland with their daughter, also called Mary. Following in the footsteps of James Barron, Thomas invested in a shop in the centre of town, which was listed in directories as being in Market Place, so the family may well have lived above the shop.

Market Place was right in the commercial centre of the town where the wealthier inhabitants were clustered, cheek by jowl with local shops and offices. The Sibbalds' neighbours were a solicitor and a surgeon, so it appears to have been a respectable part of town. Although Bishop Auckland was surrounded by mining communities, it was a relatively quiet place; and, like James Barron's customers, many of Thomas Sibbald's customers were farmers. Thomas regularly paid for advertisements to appear in the local press explaining that he was an agent for 'Kagenbusch and Co Agricultural Chemists of Leeds', selling a product that claimed to eradicate potato blight, 'which has proved so fatal to the crop throughout all Europe in these past two years'.[8]

As the years passed, Bishop Auckland began to grow, especially after the town was connected by rail to the coast in 1843. In 1801 the population comprised fewer than 2,000 people, but by 1851 it had more than doubled, to exceed 5,000. This population growth was mostly made up of ironworkers and colliers and their families. The expansion increased the demand for land, and by 1865 Thomas Sibbald had to move some of his stock from nursery grounds that he held near the railway station because the landowner, North Eastern Railway, wanted the land for other purposes. He offered the stock for sale, and the advert gives some idea of the scale of his operation, which Thomas was in sole charge of, after the death of his brother Robert in 1847. The advertisement outlined that Thomas Sibbald was putting up for auction stock consisting of:

about 32,000 Fruit and Forest Trees, Ornamental Shrubs &c. &c. two greenhouses, stove and propagating house. The stock comprises choice and well grown varieties of Peaches, Apricots, Cherries, Plums, Pears, Apples, and other Fruit Trees. The Forest Trees consist of Larch, Spruce, Fir, Lime, Beech, Poplar, Oak, Chestnut &c. &c. Amongst the Pines are fine specimens of Wellingtonia Gigantea, Deodora Cedars, Araucaria, Abies Albertiana, Picea Nobilis, Pinas Excelsa, Cedrus Atlantica &c. Amongst the Shrubs are Abor Vitaes, Yews, Hollies, Rhododendrons, Junipers, Laurels, Heaths, Roses &c. &c. The whole of the stock is in fine healthy condition and will be sold without reserve, as the ground must be cleared. The sale affords an excellent opportunity for Noblemen, Gentlemen, Nurserymen, Gardeners and Amateurs.

To reassure his customers, Sibbald took out an advert below the auction details to explain that:

> the sale by Auction advertised by the North Eastern Railway does not comprise the whole of his stock, but only a small portion namely 2 and a half acres and from which a large portion of the Stock has been removed to his new grounds, while his remaining stock covers upwards of 15 acres, so that he is in a position to execute orders as usual.[9]

However, it was not essential to set up business on the fringes of a large town or city; there were opportunities even in seemingly remote places. Neil Wilson grew up in the small village of Kingarth on the Isle of Bute off the coast of south-west Scotland. His father, Colin Wilson, was forester to the enormously wealthy John Crichton-Stuart, second Marquess of Bute, and Neil served his apprenticeship in the marquess's garden at Mount Stuart House. His time at Chiswick was not straightforward. In February 1829, ten months after he entered the Garden as a student, he was promoted to under-gardener in the Ornamental Experimental Garden on a three-month trial. However, on 31 August 1829 Joseph Sabine reported to the Garden Committee that Wilson 'had not yet given such satisfaction as was expected of him', so he was not confirmed in the appointment. Despite this setback, he still managed to acquire an enviable position as head gardener at Gopsall Hall in Leicestershire after leaving Chiswick.

Gopsall Hall was the grandest Georgian country house in the county, overlooking a park that covered 724 acres (293 hectares) and featured two lakes, a walled garden, a Chinese boathouse and a temple. George Frederic Handel was a visitor and composed the *Messiah* while there. This was a significant and responsible position for Neil Wilson, which many gardeners would have been happy to stay in for life. He married a girl from his home village of Kingarth in 1836 and they lived at Gopsall for around twenty years, raising eleven children there. However, at some point in the 1850s, when Wilson was in his late forties or early fifties, he moved his family back to the little village of Ascog on the Isle of Bute to set up business as a seedsman, nurseryman and florist. Notwithstanding the couple's family ties to the area, on the face of it, this appears a strange business decision. The population of Ascog was only just over 1,000 and even Rothesay, the largest settlement on the Isle of Bute, consisted of well under 10,000 people. However, what the area lacked in population size, it made up for in horticultural enthusiasm. The local climate benefitted from the Gulf Stream and winters were relatively mild. The climate, together with the stunning scenery, attracted a wealthy set of residents and the Isle of Bute had many large houses with impressive gardens.

By far the largest and most impressive property was Mount Stuart Castle owned by the Marquess of Bute, where Wilson had worked as a young apprentice before arriving at Chiswick. By this time the owner was John Patrick Crichton-Stuart, third Marquess of Bute. He inherited his title and vast family estates in Scotland and Wales at the age of just six months, on the death of his father. It was estimated that he had a gross annual income of around £300,000 (around £275 million in today's terms).[10] This vast inheritance reportedly made him the richest man in the world. His chief passion was architecture, and he will be best remembered for his restoration of Cardiff Castle and the fairytale creation of Castell Coch, built above the village of Tongwynlais in South Wales. Mount Stuart Castle is an incredible red-brick Gothic mansion set in more than 300 acres (121 hectares) of gardens and woodland.

It was not just Mount Stuart that offered business opportunities for Neil Wilson. There were other keen plant collectors, including Alexander Bannatyne Stewart, a prosperous Glasgow merchant and orchid enthusiast. Bannatyne commissioned Edward La Trobe Bateman – who had designed the Carlton Garden in Melbourne, Australia, and some of the interiors of the Crystal Palace – to landscape his house, Ascog Hall, and design a fernery.

Other fine Victorian villas, all set in substantial grounds, include Ascogbank, Balmory Hall and Millburn House, which meant that Wilson had access to a clientele that, whilst it might be relatively small, was able to spend large amounts on garden plants. This select group of customers was also supplemented in the summer months by tourists and day-trippers. Despite the remote location, new rail and sea links meant that Wilson boasted 'a large and select stock of Vegetable and Flower Seeds and Bulbs, direct from the best British and Continental Growers'.[11]

The market for these nurseries was a growing one, but it was also demanding. There was an enormous number of small nurseries, not to mention the market gardeners who would dabble in the sale of plants and seeds as a sideline to the sale of fruit and vegetables. In this competitive environment it was important to be able to differentiate your business from competitors by selling 'better', or at least newer, varieties.

People had known for many years that plants could breed with each other like animals and produce new varieties. Farmers and gardeners did not hesitate to use naturally occurring 'sports' or mutations, if they showed favourable characteristics. However, the idea of crossing plants on purpose took a long time to emerge. The 1830s and 1840s, when our men were establishing their businesses, was a time of tremendous expansion in plant-breeding experiments, spearheaded by the president of the Horticultural Society, Thomas Andrew Knight. At first plant breeders were operating without much understanding of what was actually happening. Whilst the development of microscopes had made it possible to understand how pollen fertilized the ovaries of plants, gardeners still did not fully comprehend the process by which traits were transferred. Instead they relied on close observation of the seedlings that resulted from their efforts to cross different varieties, and on persistence, until they achieved a plant that looked commercially promising. Everything was done empirically and it was a lengthy hit-and-miss affair.

However, there were so many nurseries and head gardeners keen to develop new plants that almost as soon as a new species appeared in commerce, often only a season or two after Chiswick or another botanic garden had first got it to flower, hybrids would be developed and raised. Adverts would be taken out trumpeting the virtues of the newly named variety. Even small nurseries could hope to develop a variety that would find favour and increase their profit. Growers would start selecting and propagating plant stock that showed promise in germination, vigour, yield or aesthetic quality. They would then give it a name and propagate it as a cultivar. Often there was very

little difference between the selection and the typical form of
the species, but the pressure to have something 'novel' or 'new
and improved' to sell each season was high. The naming process was often an opportunity for a bit of self-advertisement.
The adverts for George Harrison's nursery at Downham Market in *The Floricultural Cabinet* listed six varieties of dahlias with
names prefaced by his surname, including 'Harrison's Gem',
'Harrison's Don John' and 'Harrison's Mary Queen of Scots'.

In drawing attention to the Harrison name, George may
have been trying to capitalize on the fame of his elder brother,
Joseph, who worked at Wortley with their father Charles
until 1828, when he took over from him as head gardener after
Charles left to work at Petworth in West Sussex. As Wortley
was close to Sheffield, Joseph Harrison may well have known
James Barron and may even have been a customer. In 1830
Joseph Harrison was on the organizing committee of the Sheffield Horticultural Society's flower show. Joseph Paxton was
also a member of the committee, and it may have been here
that the two men met and planned to start a new gardening
magazine called *The Horticultural Register*. This was first published on 31 July 1831. The two Josephs, Harrison and Paxton,
shared the editorship of the first volume, which covered horticulture, natural history and rural economy. It was intended
for all classes of society and sold for just one shilling monthly,
compared to the three shillings and sixpence that Loudon
charged for his bimonthly *Gardener's Magazine*.

Around a year later Joseph Harrison left *The Horticultural
Register* to set up his own magazine, *The Floricultural Cabinet*.
Focusing on flowers, as the name suggests, the magazine was
extremely successful and, in his preface to the first volume,

Joseph stated that he had sold 50,000 copies in just nine months. Writing in magazines was an opportunity to encourage and support potential gardeners to try new plants, and it was also an excellent vehicle for a little bit of subtle self-promotion. For instance, in June 1833 George Harrison, who was a regular contributor to the magazine, wrote an article entitled 'On the Treatment of the *Crassula coccinea* and *Crassula versicolor*'. He gave hints on growing *Crassula* to help the amateur and happened to mention that he had himself 'for several years flowered one to two hundred of these plants every season, specimens of which have been exhibited at different floricultural meetings. In June 1831 I turned out 36 large plants into a bed in the flower garden which was one complete mass of bloom for several weeks.'[12] Likewise, in an article promoting the growing of chrysanthemums, George Harrison explained that he had plants blooming in December, and 'several eminent floriculturalists came from town to see the plants when in bloom and they declared that they had not seen such a sight before, nor was there anything likely to compete against the display of bloom and plants in the neighbourhood of London'.[13]

James Barron's name also graced the horticultural press. In 1836 he provided a specimen of *Mahonia repens* for illustration and description in *The Floricultural Magazine and Miscellany of Gardening*.[14]

The other crucial publication for every nurseryman was his plant list or catalogue. This was the period when nurseries began issuing catalogues on an annual basis, but at this time the format was still very basic. At first nursery catalogues were simply lists of plant names, with no descriptions, prices or illustrations. It was felt enough to tell purchasers what was in stock; they would be relied upon to know the appearance and qualities of the plants from other sources. However, as the pace of plant introductions accelerated and the market broadened to encompass less horticulturally-informed customers, astute nurserymen realized that they needed to at least describe the attractive properties of the varieties they sold. Thomas Sibbald was issuing a descriptive catalogue from at least the 1850s, though unfortunately none of them seem to have survived.

Paid advertising was another, more direct way of promoting a nursery business, and all the ex-Chiswick nursery and shop owners actively took out advertisements in local newspapers and the horticultural press. However, word of mouth could be just as powerful and it was good business to create and maintain strong networks. One very effective way of doing this was to be active either as a competitor or judge in the plethora of local horticultural and agricultural shows that thrived across the country.

In 1837 the curators of the Sheffield Botanical Garden noted that 'Horticultural and Floricultural Exhibitions... have within these few years been working a change in the tastes and recreational pursuits of the inhabitants of this densely populated island', replacing 'bear baiting, a cock-fight, a dog fight or mayhap two animals in human form similarly engaged'. Whilst the Horticultural Society's shows at Chiswick were the most prestigious and their medals were the ultimate horticultural accolade, other shows were also excellent meeting places and showcases for nurserymen to demonstrate their skill and display their wares. All our nurserymen were active participants in flower shows.

On 5 August 1835 James Barron acted as a judge at the Sheffield Horticultural Society's fourth flower show, which was held inside the city's music hall. Paxton's *Horticultural Register* reported on the first show, which took place in May 1832, and this account gives an idea of the type of show in which Barron participated:

> It is gratifying to state that it was attended by a very numerous and highly respectable company. The show of auriculas and polyanthuses was of the most splendid description, while the collection of hyacinths, herbaceous plants, cut flowers &c. was such as afforded general satisfaction. The display of stove and green house plants and fruits was of the most extensive kind and afforded a rich treat to the lovers of horticulture.[15]

And *The Penny Magazine of the Society for the Diffusion of Useful Knowledge* recorded that:

> The Sheffield Horticultural Society has awarded prizes of the value of £150 at one of its exhibitions – they consisted of silver cups of the value of £5, £10 and £15 and smaller prizes in money and the competition was opened to exhibitors from any part of the country. The exhibitions of fruits and flowers by the Horticultural Societies established in nearly every town in England are most agreeable proofs of the beneficial direction of the public taste.[16]

By acting as a judge, James Barron received public affirmation – reported in the local press – that he was a significant

figure in the local horticultural community. Up in Bishop
Auckland, Thomas Sibbald was also heavily involved in local
horticultural shows. Throughout the 1850s and 1860s he acted
as a judge and contributed prizes for dahlia displays at the
annual Tudhoe Flower Show and the Shotley Bridge Horticultural Society Show. However, the main event was the Bishop
Auckland Floral Exhibition, which was established in 1853 and
rapidly became one of the most significant provincial shows
in the country. Special cheap trains were put on by the North
Eastern Railway, bringing enormous crowds from Stockton,
Barnard Castle, Durham, Sunderland, South Shields and Newcastle. Although the transport did not always run smoothly
(in 1858 there was a complaint that 'the duties of the railway
company could not have been more inefficiently discharged'[17]),
it was estimated that crowds in excess of 25,000 visited the
show, which cost £1,000 to stage, and provided the weather
was fine, the organizers would make a profit.

This show offered the biggest prizes in the North of England, including 'silver plate, consisting of inkstands, cups,
goblets and c.' The high awards had the effect of attracting
exhibitors from far and wide. In 1862 exhibitors were recorded
as coming from Middlesex, Salisbury, Saffron Walden, Manchester, York, Bedale, Birmingham, Derby, Hexham and Thirsk,
and it was said that 'Entering the professional tent the display
was one that could not be surpassed in England.'[18] Despite
this tough competition, Thomas Sibbald entered exhibits
and did well. In 1855 he won a special extra prize for verbenas, and a seedling scarlet geranium was highly commended.
In 1858 he won second prize for a display of twelve varieties of
roses.[19]

Spilling out of the grounds of the Bishop's Palace and into the town, the show took over the square where Thomas Sibbald's seed shop was based, and it was engulfed by a carnival atmosphere:

Many of the windows of the shops and places of business displayed a considerable amount of bunting and flags bearing various mottoes and devices. The Market Place, in which were stationed various menageries, Thespian booths and exhibitions naturally attendant on occasions of this character, presented a most animated appearance.[20]

The exhibitions and entertainment in the Market Place were certainly eclectic: 'There were exhibited wonders of all kinds, from the performing elephant to those anomalies – the fat Scotchman and a learned pig.'[21] Provided the public could tear their eyes away from elephants, fat Scotsmen and performing pigs, horticultural shows were a great place for a nurseryman to showcase his wares and horticultural credentials. They were also good places to meet up with fellow growers and nurserymen.

Though they could be in fierce competition, most nursery gardeners were part of a community, swapping information, trading stock and recommending and developing staff for each other. When big orders for certain plants caused shortages, they could rely on ordering stock from other nurseries to fill the gaps. Many plants changed hands through auction and sales following the death or financial difficulties of other nurserymen, private collectors or the owners of notable gardens, so good contacts and an ear for gossip picked up in the show tent could ensure that a nurseryman would be first on the scene to take the pick of the collection. Astute nurserymen were also willing to buy and sell on good plants raised by amateurs, and a flower show was an ideal place to see what was on offer.

Although local links were essential, the Horticultural Society was still the most valued source of horticultural information and ideas for nurserymen. It offered a vital link to gardeners and nurserymen across the country – its shows and meetings were the best place to gain attention for a new plant, because all the gardening magazines slavishly reported their proceedings. When James Barron visited London for his stock-buying trip, it is highly likely that he paid a visit to the Chiswick Garden to see what newly arrived plants were being grown or what horticultural techniques were being tested. The valuable seeds and cuttings regularly distributed to Fellows were another reason to maintain close links to the Society. In 1832 Thomas Sibbald's association with the Horticultural Society was marked when he was listed as a 'Professional Gardener Admitted to the Privileges of Fellowship'. This was a special status given to professional gardeners who had been awarded a medal or had communicated a paper, who were able to be Fellows of the Society at a reduced fee of one guinea per annum.

All this effort was essential in order to nurture and protect the nurseryman's most important business asset: his reputation. A reputation for expertise, quality of product and reliability was crucial to commercial and professional success. A reputation for honest dealing was particularly important if a nurseryman was to have any long-term success selling seeds, and to a lesser extent bare-root plants, as they were sold on the promise of the plant they might become – a promise based in large part on the supplier's good standing. Buyers were advised to be wary, because it was a dirty business. Unrealistic promises could be made about new varieties; and old varieties could be given new names, fooling buyers into thinking they were trying something novel. Even worse, seed could be adulterated. It was common practice to add killed mustard seed to pad out more expensive, but very similar-looking, cabbage or cauliflower seed. This was why when Thomas Sibbald advertised his 'splendid stock of Turnip seeds', he was at pains to point out that the seeds had been 'specially grown for him' and were 'quite true to name'.[22]

While James Barron, Thomas Sibbald and Neil Wilson were selling seeds, there were no official trials or traders' associations to police the trade. It was not until later in the century that there was a move to government and industry-wide regulation of the seed industry. Furious letters to the gardening press suggest that fraud was relatively common. In 1856 *The Gardeners' Chronicle* published an article on the subject of seed adulteration, explaining: 'It is notorious that some seeds are indistinguishable by the eye, although they produce totally different plants. No one for instance can tell the varieties of Carrot, Beet, Turnip, Cabbage, Radish & c., for each other by their seeds.' The magazine even published an extract from a circular letter sent to seedsmen by an unscrupulous wholesale supplier, offering seed for mixing: 'I have sold this day some Indian Rape Seed for mixing with Turnip seed... If you want some seeds for mixing, I shall be happy to serve you.'[23] In this environment, the ability to convince buyers of the reliability of the seed you were supplying was a crucial business advantage.

As the century progressed, larger firms began to exert a significant lead on smaller firms in this regard. In 1840 Suttons Seeds established its first laboratory to test seeds for germination and purity. In the 1850s it also began to sell seeds in labelled packets. This branding, together with a careful and well-publicized focus on quality assurance in aggressive advertising campaigns, meant that consumers felt they could trust and rely on branded seed, in preference to seed provided by small independent suppliers. The advantage of brand recognition was amplified by the money that larger firms spent on producing ever more elaborate catalogues. As the railway network expanded, it was possible to deliver bare-rooted plants, seeds and bulbs to all parts of the country, and small local nurseries found themselves in competition with much larger firms.

On 10 January 1840, with the implementation of the Penny Post, money orders for sending small sums of money through the mail became available. This meant that companies were able to ask for payment up front and could send out plants and seeds reliably and speedily. Firms like Suttons, Carters and Barr & Sugden expanded to become massive mail-order companies. They were able to increase the size and number of catalogues they produced, and shipped catalogues to customers free upon request. Catalogue covers became more elaborate and, as colour printing processes developed, more space was devoted to illustrations, descriptions, testimonials, contests, special offers and awards won at horticultural fairs or exhibitions. As a result, it became harder and harder for small firms to compete.

Another key pressure was the rising cost of land. To be successful, our men needed good-quality land with access to water, ideally close to good transport links and metropolitan areas. This was prime development land and, as demand for it increased, nurserymen and market gardeners were faced with higher land rental costs. The need to carry large stocks and to spend money on greenhouses and skilled labour also made nurseries expensive businesses to set up and run. Moreover, it was a high-risk business, with a whole host of factors that could go wrong, even for the most experienced horticultural businessman. High-stake decisions needed to be made each year about what varieties to grow or develop. In a crowded marketplace, everyone was trying to develop new and better varieties to steal a march on their competitors. If successful, one of these new versions would make last season's varieties obsolete, and a nurseryman could find himself lumbered with a large amount of stock that simply would not sell.

Another key problem was the high cost of developing a new plant in sufficient quantity to sell well, and the difficulty of recouping that investment quickly enough. With the state of knowledge of inherited characteristics, evaluating new crosses took up huge amounts of time and space, tying up resources that could have been used for raising tried and tested varieties. Only a tiny number of many thousands of crosses would pass muster and be preserved. Furthermore, whether bred inhouse or purchased as seeds from other suppliers, all the bedding plants propagated and overwintered under glass had to be planted out and sold in a very short period of time. The market for bedding plants lasted only from June to September, so a spell of really bad weather at the wrong time and the whole year's income could be at risk. If for any reason his stock did not sell, an unlucky nurseryman could face major cashflow issues.

* * *

We do not know which of these pressures hit George Harrison, but in November 1834 the business he was running with his brother was in serious trouble. An advert in the *Norfolk Chronicle* notified readers of the Assignment that had been drawn up relating to the business. Insolvent debtors were individuals unable to pay their debts and could be kept indefinitely in a debtors' prison if their creditors so wished. To avoid this fate, a debtor would set up an Assignment that put in place a formal arrangement that paid any proven creditor monies owed from the proceeds of the sale of the debtor's assets, or collection of any income that they themselves were owed. The announcement in the paper declared that the Harrison brothers had 'Assigned all their personal estate and effects to trustees for the equal benefit of such of their creditors as shall execute the same indenture within 2 calendar months from the date thereof'.[24] The trustees in charge of the Assignment (two Downham Market solicitors) lost no time in releasing the value of the assets, because the same newspaper also carried an advert that read:

> To Nurserymen. To be sold by Private Contract. All that valuable assortment of Nursery Trees late the property of Messrs John and George Harrison in the Nursery Grounds at Downham Market and Stow Bardolph in the County of Norfolk. The above consists of several thousand Oak, Ash, Beech, Fir, Elm and other Plants in a most flourishing state. A lease of the Nursery Ground for any length of time may be had.[25]

It seems that this sale satisfied the creditors, but there is no further reference to George Harrison in the nursery trade,

and his article-writing days for his brother's publications seem
to have stopped at the same time. The 1841 census includes an
entry for a George Harrison, aged thirty-one, farmer at Stow
Fall, Stow Bardolph, Downham in Norfolk, so it may be that
he took up farming instead.

Even the self-confident James Barron was not immune. By
1842 something had gone badly wrong for his business. Perhaps he overspent during the shopping trips to London and
Scotland, and could not sell his stocks of expensive plants and
agricultural machinery quickly enough to pay his creditors.
Perhaps the competition was just too stiff. Barron faced several competitors: *The Floricultural Cabinet* for the years 1834–7
carried adverts for Thomas Beighton (tulips), James Levick
(florist), R. Turner (seedsman), all based in and around Sheffield. He fared even worse than George Harrison, as his name
appeared in *The London Gazette* 'Under the announcements of
the Court for Relief of Insolvent Debtors'. In a list of people
who had petitioned to be debtors, we find 'James Barron late
of Norton Hammer near Sheffield, Yorkshire, nurseryman and
seedsman – in the Gaol of Sheffield'.[26] His troubles seem to
have dated back to the summer of 1839, when he was forced
to give a notice of Assignment and attempted to sell 'the well
selected stock of Garden & Agricultural seeds and the shop
in Broad Street near to the Corn Exchange may be taken'.[27] It
does not appear that the sale went through or raised enough
money, for in October 1839 another advertisement appeared:
'To be sold by Private Contract "The Old Established Nursery at High House, late in the Occupation of Mr James Barron
and formerly of Mr Nicholson and now in the best condition"'
and 'to let the shop'.[28] Eventually it seems his creditors lost

patience and took him to court, and Barron ended up having
to spend some time in jail. In order to be released, he needed
to apply to the Court for the Relief and Discharge of Insolvent Debtors, in Portugal Street, Lincoln's Inn Fields. The
court would agree to a release provided the debtor could come
up with a convincing plan for satisfying his creditors. Charles
Dickens gave a vivid picture of the atmosphere of the court
in *Pickwick Papers*:

> In a lofty room, ill-lighted and worse ventilated, situated
> in Portugal Street, Lincoln's Inn Fields, there sit nearly the
> whole year round, one, two, three, or four gentlemen in wigs,
> as the case may be, with little writing-desks before them…
> There is a box of barristers on their right hand; there is an
> enclosure of insolvent debtors on their left; and there is an
> inclined plane of most especially dirty faces in their front…
> It is always full. The steams of beer and spirits perpetually
> ascend to the ceiling, and, being condensed by the heat, roll
> down the walls like rain.

The court proceedings were viewed as a source of amusement and attracted a distinctive crowd, which seemed to enjoy
listening to the misfortunes of others:

> Some of them sleep during the greater part of the sitting;
> others carry small portable dinners wrapped in pocket-
> handkerchiefs or sticking out of their worn-out pockets, and
> munch and listen with equal relish; but no one among them
> was ever known to have the slightest personal interest in any
> case that was ever brought forward. Whatever they do, there

they sit from the first moment to the last. When it is heavy, rainy weather, they all come in, wet through; and at such times the vapours of the court are like those of a fungus-pit.[29]

This experience must have been a painful and embarrassing one for a man who had had such high hopes for his business. The process of clearing Barron's debts dragged on through 1843, and in November of that year there was yet another attempt to sell assets to pay off his creditors. An auction was advertised 'by order of the Assignee of James Barron an insolvent'. The sale was arranged to take place on the premises of the nursery at Norton Hammer at 11 a.m. on 22 November. 'The whole of the Valuable and Thriving Stock of Trees, Plants and Shrubs' included:

> Rhododendrons, Azalias, Kalmias, Ericas, Andromedas, Vacciniums, Ledums, Menziezia and other American Flowering Evergreens of the choicest and most varied kinds. Also a select assortment of Hardy Herbaceous Plants. The above stock has been collected and reared with the greatest taste and care, and comprises plants of all ages and descriptions suitable for either a Nurseryman's stock, or for private Gentlemen disposed to avail themselves of an opportunity of adorning their grounds on moderate terms.[30]

The same front page carried a chilling advert from the Sheffield Union: 'The Guardians of the Poor are extremely desirous of obtaining eligible SITUATIONS for a number of Fine Healthy Children now chargeable to the union.' James Barron was far from alone in feeling the pinch. This was a period known

as 'The Hungry Forties', and children in the workhouse were
a good source of cheap apprentices and servants.

The picture for James Barron during the rest of the decade
seems a mixed one. He managed to cling on to his nursery business, although by 1843 his old nursery shop at 10 Haymarket
belonged to a grocer and tea dealer. He still described himself
as a nurseryman in 1847, but our source for this information
is a sad one: on 17 July 1847, in the death-notices section of
the *Sheffield Independent*, we find the entry: 'aged two and a half
Elizabeth Mary the beloved daughter of James Barron, Norton
Hammer Nursery'.[31] By the 1851 census, James Barron was living with his wife Sarah and his daughter Charlotte, aged ten,
in Matilda Street in the centre of Sheffield. His occupation was
given as 'landscape gardener', so sadly it appears that he was
no longer a nurseryman and was just a tradesman for hire.

However, despite all the difficulties, the picture was not universally grim. Both Thomas Sibbald and Neil Wilson were able
to pass on their businesses as thriving going-concerns to members of their family. They had managed to carve out a place
for themselves serving their very different clientele – farmers,
miners and ironworkers, in the case of Thomas Sibbald; and
the wealthy leisured classes of the west coast of Scotland, in
the case of Neil Wilson.

Whether fleeting or long-lived, these small businesses were
an essential part of the nineteenth-century horticultural
boom. They were part of an ecosystem of businesses serving
every type of gardener, and an essential link in the chain that
brought a rich variety of plants into gardens up and down the
country. Every town was ringed with nursery grounds and
they were a natural part of the transition between urban and

rural spaces. Whilst plant collectors grab the headlines, when it comes to charting the story of plant introduction, after a plant had been 'discovered' in the wild and sent back home, it still had a long journey to travel before it made its way safely into the confines of the garden.

Nurserymen are the forgotten heroes of the transformation of a plant from the wild to the garden. It was they who had the task of creating the right conditions in which new plants could grow, on a scale that would make them accessible and affordable to ordinary gardeners. They invested years of labour in raising stocks, hoping that gardeners might find the new plants desirable enough to buy, at a price that made this investment worthwhile. From seed to sale often took many years of patience and skilled work in the nursery seedbeds and glasshouses. They had to second-guess taste and fashion, and the decisions they made, the variants they selected or rejected for breeding, and the plants they chose to stock and sell did much to determine the cultivars that we now grow in our gardens today.

By and large, these skilled and enterprising men have not received the attention or credit they deserve. This is largely because the way of raising and selling plants that they perfected is long gone. Until as late as the 1950s, most gardeners still bought plants from nurseries, where they were grown from seed, much as Thomas Sibbald and colleagues had done. The plants were lifted, delivered and planted whilst still dormant or (in the case of bedding) still young. However, from the early 1960s that world was overturned by the introduction of lightweight plastic plant pots and the fact that more families could afford private cars. Plants could now be easily transported and replanted at any time of the year. Very rapidly a brand-new concept arrived: self-service 'garden centres'; the mail-order nursery catalogue became almost a thing of the past. A few specialist nurseries clung on, but many small family businesses simply disappeared. Today the Internet offers hope to small specialist growers, and there is an increasing willingness among keen gardeners to seek out new and unusual plants, so hopefully new Thomas Sibbalds, George Harrisons and James Barrons can thrive in their place.

CHAPTER NINE

'A solitary wanderer':
The Australian Adventurer

John Dallachy admitted 21 June 1826 upon the
recommendation of the Earl of Aberdeen

ON SATURDAY 2 SEPTEMBER 1871, THE CITIZENS OF
Melbourne opened their weekly copy of *The Leader* to read
an article which, amongst other things, made mysterious reference to 'the late Mr Dallachy'. The writer of the article
declared:

> It may astonish many of Mr Dallachy's old friends thus to
> hear of his death, but it will surprise no one in the Botanic
> Gardens. His death, we understand has been well known
> there for some considerable time past, but there has been no
> public notice of it. Why is this – we would ask Dr Von Muel-
> ler? Where and when did Mr John Dallachy die? Why has he
> been exiled in his old age for so many years under the burning
> Sun of North Australia in the neighbourhood of Cardwell?[1]

The journey that John Dallachy took from a small Aberdeenshire village to 'exile' and death in the wilds of North
Queensland was a remarkable one, but there are clues to the

path that his life took, in the record of his time at Chiswick. Dallachy's entry in the Handwriting Book has some of the poorest spelling in the book. It looks as though his formal education stopped at fourteen, when he went to work as a farm boy on a local farm in Banffshire. As 'Town's Officer', his father was employed by the town council to patrol the streets, fetter prisoners and guard the jails. Although a responsible position, this role was not well paid and did not enjoy high social status. We do not know how or why John Dallachy moved from agricultural work to working in gardens, but his early career went well. The key appointment in his Handwriting Book entry was eighteen months spent at Haddo House, the great estate owned by the Earl of Aberdeen, and it was the earl who recommended Dallachy for a place at the Chiswick Garden.

In March 1827, after being at the Garden for nearly a year, the night watchman James Holder left his job, and Dallachy obligingly stepped in for a month until a replacement could be found. He was asked to stand in again during the winter when the new watchman, Devereux Fuller, left to work for the new Zoological Gardens. Acting as a night watchman was a lonely and thankless task, especially in the depths of winter. Many experienced gardeners would have regarded it as beneath them, but John Dallachy does not seem to have minded. Indeed, as a sign of deference or gratitude to the Horticultural Society, he later gave his eldest son the middle name 'Sabine', in honour of the Society's unpopular and overbearing secretary. The impression given is of a capable man of humble origin, obliging and deferential to his social superiors.

Some accounts say that Dallachy worked for a while at Kew on leaving Chiswick in August 1829, but I have not been able to find any evidence to corroborate this. What is clear is that he was back in Scotland working at Haddo House by 1836. He married a local girl, Ann Matheson, at Methlick, near Haddo House, on 6 March that year. She was twenty-five and he was thirty-two. At this time the owner of Haddo House, the fourth Earl of Aberdeen, was embarking on a programme of massively ambitious estate development and this must have been a busy time for John. Not only was the earl planting an enormous number of trees in his parkland (by his estimate, around eleven million), but he also ordered that the formal gardens around the house be redeveloped. As head gardener, John Dallachy oversaw the replanting of the eighteenth-century terraces around the house. A series of sketches and paintings by James Giles depicts the evolution of the terrace from a simple lawn with central fountain, to a colourful symmetrical garden of parterres, seats and flowers. It seems that Dallachy had a comfortable life in the purpose-built gardener's house, positioned just outside the walled kitchen garden. He and his wife had four children – two boys (Joseph Sabine and John) and two girls (Mary and Eliza) – and, as would be expected of a competent gardener working on a great estate, he upheld the reputation of his employer with a regular smattering of awards at national and local horticultural shows.

Then, in 1847, completely out of the blue, Dallachy revealed another character trait that was to reappear throughout his life – a thirst for adventure. He decided to leave the comfortable set-up at Haddo House, emigrate and take his young family to Ceylon. Like most of our gardeners, he left no diaries, correspondence or other clues to help us work out his motivation, but the most likely explanation is that he was gripped by 'coffee mania'. The 1830s and 1840s saw a combination of factors come together that convinced a large number of enterprising (and sometimes desperate) men that a fortune could be made setting up coffee plantations in the British colony of Ceylon.

The British authorities had managed to put down a rebellion and assert their control over the colony by building new roads, which opened up the interior of the island for development for the first time. The experiments with the crop in the Peradeniya Botanic Gardens under James Watson had shown that the lush highlands provided perfect growing conditions for coffee, and an Act of Parliament asserted the right of the Crown to sell uncultivated land over the heads of the local population. The final piece of the jigsaw that made Ceylon seem a land of opportunity was the abolition of slavery across the British Empire in 1833. This denied the coffee growers of the West Indies access to cheap slave labour; supply faltered and coffee prices rose. Suddenly there was an opening in the market and Ceylon had the advantage of proximity to the impoverished populations of southern India, a ready supply of cheap labour to work for wages, and conditions not far removed from slavery itself.

The Dallachy family left in 1847, armed with a letter of introduction from the Earl of Aberdeen. Having served as foreign secretary, the earl was formidably well connected and John must have hoped that this letter would open doors for him. However, something must have gone wrong, because on 15 October 1848 he and his family boarded a ship named *Torrington* that left Colombo in Ceylon for Melbourne.[2] Perhaps life on a remote plantation did not suit him and his family, or perhaps he heard news of even richer pickings in the wide-open spaces of Australia. Since 1815 the Colonial Government of Australia had actively encouraged free settlers, to reduce the influence of convict settlers and 'squatters' – businessmen who had unilaterally claimed large swathes of land. Journalists known as 'boosters' were paid to write complimentary accounts of Australia as a land of opportunity, where anyone prepared to work hard could prosper. Dallachy and his family may have been attracted by the accounts of a rapidly developing colony, where growing settlements created opportunities for skilled horticulturalists. We do know that he worked briefly as a gardener to one of the wealthier settlers, a stockbroker called Jonathan Were in Brighton, Victoria, now an affluent beachside suburb of Melbourne.

In 1849 John Dallachy was appointed as curator of the Botanic Gardens in Melbourne. He took over from the recently deceased John Arthur, who had been curator since the gardens were founded by Governor Charles La Trobe in 1846. Dallachy arrived to find the new Botanic Gardens an unpromising, swampy site. It seems that the burghers of Melbourne's commitment to botanical science extended only to sparing a piece of unwanted land with hills too high and too steep for housing, and which drained into a chain of useless marshes. Where the land was not marshy, it was rocky. Indeed, contrary to the 'booster' articles, Melbourne as a whole does not sound as though it had much to recommend it. A book called *The Chronicles of Early Melbourne* by 'Garryowen' describes a boom town rapidly thrown up around a growing shipping trade, with 'a vilely smelling row of slaughter houses jumped up along the river banks… commencing that Yarra pollution which has grown into a huge and irredeemable abomination'.[3]

Before he died, apparently from drinking cholera-contaminated water from the Yarra River, Dallachy's predecessor, John Arthur, had managed to fence in five acres (two hectares), into which he had planted a range of shrubs and trees. However, there was still an enormous amount of work to do to make this unpromising plot into anything like a garden. One of Dallachy's first tasks was to tackle the 'lagoon' – really just a string of marshy ponds surrounded by dense thicket of tea trees. He excavated to create a proper lake and set to work planting in the surrounding soil, which was a rich accumulation of alluvial sediment, enriched with centuries of decayed swamp growth. There was a huge amount of carting of soil and manure, and hard labour to create paths and drains, and it seems that Dallachy was very hands-on.

Obtaining sufficient supplies of water to keep the plants alive during Melbourne's long, hot summers was a constant struggle. Water had to be carried by hand up the steep slopes throughout the summer. Once the drought was over, the next challenge was flood, the river many times bursting its banks. The gardens lacked even the most basic facilities – there were no potting sheds, no glasshouses, no shelter sheds or changing rooms for the gardeners. Dallachy's propagation work was carried out in a small hut that he made himself from tea-tree branches gathered at the nearby Gardiners Creek. Having been used to running a lavishly appointed garden, backed by a wealthy and enthusiastic patron, with a team of trained garden staff at his beck and call, this must have been a shock to John Dallachy.

Gradually, John and his small team of labourers made progress, and the margin of the lake was embellished with a continuous bed of flowers and shrubs a mile long. A report to the Legislative Council boasted that in 1851 the gardens contained 5,000 varieties of exotic plants and 1,000 indigenous species.[4] The emphasis on 'exotic' rather than local plants is telling. Botanic gardens across the British Empire served as a respite from local conditions, a reminder of home and sometimes even an explicit instrument to 'civilize' the colonies by introducing genteel and educational leisure opportunities. In contrast to Kew, which over the course of the nineteenth century developed a rigorously scientific approach, eschewing ornamental plantings and restricting public opening hours, many colonial botanic gardens made a deliberate attempt to emulate the British public parks pioneered by Paxton, complete with rolling green lawns designed to evoke memories of the motherland.

Whilst the Melbourne Botanic Gardens under John Dallachy did feature local plants, he also made an effort to present the latest bedding plants, trees and shrubs in the neatly laid-out beds, exactly as he would have done at Haddo House. This proved popular with the people of Melbourne. The average attendance on a Sunday was reported to be 800 visitors, and even higher on a day when the Melbourne Horticultural Society staged one of its flower shows. This achievement was ideally timed, as Melbourne was about to experience an unprecedented burst of civic pride. On 15 November 1850, Queen Victoria proclaimed that the state of Victoria should have its own government, independent of the remote legislature in Sydney. A public holiday was declared, and John Dallachy's lakeside gardens provided the ideal backdrop for celebratory speeches and music. The spot, under an ancient gum tree, is still marked with a plaque.

Following this successful start, Dallachy was promoted to the newly created post of superintendent. Statements of account show that he was paid the respectable salary of £100 per annum with free accommodation. He had two gardeners, two under-gardeners, a carter and eight labourers working under him. He was well settled with his family in the specially built gardener's house within the walls of the Botanic Gardens. He had a group of close friends in the local horticultural community, and arranged for a 'rustic thatched shed' to be erected so that the Melbourne Horticultural Society could hold their convivial monthly meetings there. In later years one of the members of the committee fondly remembered, 'On wintry nights, along with Mr Dallachy, I have frequently piloted our way through the crabholes in Richmond Flat, steering as straight as we could for the new bridge across the Yarra at Chapel-Street.'[5]

Melbourne was gradually emerging as a proper settlement, with stone houses replacing shacks amidst tea-tree scrub, and paved streets replacing rutted tracks. By 1851 the population had grown steadily to the point where 23,000 people lived there. The local worthies must have felt they were making real progress as they sought to put the colony's penal past behind it. The Botanic Gardens, with their flower shows and tree-planting ceremonies, were the jewel in the crown.

However, this new-found gentility was to be smashed to bits as effectively as if a tornado had visited the streets of Melbourne. In many ways it *was* a tornado: a tornado of greed and gold-lust. In February 1851 a local man named Edward Hargreaves struck gold near Bathurst in New South Wales. He had joined the California gold-rush in 1849, had noted the similarities in landscape between the gold-fields of California and his homeland, and had returned home with dreams of striking it rich. His hunch proved spectacularly correct and news of the discovery flooded out, filling the Australian press with fantastical stories. In August, fabulously rich gold-fields were found in Victoria, in the Buninyong Ranges near Ballarat. Almost overnight, Melbourne became a ghost town as men and women from all walks of life dropped what they were doing and rushed to the gold-fields. This led to a chronic labour shortage, and wages went through the roof as employers struggled to keep their workers, who were all seized with the dream of overnight riches. One observer described how 'Slim shopmen, stout calved butlers, government clerks, doctors, lawyers, runaway sailors, deserting soldiers, self-ordained divines and strong minded females in ultra-bloomer costume, flocked to Forest Creek like flies around a treacle butt.'⁶ 'Ultra-bloomers' were baggy trousers gathered at the ankle. If women were donning trousers in the rush for gold, the world was truly turning upside down.

And yet amidst all this, it seems that John Dallachy loyally stuck by the Gardens, unmoved by tales of miners riding gold-shod horses or eating sandwiches jammed with £10 notes. However, he could not have failed to notice the changes around him. The dust had barely settled on the road out of town when the locals were followed by a massive inrush of foreigners, drawn to Australia by tales of gold. Now Melbourne morphed into a transit camp, the jumping-off point for immigrants disgorged from ships that had travelled thousands of miles. The town was ringed with tents, and the beaches around were littered with the possessions of desperate immigrants who had jettisoned them when they discovered the extortionate fees that would be charged to transport them to the diggings. Even worse, the streets were thronged with drunken gold-diggers, newly returned from the hard life of the gold-field and ready to rip up the town with their new-found wealth. Swaggering bearded men, carrying Colt guns and a bowie knife to protect their bounty from thieves, were hardly the target market for flower shows in a botanic garden. The preferred amusement was to watch a miner's lavish wedding, which had become a craze among those who wanted to celebrate their bonanza. Miners paraded through the street in carriages bedecked with feathers and attended by liveried servants, their lady of choice festooned with the latest fashions and jewellery.

Life must have been difficult as these free-spending new-comers tempted tradesmen to hike their prices, and public servants like Dallachy on fixed incomes must have struggled. Many of his garden staff deserted him, and Dallachy was forced to rely on untrained farm boys. Twenty years later his loyalty was still remembered and appreciated in Melbourne: 'When others rushed off to the diggings, and secured wealth, he remained at his post, and took care of the gardens.'[7]

Whilst Dallachy was undoubtedly loyal, this version of events fails to mention that all the while he was actually busy undertaking his very own treasure hunt. Like the gold-diggers, Dallachy was drawn to Australia's wide-open spaces, but for him it was the promise of exciting botanical discoveries that was the draw, rather than the prospect of gold. For several years he had been in the habit of leaving the tending of the gardens to his under-gardeners, whilst he went off for long tours of what was then largely uncharted country, including an expedition to the marvellously named Mount Disappointment in January 1850. Just like his fellow Chiswick student Thomas Bridges, the best of the specimens he gathered went straight to William Hooker, the director of the Royal Botanic Gardens at Kew, and duplicates were added to the collection at the Melbourne Botanic Gardens, where, being local and more familiar, they were likely to cause less of a stir.

Chenolea Dallachyana, 'Dallachy's Saltbush', one of many
Australian plants collected and named after John Dallachy.
This species (now known as *Maireana trichoptera*)
was described as a 'capital forage plant' for sheep.

It is not clear whether Hooker paid him for these specimens or whether Dallachy did it simply for his own satisfaction and to support botanical science. Most Australian flora was startlingly different to European eyes, and there was a high demand for plant material from this strange and distant continent. Dallachy's erstwhile employer, the Earl of Aberdeen, had collected trees and shrubs from 'New Holland', and William Hooker regularly sent Australian seeds and plants to Haddo House. Whilst at Chiswick, Dallachy would have handled the consignments of exotic plants from plant hunters in far-flung places. It seems likely that these early experiences fostered in him a desire to taste at first hand the excitement of 'discovering' new plants. Having ridden the storm of the initial gold-rush disruption, all looked set fair for John Dallachy to enjoy a respectable career, with a tied cottage in the gardens for his young family, steady improvement of the Botanic Gardens, and the intermittent excitement of a plant-hunting expedition to earn him the respect and esteem of the horticultural and botanical community.

* * *

It fell to a 'lean, weak chested' young German to disrupt Dallachy's life far more than thousands of burly, gun-toting gold-diggers had managed to do. In 1847 Ferdinand Jakob Heinrich Mueller arrived in Adelaide. This was the villainous-sounding 'Dr Von Mueller' whom twenty years later the anonymous letter-writer was to accuse of 'exiling' Dallachy to a lonely death. Mueller was a doctor of philosophy and a keen student of chemistry and botany. He had a passion for exploration, which belied his rather puny physical appearance. Over his lifetime Mueller was to be responsible for more than a thousand publications and become the world's leading authority on the flora of Australia.

He started as he meant to go on, making his first Australian plant collection by leaning over the railings of the ship to gather samples of seaweed as it came into dock. In 1852, the same year that Dallachy was made superintendent of the Gardens, Governor La Trobe created the new post of Government Botanist and appointed Mueller. He was a hypochondriac, a martyr to piles and was frequently seen with a woollen muffler around his chest to protect him from chills. Nevertheless, he was physically hardy enough to throw himself into arduous and often solitary expeditions.

Within days of his appointment, Mueller embarked on a dazzling series of inland expeditions which earnt him the title of 'the last explorer of Victoria'. Gathering specimens as he went, these missions far outshone those of John Dallachy. Mostly Mueller travelled alone, though on at least one occasion Dallachy accompanied him (for instance, in 1853 Dallachy joined him on one of his expeditions to the Ovens valley and Mount Buffalo). With single-minded ambition, Mueller threw himself into creating one of the world's most important herbariums. Within five years of his appointment he had amassed more than 45,000 specimens representing 15,000 species. His reputation as the authority on Australian plants grew rapidly. Over time, the Government Botanist inserted himself more and more actively in the day-to-day decision-making of the Melbourne Botanic Gardens, eventually joining the management committee. He was active in giving John Dallachy advice and acted as an intermediary for him with Kew, asking for plants and seeds on the Gardens' behalf. In September 1853, Mueller wrote a report for the governor on the Botanic Gardens, confidently asserting what, in his view, the objectives of the gardens should be: acclimatization of foreign plants, research on native plants and, firmly in last place, healthy recreation for Melbourne's citizens.

At no point did Mueller pass on any negative comments on Dallachy's management of the Gardens; when he wrote to William Hooker he commended 'the well-known Mr Dallach [sic] under whose able management the young bot. garden of this colony is growing rapidly'.[8] Nevertheless, whether deliberately or not, with his greater social standing and higher standard of education, Mueller gradually edged the humble John Dallachy to one side, as the gardeners deferred to him rather than the actual superintendent.

Mueller's collecting activity added more and more plants to the Gardens, which increasingly began to resemble a showcase for his own collections, laid out with Teutonic thoroughness according to the principles of systematic botany, with few allowances made for aesthetic appeal. La Trobe basked in the reflected glory of the Government Botanist's achievements, and in August 1857 Mueller was officially appointed as director of the Gardens as well. On 18 August 1857, Dallachy received a bombshell of a letter from the Inspector-General of Public Works, which stated that he must 'obey all instructions as he may receive from the Director, without whose knowledge and consent he will not commence on any new work'.[9] To add insult to injury, Dallachy was to submit a weekly report to the new director, and was not allowed to fell trees or issue any plants or seed from the gardens without his written permission. Essentially, he was stripped of any effective control of the gardens that he had managed for nearly a decade.

It seems that John Dallachy slipped into a more subservient role with little objection. He undertook more plant-collecting trips for the Botanic Gardens. In 1858 he collected drought-resistant species along the River Murray near

Wentworth and along the Darling River as far north as Mount Murchison near Wilcannia. In 1860 he investigated the Wimmera River and Lake Hindmarsh. By 1861 the state decided it could dispense with the role of superintendent completely, and Dallachy was laid off with a compensatory payment of £300. It seems that he tried his luck setting up a nursery, although there is some disagreement as to the location – the *Australian Dictionary of Biography* says it was at Prahran, but other accounts say Mount Erica. Either way, the venture failed and it appears that Dallachy was in real financial difficulty, so he turned again to the Melbourne Botanic Gardens. Mueller engaged him as a 'Collector for the botanic Garden', at a rate of ten shillings for each working day, 'no personal travel expenses being allowed'.[10]

View of Melbourne Botanic Gardens from a photograph taken around thirty years after John Dallachy worked there.

In 1864, at Mueller's request, Dallachy joined a party led by the explorer George Dalrymple to form a settlement at Rockingham Bay in North Queensland, with a view to collecting plants in this unexplored region. Aged just thirty-eight, George Augustus Frederick Elphinstone Dalrymple was twenty-two years younger than Dallachy, yet had already managed to pack a lot into his life. Like Dallachy, he was born in Scotland and left in the 1840s, intending to become a coffee planter in Ceylon; but also like Dallachy, he was diverted to the opportunities of Australia. He arrived there in around 1856 and headed for the undeveloped north. He set up a syndicate to fund expeditions to explore and establish new settlements in Queensland. There appears to have been some sort of scandal involving a friend's wife, which somehow resulted in Dalrymple assaulting a police magistrate. Nevertheless, in 1864 his company, with official backing, organized an expedition to establish a new settlement on Rockingham Bay. The aim was to find a good location to act as a port for inland cattle stations north of Bowen.

Crammed together on two small boats was all that was needed to set up a miniature town. Alongside John Dallachy and his collecting kit, the party consisted of G. E. Dalrymple himself, the land commissioner W. A. Tully, Lt Marlow of the Queensland Native Police and three native troopers, a hotel keeper, a storekeeper, a carpenter, a market gardener, three farmers, two bushmen, a translator called James Morrill, twelve horses, twelve sheep, two goats and some fowls, together with stores and building materials. The official record of the expedition shows that the party anchored on Rockingham Bay in *The Policeman* on 22 January 1864. They disembarked, raised

Hoya pottsii grown at Chiswick from a single leaf brought back from China by the Society's plant collector, John Potts. Before he left Chiswick to work in Egypt, James Traill described how the plant was 'carefully planted and anxiously attended to' by the Chiswick gardeners.

(*Left*) Self portrait of Harmanis de Alwis, a talented botanical artist who was working at the Peradeniya Botanic Gardens in Sri Lanka when James Watson arrived to take up the post of superintendent of the gardens in 1832.

(*Below*) The house in the Caledonian Horticultural Society's garden that James Barnet was suspected of vandalizing in 1836. Today the building is a café in the Royal Botanic Garden Edinburgh.

The Dutch Codlin apple painted in 1820 for the Horticultural Society by William Hooker.
This was one of hundreds of apple varieties in the Chiswick garden cared for by Robert Thompson.

1. Coes Golden Drop.   2. Reine Claude Violette.
3. Kirkes.   4. Jefferson.

An illustration of plums from Robert Thompson's book titled *The Gardener's Assistant*.
The plum on the bottom right of the picture is a Jefferson Plum, the variety sent to
Thompson by his erstwhile colleague, James Barnet.

This illustration from *The Horticultural Magazine*,
1837, shows a yellow calceolaria and a rose
supplied by 'Mr Barron, Nurseryman High
House near Sheffield'.

The much-decorated Australian botanist
Ferdinand von Mueller – friend or foe to
ex-Chiswick gardener John Dallachy?

John Dallachy's entry in the
Handwriting Book. The
poor spelling and grammar
suggest John Dallachy only
enjoyed a basic education.
This was to be decisive in
the course of his career
after leaving Chiswick.

*John Dallachy admitted 21 June 1826, upon the
recommendation of the Earl of Aberdeen*

*I was Born on the 28 of August 1804 in the Parish
of Keith Banffshire. My father was Towns
Officer in Huntly. Nov 1818 when 14th I was
employed by Mr McPherson near Huntly on
his farm, Nov 1821 when 17th I was engaged as an
apprentice to the Gardens of Huntly Lodge where
I stoped 2 years. I went in Feby 1824 to Aberdeen
was employed by Mr Walker in his nursary for
3 months. In May 1824 I engaged to Haddo Hous Garden
belonging to the Earl of Aberdeen In Nov 1825 I left it and
lived with my father till Feby 1826 then I came to London
and was employed by Messrs Malcolm Gray & Coy in thei
in there nursary At Kensington nearly 3 months I was sen
by Mr Malcolm to Kew Hall Gardens where I stoped one mon
th. on The 21st June nearly 22 years of age And Unmaried
John Dallachy*

(*Left*) This illustration of a Douglas fir, *Pseudotsuga menziesii*, gives an indication of the impressive conifer specimens to be found in arboreta like the one John Slowe cared for at Bayfordbury in Hertfordshire.

(*Below*) Cartoon showing a rain-soaked flower show at the Chiswick Garden in 1828. These fetes became popular events in the London social calendar, even though some members of the Society worried they might set a bad example of moral conduct to the young gardeners.

Seeds of *Pentstemon ovatum* were amongst those stolen from the Chiswick Garden by Reuben Hale and John Frederick Wood in 1828.

Joseph Sabine, the Secretary of the Horticultural Society, was blamed for its financial difficulties. Here he is depicted outside the Chiswick Garden as a poor gardener forced out of work by freezing weather – a common occupational hazard.
(© *The Trustees of the British Museum*)

Cartoon by George Cruikshank of a Horticultural Society meeting in 1826, with Joseph Sabine and fraudster John Turner flanking the chairman.

Illustration of Bow Street Police Court, Westminster, in 1808. The bottom right of the picture shows a Bow Street Runner with a suspect. (*London Metropolitan Archives, City of London*)

A view of the Society's garden at Kensington, published in 1863. When this garden opened in 1861, the Chiswick garden was very quickly over-shadowed and its decline accelerated.

the Union Jack flag and, after scouting the beach, chose a site for the settlement, rapidly marking out streets and plots for houses and shops with wooden pegs and string. This settlement was to become known as Cardwell, and today is a popular tourist centre for visitors to the World Heritage sites of the Barrier Reef and the Queensland Wet Tropics.

By this point John Dallachy was sixty years old and the expedition was by no means an easy one. While most of the party concentrated on building shelters and clearing scrub, Dallachy joined scouting parties that attempted to find a route over the Cardwell Range to link this new port with the grazing land and settlements inland, all the while keeping his eyes peeled for interesting specimens. This was arduous and dangerous work. The accounts of the first days of the settlement frequently mention close encounters with alligators and tiger sharks. The rhetoric of exploration in this period suggested that explorers, settlers and botanists alike were entering 'virgin' territory, completely ignoring that this was land that had been occupied for millennia by Aboriginal communities. When Aboriginal peoples understandably resisted this occupation of their home territories, the white settlers reacted as if these acts of resistance were unwarranted acts of 'savagery'. Some of the settlers were honest enough to state clearly what was happening. Arthur J. Scott, who was in the party with John Dallachy, openly admitted 'the fact that occupying their country is at once a declaration of war'.[11]

Dallachy never left Cardwell, staying as the town rapidly developed along the foreshore, sandwiched between the white-sand beaches and the mangrove forests. He continued to make his living by sending back plants to Mueller in

Melbourne. This involved making many unaccompanied trips into the surrounding countryside, and he seems to have been completely unconcerned about the danger involved. The dense rainforest was a botanical treasure trove, home to many rare species found nowhere else on Earth, but it was also a dangerous environment. Rainfall of more than twenty-three feet (seven metres) a year made for difficult and treacherous conditions. Contemporary government surveyors left accounts of nettle trees that stung their packhorses so badly, they 'got mad and died within two hours'.[12]

Travelling unaccompanied also left Dallachy vulnerable, when it came to encounters with Aborigines. Many years later a friend recounted:

> To my knowledge, on one occasion they staked his camp in the scrub on the Tully, when he was by himself. He had made a fire at dark on the river bank in the scrub, no tents or blankets, being tired, he had gone to sleep; in the morning when he woke up he found a sword and large wooden shield lying at his head, and almost touching it. Dallachy thought it was a present; he had not seen or heard anything during the night, and he knew it was not there when he went to sleep.

The writer claimed that the Aborigines 'never molested him, but always got out of his way, thinking him demented for gathering things that they knew were useless to them, and they thought utterly valueless to others'.[13] However, another more contemporary newspaper article recorded an encounter when 'he had to run for his life, leaving everything, and reaching the town thoroughly exhausted'.[14] Even more alarming, after Dallachy called his family out to Cardwell to join him, his daughter was caught up in an Aborigine attack whilst she was on a boating party to Garden Island. Against a backdrop of frequent and violent land clearances by white farmers, the boat was attacked and 'three of their spears took effect, two of them wounding two of the men slightly, and one of them Miss Dallachy rather severely'. Retribution for this type of assault was swift and merciless. A party went out the next day and destroyed several Aboriginal camps.

Back in urbanized Melbourne, it is easy to see why John Dallachy's loss of position and removal to remote and danger-ous Cardwell was viewed as exile. The sense that his position had been usurped by the newcomer Mueller gained ground, finding voice in a series of increasingly hotly worded letters to the local newspapers. In November 1869 one letter, signed 'An Older Gardener', painted a heart-rending portrait of Dallachy:

> I often think with pity on the sad lot of the now frail white-headed old man who bore the heat of the day and the brunt of the toil in winning from the wilderness, by aid of a very small annual grant, the only part of the gardens yet worth looking at; who stuck to his post when all hands left and joined in the rush to the newly-discovered goldfields; and picture him as he is at present, a solitary wanderer among the savage tribes about Rockingham Bay, in Queensland, employed as botanical collector to the Melbourne Botanical Gardens.[15]

To a great extent these letters, accusing the director of the Gardens of being a 'cuckoo' who had 'jumped poor Dal-lachy's claim', were motivated by a dislike for the way Mueller ran the Gardens, as much as by concern for Dallachy. Despite cementing his reputation as an eminent and knowledgeable botanist and energetically planting the Melbourne Botanic Gardens with more than 30,000 trees, the work of Ferdinand von Mueller was not popular with the good people of Melbourne. They missed their attractive pleasure grounds and had limited patience for the rigorously scientific layout of the Gardens, which had begun to take on the appearance of a three-dimensional botanical textbook, festooned with Latin labels. Even emulating Paxton's achievement by getting *Victoria amazonica* to flower at the Gardens in 1867 failed to placate the people of Melbourne.

Mueller paid little attention to his local critics, being far more concerned about how he was viewed in the international scientific community. To make matters worse, even after several decades in Australia he maintained his old-world formality and still spoke with a heavy German accent, which made him an easy target for xenophobic and anti-intellectual journalists and politicians. Meanwhile local nurserymen and horticulturists despaired of the poor horticultural standards displayed in the Gardens, and were frustrated by Mueller's habit of distributing new plants freely to other botanic gardens and foreign potentates rather than to them. One typical article in *The Leader* thundered against Mueller's 'ignorance and want of ability as a practical gardener. It is one thing to anatomise a plant, but quite another and very different thing to grow one. However transcendent Dr Mueller's ability may be with the micro-scope, the dissecting knife and tweezers, he has no knowledge of the use of the spade.' The state of the Gardens under Mueller was contrasted with their appearance under Dallachy's care: 'Twenty years ago these gardens possessed great natural beauty. This has been destroyed, and what have we in its place? A wilderness of plants stuck – not planted – in the earth – without judgement, skill or taste.'[16]

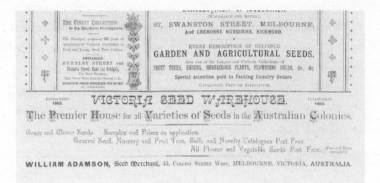

Advertisement for William Adamson's Victoria Seed Warehouse. Owners of nursery businesses like this one preferred John Dallachy's style of running the Melbourne Botanic Gardens to that of von Mueller.

The campaign against Mueller intensified when news of the death of John Dallachy reached Melbourne. He died on 4 June 1871 at the age of sixty-three at his home in Cardwell, after a short illness lasting just ten days. The governor appointed a board to look into the management of the Gardens, which reported in December of that year. The report explicitly contrasted the parts of the Gardens laid out by Dallachy with the parts laid out under Mueller's supervision, and recommended that Mueller should be relieved of the task of managing the grounds and should have his responsibilities confined to the scientific work of the Gardens. Although he maintained his position as Government Botanist, Mueller never forgave the

262 *THE HIDDEN HORTICULTURISTS*

government officials who dismissed him and refused ever to set foot in the Botanical Gardens again. Whilst the report never explicitly addressed his supposed maltreatment of John Dallachy, the accusations certainly coloured the public mood and probably forced the governor's hand in dealing with the situation.

However, before we assign roles of villain and victim to Mueller and Dallachy, it is worth pausing to examine some counter-arguments. Even whilst the criticisms of Mueller were at their most intense, there were people ready to recount a different version of events. In *The Weekly Times* for Saturday 20 January 1872, an anonymously written letter, responding to earlier correspondence in the paper, concluded:

> The statement put forward in reference to the late Mr Dallachy, viz., that he perished miserably in the bush while collecting specimens, which, when sent to Europe, assisted to 'procure for his chief a title,' is simply untrue. He died upon a station, with every comfort around him. Letters were repeatedly sent to him from Melbourne by certain parties endeavouring to urge him to agitation against Baron von Mueller.[17]

There is no evidence that Dallachy ever made a complaint against Mueller, and we know that he regularly sent letters along with the specimens he submitted. Unfortunately, only one letter from John Dallachy survives, but the tone is not only friendly towards Mueller, it is overwhelmingly positive about the experience of plant collecting in North Queensland. As with his Handwriting Book entry, the grammar and spelling are touchingly uneven. Written in November 1868 and giving his location as 'Herbert River', Dallachy explains: 'I was up on Mount Grahame on Saturday and returned to station last night I have inclosed a fragment of a tree Fern... I suppose is an Alsophila.' Even though the vocabulary in the letter is basic, his excitement at exploring the landscape shines through as he continues:

> on the tope of the above mountain is covered with the most dense scrub and high trees some of them 150 to 200 feet in hight. I could not get to the highest Point of the mountain on account of the scrub – there are miles of it here and this mountain and scrub no white man has ever been in it but myself – I have got the Bowenia spectabilis in flower for you – it grows in a bundance on the tope in Scrub.[18]

Life at a new township like Cardwell was basic, and there was frequent conflict with the Aboriginal clans, whose grounds the settlers and squatters were taking and in some cases destroying, but John Dallachy does seem to have settled happily into his new life.

It is true that he was of enormous value to Mueller, particularly as he collaborated with George Bentham on the masterwork *Flora Australiensis: A Description of the Plants of the Australian Territory*, published between 1863 and 1878. However, it was not a one-sided relationship; in March 1870, in a letter to Bentham, Mueller noted:

> Mr Dallachy's plants, as you remark, are always, or at least often, instructive and frequently completer than those of

other collectors... no one has ever in Australia enjoyed such facilities to explore a jungle district, than Mr Dallachy. He is now half a dozen years quietly and *purposely* settled at Rockingham's Bay and his plants cost me from that district alone over one thousand pounds sterling! He has nothing in the world else to do, then to collect, as he is a kind of pensioner of my department. As he is no botanist in the true sense of the word, he incurs no loss of time in any minute examinations. Besides he is stationary at Rockingham's Bay, has a cottage to dry and keep his collections in, and commands the sea port & the dense forest in one hours walk.

In this letter Mueller jealously contrasts Dallachy's comfortable berth with his own experience as a plant hunter:

Look how I was placed for years, sleeping under the canopy of heaven, I had to shelter myself and my plants with a bid of light calico, and often to carry my collections for thousands of miles on pack horses! I could only take a few specimens of any plant just as I found it at a time, while Mr Dallachy could comfortably watch the same trees for years, until he finally found flowers & fruits for most. I have ordered him to move to Cape York... In the thousands of letters written to Dallachy I always directed him to what flowers & what fruits in each special wanting case to look![19]

Mueller's defenders also made the point that far from usurping Dallachy from his rightful place in the Gardens, Mueller was offering him a lifeline when he made him a plant collector. One anonymous letter-writer to *The Weekly Times* noted:

It should not be forgotten that it was solely through the generous intercession of Baron von Mueller that Mr Dallachy's
removal from office was prevented in 1857. Eventually, however, his extreme want of steadiness led to his removal in
1862 with compensation, the office of curator being then
abolished. He since that time was well supported as a plant
collector in Queensland, where he was left, as regards his
movements, to his own discretion – in fact, being looked
upon in the light of a pensioner.[20]

Another reference to John Dallachy having shortcomings
was made by one of his supporters, who admitted that Dallachy unfortunately had a 'failing', and that this unnamed
weakness 'was intensified and developed by domestic sorrows.
How the domestic troubles and sorrows originated, it is not
now my intention to enter into. It is a sad story.'[21]

Combing through the archives and records of Melbourne
for the late 1850s and early 1860s reveals some 'domestic
troubles and sorrows'. The first is the fact that his wife Ann
Dallachy is nowhere to be seen in any official record after the
family's arrival on the *Torrington* in 1848. On John Dallachy's
death certificate, his children are listed in the margin and the
list includes the sad note 'female child (deceased)'. It is possible that Ann Dallachy died in childbirth at some point. A
history of the Melbourne Botanic Gardens also mentions in
passing that Ann Dallachy died in 1857.[22]

With a family of young children to look after and a difficult job to keep up in a gold-rush town, John Dallachy would
have been under considerable pressure. The list of children on
the death certificate holds one other clue to domestic strife.

Alongside Joseph Sabine, John, Eliza and Mary, there is the name William Dallachy and his age is given as twelve in 1871. Although listed as John Dallachy's son, a search for William's birth certificate revealed that William was in fact his grandson; the mother was Mary Dallachy, the father unknown. To add to his worries, John Dallachy's eldest son, Joseph Sabine, appears to have gone off the rails too. On 1 February 1868 *The Age* newspaper carried the notice 'Sabine Dallachy is charged on warrant with obtaining goods on false pretences from Robert Bullen.' The description given in the newspaper paints Dallachy's eldest son as a rough-sounding character. 'He is Scotch aged 25, 5 feet 6 or 7 inches high, slight build, brown hair, small billy-goat beard, small moustachio, fair but sunburnt complexion; wore new pilot-cloth coat, old moleskin trousers, drab felt hat, puce shirt, and bluchers.'[23]

To complete the picture, whilst critics of Mueller might have viewed Dallachy's time in control of the Gardens through rose-tinted spectacles, there are signs that all was not well. In 1855 there were complaints that gunshots could be heard in the Gardens at night. Local South Yarra residents noticed that the number of waterfowl in the Gardens had dramatically diminished, and in August the local papers carried an accusation that garden staff were either shooting the ducks themselves to sell or were taking payment to turn a blind eye whilst others shot the birds. John Dallachy hotly denied the charge, but the accusations were repeated by another witness under the alias 'Veritas' and the paper concluded, 'Mr Dallachy must, therefore, either be culpably ignorant of what is passing in the locality committed to his charge, or possesses unqualified assurance to give a matter of such notoriety a flat denial.'[24]

So we have a picture of John Dallachy struggling with a young family, an illegitimate grandson, a son in trouble with the law, and he himself possibly caught engaging in illicit money-making sidelines. Perhaps it is little wonder that he was happy to take a commission as a plant hunter, to do something he clearly enjoyed and place himself as far as possible from the scene of his troubles. Although Mueller's enemies liked to paint Dallachy as a victim of the German botanist's undeniable ambition, it looks as though the truth was more complicated.

Mueller was lauded during his lifetime with honorary doctorates, titles and medals, but Dallachy was not entirely overlooked by history. He was commemorated in the name of the genus *Dallachya* (now, thanks to the vicissitudes of taxonomy, *Rhamnella*, Rhamnaceae) and more than twenty Australian plant species, including *Acacia dallachiana* and *Austromyrtus dallachiana*. Ultimately, it seems John Dallachy was used as a figurehead for one side in an argument that he had little part in. It was an argument between two different responses to the Australian landscape. Mueller personified the scientific response to exposure to a whole new world of plants – the drive to collect and classify and bring the flora of this new land under the control of science. The pleasure gardens that Dallachy became associated with were a different way to colonize and control this strange new world – by supplanting it with a European-style landscape park.

It seems that personally John Dallachy was perfectly happy to work within either world, whether planting out bedding plants in the middle of Melbourne or roughing it in the bush, collecting specimens. He and Mueller were partners for decades. Despite the gap in their social standing and education, they shared a passion for collecting the fascinating and unique plants of Australia. They also shared another characteristic of their time: when out in the field, neither showed the least inclination to consider or listen to the people who knew the indigenous plants and wildlife best – the Aborigines whose way of life was so intimately bound to the landscape.

CHAPTER TEN

'Habits of order and good conduct':
The Rise and Fall of a Head Gardener

John Slowe admitted 27 May 1829 upon the
recommendation of Wm Wells Esq.

READING THROUGH THE ENTRIES IN THE HAND-
writing Book and following the gardeners' subsequent life
histories, it is tempting to assess each gardener and catego-
rize them as 'successes' or 'failures'. However, the life of John
Slowe, the last gardener to make an entry in the Handwriting
Book, shows that things could be much more complex than
that simple binary division. The son of a gardener, he was born
at Broad Green, just outside Liverpool, which was the country
retreat of Thomas Staniforth, a merchant who had made his
money chiefly in the slave trade. As a young boy, John Slowe
moved to Ireland with his father, who had obtained a position
as head gardener to Robert Gun on his large estate in County
Wicklow. This is where Slowe started his apprenticeship, until
at the age of eighteen he was deemed ready to make the move
up to journeyman gardener at another garden.

The garden that he was sent to, Redleaf in Kent, was celebrated throughout much of the nineteenth century as a highly
innovative one. It was owned by William Wells, a retired

shipbuilder and enthusiastic art collector, and the head gardener was Joseph Wells (no relation to William, but actually
grandfather of the author H. G. Wells). The garden was known
for its use of native and imported trees and plants, which were
arranged within a carefully constructed landscape, featuring
natural and artificial rock formations. Slowe was only placed
in the garden for a matter of weeks before William Wells recommended him to the Horticultural Society, but the fact that
he was associated with Redleaf will doubtless have counted in
his favour.

We do not know exactly how long John Slowe stayed at
Chiswick; but he must have left before April 1833, because
on 31 April he married twenty-year-old Caroline Powell at St
George's Church, Hanover Square. Then as now, St George's
sat in one of the most fashionable and wealthy areas of London, and the church with its elegant Corinthian portico was
seen as a most desirable place to get married. The parish of St
George covered an area stretching from Regent Street west-
wards to the Serpentine, and southwards from Oxford Street
to include the whole of what is now Mayfair, Belgravia and
Pimlico. It is possible that Slowe was employed as a gardener
to one of the grand houses in the area, or perhaps he was working at one of the nurseries or market gardens that still covered
this part of London. Caroline Powell was born in Turnham
Green, so they may well have met whilst John was still working
in the Chiswick Garden. Gardeners' wives scarcely get a mention in the historical record, but for head gardeners, whose
family home was actually in the workplace, their wives must
have been intimately connected with their working lives. Certainly Joseph Paxton's wife, Sarah, is widely acknowledged as

a strong woman who played an important role in keeping the daily management of the garden going whilst her husband took on myriad other projects. John Slowe's marriage to Caroline and their subsequent family life together were to be even more decisive with regard to the course of his career, though in a much darker and more disturbing way.

By September 1836 Caroline and John had left London and moved to Hertfordshire, by now accompanied by two young children: Thomas, aged nearly two, and John Joseph, who was born on 10 September in Hertingfordbury. The reason for this move was that John had been appointed head gardener at another influential Home Counties garden – Bayfordbury, belonging to William Baker. The fortunes of the Baker family were founded by William Baker's great-grandfather, Sir William (the Baker family was one of those that stuck to a narrow range of forenames, to the lasting confusion of historians and genealogists). Sir William was a merchant specializing in trade with the North American colonies, and in the 1750s and 1760s he had secured lucrative contracts for supplying and paying British troops in the region; he was also one of the city financiers to whom the government turned for large-scale loans. He used the resulting wealth to buy the Bayfordbury estate in Hertfordshire, build a new house there and lay out the grounds in a grand style, establishing an interest in gardening that was to run down through several generations of the Baker family, with each successive descendant adding to the stock of trees on the estate. John Slowe's employer was no exception.

In 1837 work began on establishing a 'pinetum', a newly fashionable horticultural feature that was a plantation of conifers planted expressly for scientific or ornamental purposes.

Ground in the north-west corner of the park was cleared and trenched, ready to take the new trees. With advice from John Claudius Loudon, William Baker instructed Slowe to lay out a semicircular area of around three acres (1.2 hectares), laid out with walks and planted with labelled specimen trees, placed on mounds to avoid damage from ground frost. A collection like this was the equivalent of a 'museum of trees', arranged according to a classification system that aimed to show the interrelationship between different species. It was created to satisfy a desire for collecting and display, but also to demonstrate the owner's discernment and learning. In choosing this project, Baker was in good company. He was following in the footsteps of the Duke of Devonshire, who in 1827 had instructed Joseph Paxton to create a pinetum with more than fifty species of conifer at Chatsworth, one of his first big horticultural projects.

Today, many people dismiss conifers as dull plants, influenced perhaps by memories of 'low-maintenance' dwarf conifers shrivelling in bleak isolation on 1970s front gardens. If they are not seen as dull, they are scary – the misuse and mismanagement of the Leyland cypress (× *Cuprocyparis leylandii*) has left its mark as well. The result is that it is hard to imagine the Victorian enthusiasm for conifers. But if we can put these prejudices to one side, it is easy to see why the Victorians became so entranced with these trees. They are a group prone to extremes: conifers can count amongst their number not only the oldest living plant in the world (the ancient bristlecone pine, *Pinus longaeva*, a 4,500-year-old specimen in the White Mountains of California), but also the tallest, the coast redwood, reaching over 390 feet (120 metres). They can be deciduous or evergreen and come in a huge variety of shapes, sizes and colours – from powder-blue to lime-green and even crimson. At the time William Baker was acquiring his specimens, they also had the benefit of novelty.

Pinus sabineana. Named to commemorate Joseph Sabine and introduced to Britain by David Douglas, this was one of the rare conifers cared for by John Slowe at Bayfordbury.

From the 1820s onwards, plant collectors David Douglas, Robert Fortune and William Lobb brought a steady stream of new species back from North America, Asia and South America. There was great competition between estate owners to be the first to have some of these conifers, to show off to visiting royalty and dignitaries. John Slowe will have had good opportunities to learn about these new plants at Chiswick, where David Douglas' introductions first arrived. He also will have had the chance to work alongside another Chiswick student, Irishman George Gordon, who had joined the Chiswick Garden in February 1828. Like Robert Thompson, Gordon was a Chiswick student who remained at the Garden for the whole of his working life. He was in charge of the arboretum and in 1858 published the first edition of his book *Pinetum*, which was considered 'the most useful one on the subject in this country'.[1] The pinetum that John Slowe helped develop at Bayfordbury was particularly fine. Loudon declared, 'There is indeed no species of Abietinae or Cupressinae in the country of which there is not one or more plants in the collection here.'[2]

Given his own involvement in planning the pinetum, it is hardly surprising that Loudon approved. However, he also lavished praise on the rest of the garden that was under Slowe's care. He described the flower beds in glowing terms: 'They are almost all planted with low flowering shrubs and with occasional low trees, such as rhododendrons, azaleas and heaths, and the shrubs have almost everywhere spread sufficiently to cover the dug surface and brake the boundary lines which is exactly what is desirable in such a situation.'[3]

Slowe also had charge of a large conservatory, a rock garden (designed by the famous maker of artificial rock features, James Pulham) and a kitchen garden a mile from the house, which was praised as 'well managed', as were 'the numerous forcing houses pits and frames and the adjoining tree nurseries'. Loudon, being also something of an authority on domestic architecture, commented on the house: 'nothing to recommend it'. However, it does seem to have been set up for entertaining on a grand scale, with 'a wing for family, another for bachelors and gentlemen without families, and that in the centre for strangers with families and stranger ladies'.[4] Judging by the estate record book documenting activity in the garden, it seems that Slowe will have been kept far too busy ever to have had much to do with any of 'the stranger ladies' or other house-guests.

One of his tasks was to make herbaceous grafts in order to propagate additional specimens from rare trees. Grafting is a technique whereby a portion of a parent plant (known as a scion) is removed and fixed (or 'grafted') to a seedling (known as a rootstock) with an existing root system. The two knit together and eventually the top of the seedling is removed, leaving the new scion to grow on its own, using the seedling roots. The tree produced is a clone of the original parent plant, with none of the unpredictability that can come with raising plants from seed. Many conifers are difficult to root from cuttings, so grafting is the most practical way to raise new trees. Careful selection of the rootstock can result in trees with a stronger root system and better tolerance to local conditions. In 1840 Loudon reported on the conifer-growing techniques used at Bayfordbury, writing:

Mr Baker has tried with success the 'greffe herbace' (herbaceous grafting) and intends next year to make a great many trials on the summits of Scotch pines, common spruces and silver firs of 10 or 12 feet in height. Perhaps *Picea Webbiana* grafted at this height, or even at a greater height, might escape the spring frosts.[5]

It is typical that it is the garden owner, rather than the gardener, who is given sole credit for this experimentation, when in fact we can be pretty certain it was not William Baker teetering on a ladder twelve feet (3.6 metres) up in the air, trying to make a good graft. The success of grafting and other aspects of tree cultivation at Bayfordbury relied at least as much on the technical expertise of John Slowe as it did on the spending power and ideas of William Baker.

Grafting was not the only procreation that Slowe was involved in during these years. The census of 1841 recorded that John and Caroline were living in the Garden House with four children: Thomas, aged five; John, aged four; Elizabeth, aged three; and one-year-old Charles. Over the course of the next thirteen years Caroline was to have a further seven children, bringing the total to eleven – three boys and eight girls. The gap between births was very short and the Garden House must have been a crowded, noisy place. Like many large Victorian families, not all the children survived early childhood; unfortunately, Charles died at the age of nine in 1849. Nevertheless, as far as the outside world was concerned, John Slowe's career went from strength to strength in the 1840s and 1850s. Between 1846 and 1851 he won a remarkable forty-three awards from the Horticultural Society for exhibiting plants and fruits at flower shows, including four Gold Banksian medals. The majority of his medals were for rose exhibits, but he also won prizes for producing fine examples of hothouse fruits, including melons, pineapples and 'Black Hamburg' grapes.

His competence and expertise were clearly appreciated by William Baker, because by 1861 John Slowe was not just head gardener at Bayfordbury, but was also the land steward. This meant that he was responsible for collecting rents and under-taking all those activities associated with making the estate profitable, which at Bayfordbury revolved largely around for-estry management. A land steward was regarded as one of the most senior members of the estate's staff, and it suggests that Baker had a high degree of trust in Slowe's honesty, as large amounts of money frequently passed through a land steward's hands. The bailiff or land steward was also often at the front line of the conflict of interest between landowners and the wider rural population.

The 1834 Poor Law was much more oppressive than the old Poor Law regime, and the workhouse was made a deliberately punitive option. In hard times like the economic depression of the 1840s, people would resort to desperate measures to avoid having to go into the workhouse, and these measures included poaching, which the land steward was expected to clamp down on. John Slowe was a large and physically strong man and this will have given him a certain degree of personal presence, a valuable aid in imposing his authority on the local rural community. By the early 1860s he was entering his fifties and seemed to be at the height of his career: a prize-winning head gardener at a highly regarded garden, blessed with an enthusiastic and supportive employer. However, in 1865 he was hurriedly to leave Bayfordbury, his home of nearly thirty years – a figure of public shame and condemnation.

* * *

The story starts in 1860, when it would be expected that life in the Slowe household was becoming easier. The older children had left home to work or marry, and there were now only three children to look after – Anna Sophia, aged thirteen, and her younger sisters, Mary Ann and Agnes Florence. The family had moved in 1856 from the Garden House, adjoining the coach house at Bayfordbury, to a more secluded cottage a quarter of a mile from Roxford Farm, which was also part of the Baker property. The family could even afford a charwoman to come in each day to help Mrs Slowe. However, the teenage Anna Sophia, known within the family as Annie, was to be the source of considerable turmoil within the family. In the summer of 1860 she was expelled from the local Hertingfordbury school, accused of 'teaching other girls to steal'.[6] The family responded by sending her away from home to Sheffield to stay with her older brother Thomas, who was recently married and working as a railway clerk for the Sheffield and Rotherham Railway. However, it appears that Annie managed to get in trouble in Sheffield, apparently being accused of stealing a penknife and a hymn book, and after a year she returned home to Bayfordbury.

In September 1863, at the age of sixteen, she ran away from home, taking with her eight shillings and making for London, hoping to find her older sister Elizabeth and, like her, a job as a domestic servant. Unfortunately, Annie did not have her sister's employer's address and she had to spend the night in a coffee shop opposite the Red Cap public house in Camden Town. The story of a teenage girl running away to the metropolis was a familiar one in the popular fiction of the day, and generally ended in destitution or life as a 'fallen woman'.

Annie decided that the thing to do was find a job, but when she applied for a 'situation' the next day, she was turned away because she had no references. Luckily for her, the lady she applied to told her about a female servants' home on Blackfriars Road where she could find safe and affordable accommodation until she landed a job. Mrs Jarrett, the matron at the home, who presumably had dealt with runaways in the past, persuaded Annie after a couple of weeks to write to her father to let him know her whereabouts.

As soon as he received the letter, John Slowe rushed to London 'in great distress of mind' and paid the bill for her lodging and arranged for Annie to stay with her aunt (her mother's sister), who was living nearby in King Street, Camden.[7] At some point mention was made of sending Annie to a 'reformatory', which was a residential school run by a religious organization or charity, designed to steer children away from a life of crime through strict discipline, religious instruction and training in useful occupations. Annie did not like the sound of this one bit, and ran away from her aunt's house while her father was in another room, leaving in such a rush that she did not even stop to put on her bonnet. By this time she had Elizabeth's address in Haverstock Hill and was allowed by Elizabeth's employers, Mr and Mrs Bussey, to stay with them until she managed to get a job herself. Annie worked as a maid in Covent Garden for three months until she fell ill with smallpox and was forced to return to her aunt's house once more to recover. However, there was no question this time of a reformatory or even of returning to Bayfordbury, for at some point in early 1864 Annie confided in Mr and Mrs Bussey that the reason she had run away was that her father had beaten and mistreated her.

The details that she recounted were so shocking that the
Busseys contacted the Society for the Protection of Women
and Children. This charity, established in 1857, employed bar-
risters and solicitors to provide legal advice and assistance in
cases of bigamy, abduction, neglect, desertion, sexual assault
and cruelty. Lacking economic resources and in the absence of
an official prosecuting agency, such as the modern Crown Pros-
ecution Service, women and children were often in no position
to seek justice without help from philanthropic bodies like
this one. Annie's accusations were sufficiently convincing for
the Society to agree to take the case to court on her behalf. It
caused a sensation and made headlines in newspapers up and
down the land. For example, under the heading 'STRANGE
PARENTS', *The Monmouthshire Merlin* reported verbatim
Annie's testimony at the first hearing of the case at Hertford
Town Hall, where she said that:

My father and mother have both constantly beaten and otherwise ill-used me as long as I can recollect anything. For the
most trifling offence I have been seriously beaten with whips,
ropes and sticks. When I was very young I was constantly
severely beaten by my mother because I could not say the
word temptation in my prayers. On one occasion, about four
or five years ago, I was tied quite naked in an arm chair, and
my father threw several bowls of cold water over me, after
which I was taken from the chair and severely beaten. On
another occasion, my mother threw a saucepan at me because
it was not properly cleaned. She then requested my father to
punish me for it. My father then seized me by the hair of my
head, threw me down with my face on some rough matting,

and knocked my head about upon the matting till it bled from every part.[8]

This shocking account was repeated in newspapers through-out the country, from Southampton to Belfast. As a result, when the case came to court for judgement on 2 July 1864, the Magistrates' Court in Hertford was packed with spectators. Under cross-examination, Annie Slowe once more gave her account of long-standing and frequent cruelty, and of harsh punishment for minor offences, and furthermore said that two of her other sisters, Caroline and Isabella, had received the same treatment. The magistrates decided that the case should focus on just one incident, the beating that Annie claimed pro-voked her to leave home. She recounted how her mother 'told father to get a stick and flog me well because I had not done my work before breakfast'. Her father gave her thirty minutes to clean the sitting room. When she failed to complete the task within the time, he returned with 'a kind of ash stick: 4 times as thick as my parasol handle and about a yard long; he said "you've not done your work now my lady, you'll have a beat-ing".'[9] Whilst her daughter was speaking, 'Mrs Slowe's feelings appeared almost to overcome her, but she restrained them.' Annie said she was hit with the stick about six times over the course of ten minutes and that when she cried out, her father said, 'the more you holloa the more I'll beat you', and that the beating only stopped because her aunt was expected for a visit.

No detail was spared, and Mr Besley, the prosecutor on behalf of the Society for the Protection of Women and Chil-dren, even made a point of describing the Slowe family's move

to the cottage at Roxford in such a way as to make it sound
like a premeditated plan to facilitate cruelty: the house being
described as on 'a private road and at such a distance that no
screams could be heard'.[10] It seemed a damning case and the
sympathies of the spectators were clearly with Annie, who
spoke so quietly that sometimes the barrister representing her
had to repeat her answers to his questions so that the magistrates could hear.

However, Mr Woollet, the barrister defending John and
Caroline Slowe, declared the case 'a trumped-up charge'. He
produced letters that Annie had written to her parents from the
servants' home, addressed to her 'dear and affectionate Father',
in which she wrote, 'I do miss my dear mother very much' and
admitted to her determination to leave home, even though her
parents thought her too young. He also cross-examined Annie
about her earlier history of stealing, leaving the inference to
hang in the air that perhaps she was more deserving of chas-
tisement than she was willing to admit. He claimed that Annie
had been goaded into making the charge by the Busseys and
the 'do-gooders', who would 'go into every cottage every time
a father chastised his child and call him before the bench'.[11] He
declared that the reason Annie Slowe made the allegation was
that she 'was afraid of her father's threat of sending her to the
Reformatory, and then started the charge'.

However, the chief defence that John Slowe was to rely
upon was that the Act of Parliament that made beating a
child an aggravated offence specified that complaints must
be brought within six months of the event in question. Annie
Slowe had waited nearly a year before making any mention of
the incident and it was therefore not an admissible case. The

magistrates retired to consider the verdict and 'in no great time they returned' and declared the case dismissed. The crowd gathered in the courtroom was outraged: 'Hisses from the spectators followed the decision' and, as Mr and Mrs Slowe hurried from the scene in a hired coach, there were 'groans and execrations, and shouts that any one might kill a child now'.[12]

The dismissal of the case on a technicality was unsatisfactory to everyone. It is interesting that Mr Woollet's concluding remark was: 'What could be more favour of Mr Slowe than that he had been 30 years in the employment of as respectable a gentleman as any in the county, Mr Baker?'[13] William Baker was the chief magistrate for Hertford, and the other magistrates hearing the case will have known him well. They included Mr Gaussen of Brookmans Park and Mr Cherry of Lamer House, both Repton gardens. Was it unrealistic to expect this group of men, highly conscious of the desire to avoid a scandal associated with an employee of one of their peers, to do anything other than sweep the matter away as quickly as possible?

The reaction of the crowd at the hearing shows that many people felt that John Slowe and his wife were guilty and had got away with unacceptable cruelty. The attacks described by Annie crossed a line, even by contemporary standards, where 'Spare the rod and spoil the child' was more than a glib saying; it was a well-respected theory of childcare. Equally, the Slowes will not have been happy with the outcome of the hearing; since the case was dismissed as inadmissible, John and Caroline Slowe were not actually acquitted and declared innocent, so there was still a cloud over their heads.

The following week a letter from Mr Armstrong, the Slowes' solicitor, was published in a number of newspapers, putting John Slowe's case more forcibly. He criticized the Society for the Protection of Women and Children as 'a few well intentioned, but in some instances crazy lovers of their fellow creatures... searching out cases of imaginary wrongs', and complained that the dismissal of the charge meant that he had not had the opportunity to clear Mr Slowe's name by bringing forward witnesses (including his older children) to testify that the assault in question never took place, and that both Slowe and his wife 'had uniformly stinted themselves in order to bring them up respectably, and that every member of the family had been kindly and affectionately treated both in health and sickness.' He also claimed that a 'respectable person' (the charwoman Mrs Baker) had heard no shouts or screams, even though she was in the small cottage during the whole time of the alleged incident.[14] However, to set against this there was the testimony during the trial of under-gardener George Ramsay, who said that although he never saw Annie being hit whilst he worked at Bayfordbury, she did once show him bruises on her arm and shoulders.

We will never know what really happened in the cottage near Roxford Farm, but there can be no doubt that the impact of the case was dramatic for the whole family. It is not clear whether William Baker dismissed John Slowe, or whether John himself simply felt it impossible to stay in the area, knowing that every one of his employees and neighbours was aware of the case in all its awful detail. The very idea that a head gardener and land steward – a professional man of some standing – could mistreat a defenceless child was profoundly shocking. There was an expectation that this type of violent lack of self-control was the province of the lower orders, usually fuelled by alcohol. In 1850 one newspaper remarked of working-class men that:

> they are impressed with the belief of their having a right to inflict almost any amount of corporal violence on their wife or their children. Are they not entitled to do as they will with their own? These phrases are not, to their apprehension, metaphorical. The shoes on their feet, the cudgel in their hand, the horse or ass that carries their burden, the wife and children are all 'theirs' and all in the same sense.[15]

However, better behaviour was expected of a senior gardener. By the mid-nineteenth century gardening was firmly associated with moral improvement. Horticulture was promoted as a 'rational' and educational activity that offered opportunities to contemplate the wonders of the natural world or, depending on your point of view, the munificence of the Almighty, and provided an alternative to the temptations of the public house. Moreover, a head gardener was entrusted with the care and supervision of young apprentices and was also frequently a representative of his employer, expected to be able to show visitors around the grounds. The Horticultural Society laid a great deal of emphasis on the importance of good conduct and sound character in its Chiswick trainees. The Society anticipated that training in its Chiswick Garden would instil 'the habits of self-control and discipline which... would give them habits of order and good conduct, and a knowledge of the world, which would be useful to them when entrusted with the management of others'.[16] A head gardener was expected to be a strong leader, with a firm, patriarchal grip on the team of young men working under him, to ensure that order was maintained at all times. However, this need for discipline did not, in anyone's mind, encompass physical cruelty. The lurid details reported in the newspapers did not align well with the ideal image of a head gardener. Whether Slowe was sacked or left of his own accord, the family departed from Bayfordbury in the late summer of 1865.

However, despite the notoriety of the case, John Slowe was rapidly able to attain a new position at Mentmore Towers in Buckinghamshire. This was a large and well-resourced garden and would have been regarded as a very good position. The owner, Baron Mayer de Rothschild, a member of the wealthy banking dynasty, had commissioned none other than Joseph Paxton to build him a house on land he had acquired at Mentmore, near Leighton Buzzard. Several members of the Rothschild family purchased properties in the Vale of Aylesbury in the nineteenth century, and the area acquired the soubriquet 'Rothschildshire'. In addition to Mentmore, other impressive Rothschild houses included Ascott House, Champneys, Eythrope, Halton House, Tring Park and Waddesdon Manor. The technological innovations and public impact of the Crystal Palace made Paxton – although not a trained architect – the man of the moment. The result was Mentmore Towers, a vast mansion built in the Elizabethan style, influenced by Hardwick Hall and Wollaton Hall, which was completed in 1855. Joseph Paxton also designed the pleasure grounds and, in typical eclectic Victorian style, matched an Elizabethan house with Italianate formal gardens.

It is tempting to wonder whether he had any hand in Slowe's appointment. Joseph Paxton was on friendly terms with the

Rothschilds and was a regular visitor to Mentmore, and it would have been natural to ask his opinion on the appointment of a head gardener. As an expert planter of arboreta himself, it is possible that Paxton would have been aware of the high quality of John Slowe's horticultural work. Joseph had a difficult relationship with his own son, George, a spoilt young man prone to drunkenness, profligacy and idleness. Whilst there was never any suggestion of parental cruelty (quite the opposite, as George Paxton was, if anything, over-indulged), perhaps Paxton had sympathy for a family struggling with a difficult teenager. However, this is pure speculation and there is no record in Paxton's correspondence (or anywhere else, for that matter) of any involvement in Slowe's appointment. An alternative theory is that William Baker vouched for him, convinced – through his long association with the gardener – that the charge was groundless. Or perhaps Baron Mayer de Rothschild simply did not care, so long as his garden was competently cared for.

By the time Slowe started work at Mentmore, the house had been complete for eleven years and the gardens were beginning to mature. Paxton had created a broad mile-long approach road with circular clumps of horse chestnut, birch and elm, alternating with massive Wellingtonia (*Sequoiadendron giganteum*). In addition to rolling parkland, there were formal flower gardens running around three sides of the house, ornamented with statues and evergreens. The gardens were equipped with an aviary, a range of glasshouses and a subtropical garden, and there was a staff of approximately forty men to manage. However, although high standards of care were of course expected, Baron Mayer de Rothschild (unlike William Baker) was not personally concerned with gardening to any great extent. His interests were equine rather than horticultural. Despite weighing more than fifteen stone, he was a keen rider and huntsman and a lover of horse-racing.

The garden was less lavishly appointed than might be expected for a man of Mayer's enormous wealth. Paxton's original designs included a terrace and a garden along the south-east front of the mansion, but neither was executed. The estate records show that the Veitch nursery was regularly employed from 1866 to 1875, being paid a considerable amount of money (£4,645). Some of the payments were clearly for plants, but others were round figures, suggesting a consultancy approach.[17] This would suggest there was little room for creativity or initiative for Slowe at Mentmore, and his job was probably chiefly one of maintaining a garden that was already regarded as finished. There were to be no more horticultural prizes or attention from the horticultural press.

The family was still living in Mentmore village by the time of the 1871 census. John and Caroline were living with their daughter Emma, aged twenty-five, and were also looking after their two-year-old grandson Frederick Slowe (son of Thomas, whose wife had unfortunately died at some point after 1868) and two lodgers – under-gardeners John Jennings and Samuel Brown. This does lend some weight to the idea that Annie at the very least exaggerated in her accusations, as it seems highly unlikely that Thomas would have left his young son with his parents if he felt they were capable of the levels of cruelty and violence she had described.

The estate garden records suggest that John Slowe had left Mentmore by 1874, when he was in his early sixties. It looks as though he had saved enough to set himself up in business away from horticulture, as he is listed as a publican at the King's Head Hotel in Maldon in Essex in 1878. However, this venture did not last long. By the time of the 1881 census, John, Caroline and their grandson Frederick had all moved to the working-class district of Stepney in east London. It was here that John Slowe died in 1895, a long way from the ornamental forestry of Hertfordshire or the splendour of Mentmore.

Meanwhile, Annie Slowe appears to have stayed in London. Mr Bussey was reported as saying during the court case that, whatever the outcome, she could stay in employment within his household as a nursemaid. There is nothing to suggest that she was ever reconciled with her family. On 6 October 1867, aged nineteen, she married David Angell, a car man (driver of a horse and cart used for deliveries), in St Pancras Church in London. None of the witnesses listed on the marriage certificate were family members. The couple lived in Gurney Street, one of a set of tightly packed working-class terraces (since demolished), close to the present-day Elephant & Castle Underground station. This was only around four miles away from where her parents settled in east London. Annie had two daughters and in 1907 the family emigrated to Canada. Annie Angell, née Slowe, died in Montreal in 1925 at the age of seventy-eight.

Today, Mentmore is no longer a private home, and much of the park has been split up and converted into a golf course. The gardens were reworked under Baron Mayer de Rothschild's daughter, Hannah, and there is very little that can be associated with John Slowe in any way. At Bayfordbury his work has left a much more lasting legacy, although at times the survival of the planting has been a close-run thing. The Baker family retained the house and estate until 1945, when it was auctioned off in lots. The house, with its surrounding parkland, was purchased by the John Innes Horticultural Institution, a large plant and fruit-breeding organization, probably best known for its garden composts. By this time the rockery had fallen into a sad state and many of the stones had been cannibalized to make a more modern rockery elsewhere. Although very little restoration work was carried out, the John Innes Horticultural Institution did carry on the association with roses begun under John Slowe (twenty of the forty-three Horticultural Society medals and awards that Slowe won were for roses).

From 1948 to 1967 Bayfordbury was home to the National Rose Collection, one of a number of national plant collections established by the Agricultural Improvement Council after the Second World War. In 1963 the John Innes Horticultural Institution decided to move to a site near the University of East Anglia at Norwich, and Bayfordbury was sold in 1967 to Hertfordshire County Council. It passed to the University of Hertfordshire in 1992, by which time the pinetum had become seriously neglected, overgrown with elder, nettles, bracken and brambles as well as self-seeded deciduous trees. It had also suffered considerable damage during the famous Great Storm of 1987.

Fortunately, the pinetum found a saviour in Dr Eastwood, formerly a Lecturer in Environmental Biology and Natural History. In 1994 Dr Eastwood became curator of the newly named Clinton-Baker Pinetum, responsible for implementing a restoration project based on volunteer labour and donations. He persuaded those who had previously been seen as trespassers in the wood – people who used it for recreational purposes – to become volunteers. Restoration and conservation are now carried out by the Friends' Association, which boasts around 250 members, and small but dedicated working parties meet every Wednesday and on one Saturday each month. Whatever the truth about John Slowe as a father, we can enjoy the trees and saplings – now magnificent specimen trees – that, as a gardener, he left for us.

CHAPTER ELEVEN

'A very respectable-looking young man': Criminals in the Garden

John Frederick Wood admitted 28 August 1823
upon the recommendation of Jos. Sabine Esq.

Reuben Hale admitted 6 July 1827 upon the
recommendation of Mr Adam Paul

AT TWO O'CLOCK IN THE AFTERNOON ON MONDAY 13 October 1828, William Ballard, Bow Street Runner, sat in The Flower Pot inn on London's Bishopsgate Street, carefully watching the door. He was on a stake-out, having laid a trap to catch a thief suspected of involvement in the theft of valuable seeds from the Horticultural Society's garden at Chiswick. Ballard had been alerted to the crime by the Society's assistant secretary, John Lindley, who had received a letter the previous Friday from William Mackey, a Hackney-based nurseryman. Mackey had included a note that he had received, signed with the pseudonym 'Hortulanus', which read: 'I beg your attention to the following list of seeds which I have to dispose of. Knowing your capacity of appreciating their value, I make you the first offer, assured that they are not to be had from any other.'[1]

Mackey was under no doubt that the seeds could not be

purchased elsewhere, because the list included some – *Clarkia pulchella*, *Collomia grandiflora*, *Penstemon ovatum* and *Gaultheria shallon* – that had been recently sent to the Horticultural Society from North America by its most successful plant collector, David Douglas. Hortulanus said that he had five pounds (2.3 kilos) of seed, which he was prepared to sell for £12, which he considered a bargain, 'as many of the things are not in the trade at all yet and the rest very sparingly'.[2] He invited Mr Mackey to write back, care of The Man in the Moon public house in Chelsea, naming a time and place to meet and make the purchase. Mr Mackey, being an astute businessman, immediately smelt a rat. Indeed, Hortulanus himself made little attempt to hide the fact that these seeds were stolen. He admitted, 'I forbear giving my name for certain reasons which are obvious.' There was only one place the seeds could have come from, and Mackey immediately passed the note on to John Lindley, who in turn contacted the Bow Street Runners.

The Bow Street Runners were London's first professional police force and originally numbered just six men, when it was founded in 1749 by the magistrate and well-known satirical author Henry Fielding. Before this point, the law-enforcing system was in the hands of private citizens and unofficial 'thief-takers', who would solve petty crime for a fee or a reward and became infamous for corruption. In contrast, the Bow Street Runners had a formal attachment to the Bow Street magistrates' office, and received payment by the magistrate with funds from central government, though they could still claim a share of any reward available. Officers could be sent by a magistrate or hired by the victim to investigate an offence. So when the Horticultural Society contacted William Ballard, it will have been expected to pay the expenses of the investigation, presumably including a pint at The Flower Pot, cab rides across London, and so on. The Horticultural Society chose its officer well; Ballard was very highly thought of and was to rise to become a Principal Officer on the force – in other words, a detective who could be trusted with serious and complex crimes. After his retirement in 1839 he became a well-respected private detective.

Ballard knew that the thing to do was to lure Hortulanus to meet him, by pretending to be a keen buyer. He adopted the pseudonym Thomas Lane and wrote a note in reply, which read: 'I am desired by Mr Mackey... to inform you that he is ready to negotiate with you for purchase of the articles you mention. Mr Mackey himself does not wish to appear, for obvious reasons; but if you will be at The Flower Pot in Bishopsgate Street, at two o'clock on Monday, I will meet you there. Bring the seed with you.'[3] Perhaps William Ballard had a sense of humour and felt The Flower Pot was an appropriately named location to trap a garden thief; or, more likely, he knew that this well-known coaching inn, set on the North Road, would be a reassuringly busy and anonymous venue for a meeting. However, he was to have a fruitless wait. As the minutes ticked by, it was clear that Hortulanus was not going to show up. Perhaps he had got cold feet and decided that Thomas Lane was not to be trusted? Ballard reported back to Joseph Sabine and John Lindley that they would need another plan. They decided to examine the handwriting of the Hortulanus note, and declared it familiar. Of course they had the Handwriting Book as a reference point to check against. The best fit was with the writing of John Frederick Wood, and this may have come as no surprise to Lindley and Sabine, as they had had difficulties with this particular gardener in the past.

John Frederick Wood entered the Chiswick Garden in August 1823 with a relatively slim CV, only having trained at one garden before joining, that of banker Samuel Smith, MP, at Woodhall Park in Hertfordshire. After eighteen months in the Garden working as a labourer, he was considered for promotion and served a three-month probation as under-gardener and was found to be satisfactory. However, by October of the following year his performance was not at all satisfactory. On 26 October 1824 the Garden Committee Minutes recorded, 'J F Wood Under-Gardener in the Flower Garden having been reproved for improper conduct while out of the Garden by which the character of the Garden Labourers was likely to be brought into discredit.' Upon being reprimanded by Joseph Sabine, Wood 'abruptly quitted the service of the Society'.[4] The improper conduct is not specified, but it sounds like rowdy or unruly behaviour rather than actual criminality.

The Horticultural Society took the question of discipline for its garden staff very seriously. A set of seventeen rules was laid down for the labourers and under-gardeners, and in its annual report the Garden Committee sought to reassure Fellows that 'a vigilant eye is kept upon their conduct at hours and seasons not employed in the garden' and that care was taken to develop 'a knowledge of their private hours'. These rules were not without their critics, including John Claudius Loudon, who felt that the Horticultural Society should concentrate more on supporting young gardeners and went out of his way to praise them; he wrote, 'Their decent appearance, their dress and linen, compared to their wages, is at once an

index to their morality.'[5] Intriguingly, amongst the critics of
the Society on the pages of Loudon's *Gardener's Magazine* was
one 'Hortulanus', who wrote a strongly worded letter in 1827
claiming that the Chiswick Garden rules were 'held in derision
by all the nurserymen and master gardeners about London who
know anything about them, and laughed at by the young men
themselves'.[6] 'Hortulanus' – Latin for 'a gardener' – is hardly
an original alias for anyone wanting to write anonymously
about horticulture, so there is no guarantee that the critic of
the Society's rules in the *Gardener's Magazine* was one and the
same as the seed-selling letter-writer. However, the fact that
John Frederick Wood had fallen foul of those very rules does
seem a telling coincidence, to say the least.

Whatever the misdemeanour causing Wood's dismissal, he
managed to find employment afterwards at Knight's Exotic
Nursery in Chelsea. This was a prestigious place to work.
Joseph Knight was a wealthy and successful nurseryman who
had set up his business on a prime site on the King's Road in
1808. It catered for a wealthy and discerning clientele, with
spectacular showrooms featuring a monumental bronze fountain and lavish plant displays. Loudon visited in 1826 and
described in the *Gardener's Magazine* how it boasted a stock
of plants that was 'rich and superiorly managed', and 'every
part of the houses, back sheds and grounds displays that order
and neatness which have always been characteristic of this
nursery'.[7]

Even if Wood was Hortulanus, how had he come across the
seeds, given that he had not worked in the Garden for four
years? He must have had some inside help. The first step was
to apprehend Wood as quickly as possible and try to find out

what he knew. What is remarkable about this story is how quickly everything moved. William Ballard must have consulted Sabine and Lindley later in the afternoon of Monday 13 October, after his failed stake-out, and agreed a plan, because very early the next morning – together with fellow Bow Street Runner Mr Schofield – he was able to conduct a dawn raid on Wood's lodgings in Chelsea. Ballard's witness statement in court later revealed that they 'apprehended him in bed' and demanded to know whether he had written the Hortulanus letter. They conducted a search of Wood's rooms and found a quantity of seeds under his bed and in a desk.

At first Wood refused to say where he had obtained the seeds, stating simply that he had purchased them for 'a fair price'. But he quickly crumbled under the pressure of questioning, with Ballard rightly pointing out that, unless he was able to give a convincing account of how he had come to possess the seeds, Wood would be assumed to be the thief himself – a much more serious crime than simply handling stolen goods. John Frederick Wood had little choice other than to confess in full. He was hardly a master criminal; a further search of his desk uncovered a letter that he was in the course of writing, this time signed in his own name, apologizing that he had not received the letter from 'Thomas Lane' in time to make the two o'clock appointment and offering to meet there the following day.

Wood eventually admitted that he had purchased the seeds from Reuben Hale, a current student labourer in the Chiswick Garden. Hale and Wood went back a long way: though they had not overlapped at Chiswick, they grew up less than five miles apart in Hertfordshire and already knew each other from their pre-Chiswick apprentice days. Their entries in the Handwriting Book show that they had both worked at Samuel Smith's garden at Woodhall Park in Hertfordshire during 1823. Smith was the son of a wealthy Nottingham banker. He and his brothers all became Members of Parliament, his brother Robert having purchased two rotten boroughs in Wendover and Midhurst, which were kept exclusively for use by various members of the Smith family until they were abolished by the Great Reform Act (1832).

Woodhall Park was an extensive estate with walled gardens, created during the Napoleonic Wars by French prisoners of war. It was under the care of well-respected head gardener William Griffin. As well as being an expert fruit grower and an early supporter of the Horticultural Society, Griffin was well known as a good trainer. In addition to Hale and Wood, Joseph Paxton trained for a time under William Griffin. His obituary described him as 'one who acted the part of a father and friend to all the young men'.[8] Unfortunately, Griffin's fatherly guidance does not seem to have had a lasting effect on Hale and Wood. Again Ballard and Schofield moved with commendable alacrity. Stopping off on the way to drop their prisoner at the watch house on St James's, they rushed back to the Chiswick Garden to arrest Reuben Hale. They found him at work in the Garden, completely oblivious to the trouble he was about to find himself in.

Upon being accosted and accused by William Ballard, twenty-five-year-old Hale, like Wood, at first tried to deny any involvement. However, he was accompanied by Joseph Sabine to his lodgings close to the Garden and, when his room was searched, seeds were found in a chest under his bed. Hale immediately confessed, saying that he stole the seeds himself, without involving anyone else, but that 'he had been urged to do so by Wood' and that 'his own distress led him to adopt this bad advice'.[9] The source of this distress would not be hard to discern. Student gardeners at Chiswick were hardly well paid, to begin with. However, on 1 January 1827 the Garden Committee had decided to cut the wages of the labourers from fourteen to twelve shillings a week, and the wages of under-gardeners working in the Garden from eighteen shillings to just fourteen shillings a week. Whether Joseph Sabine felt any twinge of guilt as he heard Reuben Hale explain the reason for his descent into crime is not recorded.

The decision to make such a harsh cut to the gardeners' wages can be fairly described as a direct result of Sabine's mis-management. As Honorary Secretary of the Society, Sabine was the driving force behind its day-to-day management and oversaw a long period of profligate expenditure on the Garden, on plant-collecting expeditions and expensively produced publications, with very little regard for the actual state of the Society's accounts. He preferred to continue in the hope that either the government would eventually underwrite the Society, due to the clear scientific and economic value of its efforts, or new and generous private subscribers would miraculously emerge. To be fair, no one else involved in the management of the Society's finances seemed to have a much better grip on reality. The minutes of every meeting of the Garden Committee begin with the phrase 'the book of accounts was laid open on the table', and there does not seem a great deal of evidence that the financial scrutiny undertaken by the committee members involved anyone actually reading it. However, by early

1827 even the Horticultural Society could see that expenditure was outstripping income. But the ones to pay the price were the garden staff rather than the administrators. Although this belated and rather half-hearted attempt at reining in the expenditure on the Garden to match the level of income available was too little too late, it did have an immediate impact on the Garden staff. For a young gardener, losing two shillings a week was a heavy blow.

Later, when testifying in the magistrates' court, Wood took issue with the version of events whereby his erstwhile friend Reuben Hale had painted him as the initiator of the scheme, tempting the impoverished Hale with 'bad advice' to become a thief. According to John Frederick Wood, the thought of selling stolen seeds from the Society's Garden would never have occurred to him, had he not bumped into Hale in The World's End tavern in Chelsea. Wood claimed that Hale was 'in the company of a young man named Robinson, who is now in Van Diemen's Land'.[10] Apparently, Wood saw Hale selling the now (conveniently) emigrated Mr Robinson some seeds from Chiswick, to take out with him to New South Wales. Wood said he asked Hale to get some of the same sort for him, and Hale agreed. Wood tried to claim that 'he had not the least idea that the seeds were stolen when he purchased them'.[11] This defence was given short shrift by the prosecutor, who pointed out that the price Wood was charging when he tried to sell the seed, and the surreptitious way he went about arranging the sale, showed clearly enough that he knew exactly what he was doing.

* * *

Both Wood and Hale pleaded guilty when the case was tried at the Old Bailey on 28 October 1828, just three weeks after Wood sent his fateful letter to Mr Mackey. Hale was found guilty of stealing '3lbs of seeds, value £12 the goods of the Horticultural Society of London, his masters'; and Wood of 'feloniously receiving the same, knowing well that they were stolen'.[12] Both 'received good characters': Wood's reference came from Samuel Smith, MP, who, according to *The Standard*, gave Wood 'an excellent character', and many of the newspaper reports commented that John Frederick Wood was a 'very respectable-looking young man'.[13] They were both sentenced to three months' imprisonment.

In the light of the value and rarity of the material stolen, it seems they were treated relatively leniently, by the standards of the time. This may have been due to the fact that they were first-time offenders, but it may also have been due to the Horticultural Society putting in a word for them at their trial, aware that for Hale, at least, there were extenuating circumstances. A newspaper report noted that Sabine and Lindley both declared they were not seeking a heavy sentence for the prisoners, but were bringing charges simply to demonstrate that gardeners could not steal from the Garden 'with impunity'.[14] Given the enormous discrepancy between the low wages offered to gardeners of all types in this period and the enormous sums sometimes spent on the plants they cared for, it is surprising that more gardeners did not resort to theft or other dishonest methods of making money 'on the side'. To earn the £12 that the stolen seeds were valued at, Reuben Hale would have had to work for nearly six months on his labourers' wages. Surrounded as he was by valuable and highly portable bulbs, seeds and young plants, the temptation must have been enormous. However, it does appear that theft and fraud were rare exceptions. It is telling that, at the very same Garden Committee meeting where Joseph Sabine reported back on the outcome of the trial, the committee members decided to clarify rules regarding whether gardeners could take excess seeds and plants from the Garden; they resolved that gardeners working at Chiswick 'should be allowed to have seeds and other things during their residence in the garden or upon leaving it for other places, provide that it shall appear advisable to the Secretary'.[15]

Having been held briefly at Newgate while they awaited trial, Hale and Wood were sent to the Bridewell House of Correction to serve their sentence. The House of Correction was for men, women and children serving sentences from as short as seven days to a few years. The idea was to keep these offenders away from the hardened criminals who would serve their sentences in long-term convict prisons. There was a great deal of concern that prisons were lyceums or academies of crime, where hardened criminals could corrupt first-time offenders like Wood and Hale. During this period the prison system was a chaotic patchwork of local provision, with no nationally imposed standards. In some regions a prisoner with good outside contacts could pass his sentence in comparative comfort, with supplies of decent food and even alcohol and cigars. However, prisoners without these resources would have a much bleaker time, and it is not likely that either Wood or Hale had an easy ride in prison. Even if the sentences were short, punishment could be severe. One aim was to prevent prisoners communicating, so as to isolate them from bad influences and give them an opportunity to reflect silently upon their deeds and repent. Rather than go to the expense of building lots of solitary cells, this could be achieved by keeping prisoners so occupied with hard physical labour that they had little opportunity or energy for consorting with each other. At the Bridewell, beating hemp to make fibres for rope was the activity chosen to occupy and exhaust prisoners.

When he visited the Bridewell House of Correction in 1777, the prison reformer John Howard recorded that prisoners were set to work from eight in the morning until four in the afternoon during the winter months. Beds were simple straw mats and heating was notoriously absent, so Hale and Wood will have had a cold and uncomfortable time from the end of October 1828 to the end of January 1829. Insubordinate prisoners were flogged or deprived of food. Even the full diet was spartan: the daily allowance was a penny loaf, ten ounces (283 grams) of beef or some cheese and three pints of shilling beer.

By the time Hale and Wood were released, the Horticultural Society had more serious things to worry about than the loss of £12 worth of seeds. Its financial problems were becoming more serious, and it was clear that the retrenchments made earlier had been woefully inadequate. Sabine's mismanagement apparently extended beyond overspending. He had failed to spot embezzlement by a protégé of his, John Turner, who worked as the assistant secretary at the Society's Regent Street offices. Since Sabine spent most of his time at the Chiswick Garden (the Society even paying for him to have living accommodation there), he had entrusted Turner with the receipt of the Fellows' annual subscriptions and paying tradesmen's bills. This gave John Turner ample opportunity to divert money for his own purposes, such as buying a nice house near Turnham Green. Even though a clerk had spotted discrepancies in Turner's accounts as early as February 1826, Sabine had failed to inform the Council until October and had tried to hush up the whole matter as much as possible. He had even allowed Turner to return to work, after he promised to pay back the £764 that was discovered to be missing from the accounts.

Obviously Joseph Sabine was not the only one to blame, for other people were also supposed to be responsible for checking the accounts. The treasurer of the Horticultural Society in this period was Colonel John Elliot. Despite being the managing director of a brewery, he seems to have had a very relaxed approach to financial matters. A later historian of the Society remarked, 'He appears to have regarded his duties as beginning and ending with the custody of such money as was from time to time passed to him for banking or investment; the question of whether the correct amounts were being handed to him appears to have caused him little concern.'[16] News of the Society's debts and the Turner affair leaked out, and Fellows began to resign their subscriptions, worried that they would become liable for the debts. On 15 January 1830 an anonymous letter was published in The Times, which laid open the shocking extent of the Society's indebtedness: 'The Society's debt at the end of 1828 was nearly £19,000 and this year it has increased by some hundreds of pounds, but no accounts have been seen.'[17] Applying the labour value used elsewhere in this book, this equates to a debt of over £15m today.

An emergency meeting was called and a committee was set up under Robert Gordon, MP, to enquire into the management of the Society and its Garden. An unedifying process of buck-passing and recrimination followed, as the president Thomas Knight declared plaintively, 'the local management of the official business of the Society was not amongst the duties which the members who did me the honour to elect me expected me to perform'.[18] John Lindley and the head gardener, Donald Munro, complained of the overbearing and interfering management of Joseph Sabine, who had demanded endless reports and the final say on every detail of the Garden's operation. On 17 February 1830 Sabine resigned as secretary, and a new Garden Committee and a Committee of Accounts were set up to try and bring some order to the Society's affairs and get the finances back under control.

Meanwhile, when their prison sentence ended, it seems that Reuben Hale and John Frederick Wood went their separate ways. Being caught red-handed in such a high-profile and well-reported crime, their prospects for future employment in their former trade looked grim. John Frederick Wood disappears at this point, leaving no definite trace in the historical record, so unfortunately it has not been possible to find out what became of him. There is some evidence that he left the country, spending some time in France. The 1841 census shows his father and mother, Charles and Susannah Wood, living on a farm in Stapleford in Hertfordshire; and although there is no sign of John Frederick, they are living with a grandson, named Charles, who is recorded as being born in France in 1834, though of course it is perfectly possible that Charles could be the son of another of their children.

On 4 July 1837 the *Hertford Mercury and Reformer* carried a small and seemingly insignificant announcement: 'Reuben Hale, gardener to Henry Cowper Esquire awarded third prize

for Heartseases by the Hertford Horticultural Society.'[19]
Whilst third prize in a local horticultural show would not strike
many people as a major achievement, it does show that, against
the odds, Reuben Hale was able to build a secure, if modest,
horticultural career back in his home county. It seems that his
father's employer, Henry Cowper of Tewin Water, gave Reuben
a second chance. Presumably his father, Thomas, pulled some
strings for him. The 1851 and 1861 censuses show him married and living on Kentish Lane in Hatfield and later at Warren Wood, between Hatfield and Broxbourne. In both census
returns his occupation is given as 'Gardener Domestic'.

The contrast between the way Reuben Hale and John Frederick Wood were treated and the handling of the fraudster
John Turner, who was able to rely on his relatives to repay
the money he embezzled and escaped any criminal charges, is
striking. Likewise, Joseph Sabine – although he had to endure
very public criticism, once the financial crisis became public
– was able to leave the Horticultural Society and move seam-
lessly across to the London Zoological Society. Natural history
was as great a passion as horticulture for Sabine, and he played
an active role in the early years of the Zoological Society and
its new zoo in Regent's Park. The people who really suffered,
as the Horticultural Society struggled to bring its finances
back under control, were the gardeners at Chiswick. Wide-
ranging cutbacks were made, including selling off plants and
ploughing up parts of the Garden to produce commercial crops
to support its upkeep. During the furore over the mismanagement of the Society, it seems that the Garden Committee
stopped meeting, and no new students had been recruited
since May of the previous year. As part of the cutbacks

initiated in 1830, students at Chiswick were replaced with ordinary labourers, with the option for students who wanted to continue there being unpaid. The dream of a 'National School for Horticulture' was over, at least for the foreseeable future.

EPILOGUE

'Glory has departed':
What Happened Next?

ON 5 JUNE 1861 THE GREAT AND THE GOOD OF THE
horticultural world mingled with high society's finest at
a grand opening of another Horticultural Society Garden.
This new garden was to completely eclipse the poor Chiswick
Garden, which by now had been through several slumps and
mini-revivals. Under its new president, Prince Albert, the by
now *Royal* Horticultural Society (RHS) only had eyes for its
brand-new garden at Kensington Gore. This garden offered
a venue for flower shows closer to central London, which
was felt to be critical if the Society was to compete with the
shows staged at the new Crystal Palace and in Regent's Park.
It was also an opportunity to showcase the latest horticultural
fashions.

William Andrews Nesfield, the new star of garden design,
was appointed to create his signature parterres, a revival of
seventeenth-century formal garden style, complete with patterns of low box hedging, laid out against coloured gravel.
Large mature trees were uprooted from Chiswick to populate
the new garden, and holly hedging was stripped out to create

mazes to entertain the Kensington visitors. Chiswick's role was largely reduced to growing bedding plants to supply the RHS Kensington Garden. *The Gardeners' Chronicle* summed up the situation neatly:

> The old Horticultural Garden is well-nigh forgotten; its glory has departed, and the world's (we mean the gardening world's) eyes are fixed upon South Kensington. The palatial architecture, waterfalls and basins, flower embroidery and tub decoration there, have drawn attention from the humble fruit walls and plant houses, green turf, shady walks, fine trees and country air of Chiswick.[1]

Ironically, it was Chiswick's most famous 'old boy', Joseph Paxton, who could take a great deal of the credit for this change. It was the profits from the Great Exhibition (the success of which was to a large degree due to Paxton's building) that funded the purchase of the land upon which the Kensington Garden sat. Prince Albert, as well as being president of the Royal Horticultural Society, was president of the Royal Commission for the Exhibition of 1851. He was determined that the profits from the Great Exhibition should be used to establish a complex of cultural institutions, designed to educate the public in the arts, science and design. As horticulture had a foot in all these camps, it was felt appropriate that the complex should include a garden. The RHS leased twenty-two and a half of the eighty-seven acres (thirty-five hectares) owned by the Royal Commission, on land now occupied by the Science Museum and Imperial College. The Commission used its funds to pay for the earthworks and the construction of elaborate

arcades that ringed the garden, and the RHS paid for the
garden layout and planting.

Increasingly the officers and committee members found
themselves occupied with the business of running a major
visitor attraction, and subcommittees abounded, covering
everything from the purchase of statues to the management
of bands for the bandstands. In the hustle and bustle of Kensington, all the early ambitions for the Chiswick Garden were
largely forgotten. Indeed, well before the Great Exhibition and
the 'Albertopolis' complex were even thought of, the Society
had decided that the training scheme was a venture best left
in the past. The scheme set up in 1823 was dismissed as being
largely a failure. Attempts were made to reform the Society's
approach to training gardeners by introducing examinations,
but progress was faltering. Gardeners were unwilling, by and
large, to go through the arduous academic and technical work
needed to obtain a qualification that did not seem to impress
employers or earn them a higher wage than the traditional
'on the job' training. Although individual head gardeners
were well respected, the idea of gardening developing as a
fully-fledged profession was a dream that had to wait a while
longer.

The financial pressure of running the Kensington Garden
rapidly became too much for the Society, which was not on
the firmest of footings financially, to begin with. In 1888 the
Royal Horticultural Society finally gave up and terminated
its lease on the Kensington site. Chiswick was once again its
sole garden, although by this time this part of west London
no longer offered the ideal environment for showcasing the
finest plants or the latest horticultural techniques. The urban

sprawl of London had surrounded the Garden and pollution was becoming a serious issue. In 1903, when millionaire Thomas Hanbury offered to buy the late George Fergusson Wilson's Oakwood garden near the small Surrey village of Wisley, the RHS jumped at the chance to relocate and start afresh. Plants, greenhouses, fixtures and fittings were uprooted from Chiswick and sent en masse to Wisley. Anything deemed not worth keeping was thrown away or unceremoniously sold off in an 'everything must go' auction held in March 1904.

Miraculously, the Handwriting Book managed to survive and was one of the items that was transferred in the move from Chiswick to Wisley, eventually making its way to a box in my office at the Lindley Library. One of the things that infuriates archivists, librarians and curators is the deep and abiding love that the media seems to have for stories about the discovery of 'lost' treasures in storerooms. As hard as we try to explain that the latest discovery is due to careful and often laborious work to better understand an item, and that we knew it was there all along, the 'Newly discovered in the vaults' headline is a regular occurrence. Items in museums, archives and libraries are rarely lost, just under-researched. This was certainly the case with the Handwriting Book. The whereabouts of the book were known to all the team at the Lindley Library when I arrived and had been referenced by researchers and authors several times, mostly in biographies of Joseph Paxton. The rest of the men in the Handwriting Book were hiding in plain sight; it was just that no one had looked into who they were and what they did in the rest of their careers. The reasons for this are not hard to find. The sheer fame of the fifth name in the book, Joseph Paxton, clearly one reason; most people never got beyond page three, where his entry sits. One 'helpful' librarian of days gone by even scribbled a handy hint – 'Paxton page 3' – on the inside cover.

It is not just the scale and range of Paxton's achievements that meant he overshadowed everyone else – it was the fact that his life story so neatly encapsulated the idea of the 'self-made man'; as Queen Victoria is reported to have said, 'To think he rose from an ordinary gardener's boy!'[2] One of the most popular books of the mid- to late nineteenth century was William Smiles' *Self-Help*, a runaway best-seller which told the stories of people who had risen from poverty through thrift, hard work and, above all, self-education. According to this school of thought, difficulties weeded out the weak, and those that succeeded did so because they were self-reliant and had a 'pushing character'.[3] Paxton was certainly hard-working and managed to overcome a low level of early education to become a skilled and well-informed horticulturist, garden designer and architect.

To proponents of 'self-help', all the men in the Hand-writing Book who did not rise to such heights were clearly lacking the necessary qualities and had only themselves to blame. The Horticultural Society clearly subscribed to this view. On 1 May 1840 the Fellows of the Society gathered at its offices on Regent Street to hear a review of progress in the ten years that had elapsed since the financial scandal of 1830. The review covered not just the steps the Council had taken to try to rescue the Society's finances, but also how the Society was faring in achieving its objectives, one of which was 'The instruction of young men in the art of gardening'. Whilst the review was very self-congratulatory when it came to other

objectives, such as 'the introduction of new, useful or ornamental plants', the tone when it came to training was far more
sombre. It was noted that 'since the first establishment of the
garden the Council have been anxious to render it conducive
to the improvement of the Education of young men intended
for gardeners', although in reality these aims were 'but partially realised'. The review put the blame for this firmly at the
door of the young gardeners themselves. Their early education, before arriving at Chiswick, had been too poor to allow
them to take advantage of the opportunity they had been
given:

> Some were found totally acquainted with the commonest
> details of the gardener's art; others were illiterate in a lam-
> entable degree; and notwithstanding the excellent example
> set by many who are now at the head of their profession,
> upon the whole it must be admitted that several of the men
> received in the garden were little improved in consequence.[4]

This seems grossly unfair, given the range of experience
and the quality of literacy demonstrated in the entries in the
Handwriting Book. As we have seen, many of the men made
considerable progress during their career. Although Joseph
Paxton stood apart, it must be remembered that he was the
beneficiary of an enormous stroke of good luck when he caught
the eye of the Duke of Devonshire in 1826. The indulgent
patronage of an enormously wealthy employer gave Paxton
advantages and opportunities that none of his other peers
enjoyed. The fact that he married a clever and capable woman
with a dowry of £5,000 was also a contributing factor. Clearly

Paxton used his energy, charm, skills and talents to make the most of these opportunities, but it is unfair in the extreme to judge or ignore the other gardeners who did not enjoy these advantages and whose careers did not reach his heights.

However, it is not just a case of Paxton taking all the limelight. Another important reason why the other Chiswick gardeners were relatively neglected over the years is that there was a gradual but distinct downgrading of the status of professional gardeners, to the point where only the most exceptional ones were deemed worthy of notice. Our men's careers overlapped at a time when the formal science of botany was emerging and was beginning to be seen as higher in the intellectual pecking order than horticulture, which was to be increasingly relegated to the category of craft rather than science. Before the early years of the nineteenth century there had been considerable fluidity between what we now regard as separate disciplines, and terms such as 'botanist', 'botanophile' and 'student of botany' were used to describe a wide range of people with varying degrees of knowledge and involvement in plants – from complete amateurs dabbling in the subject, to individuals actually employed by institutions or private patrons as taxonomists.

Although universities were beginning to found courses on the subject, and the notion of science as a professional discipline with distinct entry qualifications was starting to form, there was still considerable scope for amateurs to contribute to the development of scientific knowledge. However, increasingly this notion of the amateur-but-expert-botanist was restricted to people from a higher social class and background. A gentleman could be an amateur and still be respected, because for him 'amateur' was not necessarily a pejorative term. In the nineteenth century amateurs were regarded as valuable contributors because they were unswayed by commercial considerations and, if they were of a high enough social status, were felt to be capable of a high degree of discernment and taste. Between them, these two groups (the qualified academic and the high-status, well-to-do amateur) began to monopolize the subject of botany – leaving little room for the lower-status professional gardeners. They were increasingly restricted to the technical process of growing plants, and their expertise on plant properties and physiology was deemed of interest only to horticulture or – even worse, if this knowledge was applied to ornamental cultivars – 'floriculture', which had a strong whiff of the working class about it. Although men like Robert Thompson undertook rigorous empirical examination of the plants they were trialling and testing, their findings were not accorded the same status.

Furthermore, the style of gardening with which the men who trained at Chiswick were associated did not enjoy a high reputation as the years passed. The introduction of exotics, and the development of new hybrids that our men perfected, was described not as the epitome of horticultural innovation and skill, but as stiff, garish and artificial, at odds with nature and even national identity. The late nineteenth and early twentieth centuries saw folk revivals in architecture, dress, music, food and gardens. Influential writers and thinkers such as William Morris, William Robinson and Gertrude Jekyll presented themselves as defenders of Old English plants against the onslaught of hybridized exotics. As garden historian Dr Brent Elliott has noted, it is ironic that some proponents of the Arts

and Crafts movement, though keen to celebrate the craftsman-
ship of everyone from wood-turners to stonecutters, paid such
little respect to one kind of craftsman – the gardener.[5] Though
Gertrude Jekyll employed a bevy of professional gardeners,
you do not find them mentioned much in her writings.

The posthumous reputation of the Chiswick gardeners has
also suffered from the fact that many of the finest examples
of their work have disappeared or decayed. Maintaining the
opulent formality of these High Victorian gardens has often
required too great a burden of resources to be sustainable. Even
landmark achievements like the Great Stove at Chatsworth,
Joseph Paxton's immense glasshouse, proved too expensive
to run in the twentieth century and it was destroyed with
dynamite in 1920.

Overshadowed, obscure and out of fashion, the men in
the Handwriting Book have been easy to ignore. Wandering
around Chiswick today, there is no sign of the garden that they
trained and worked in, other than a little cul-de-sac named
Horticultural Place. But if you weave up and down streets
north of the A4 that were built over the site of the Chiswick
Garden (Barrowgate Road, Alwyn Avenue, Wavendon Avenue, Sharon Road, Foster Road and Hadley Gardens) and look
in those front gardens that have not been relegated entirely
to car-parking space, the legacy of the Garden and the men
who trained there is clear to see, in the range of plants from all
across the globe that are growing happily together. Obscure
or famous, one way or another the men listed in the Handwriting Book can be credited with helping to create our idea
of a domestic garden.

There is one other place to find echoes of the Chiswick

Garden and the men in the Handwriting Book. Go to the RHS Garden at Wisley and you will see, clad in RHS fleeces and polo shirts, today's horticultural trainees, working and learning on the job and ready to embark on their own adventures. Perhaps, in two hundred years or so, someone will write a book about them.

Select Bibliography

Brooke, E. A., *The Gardens of England*, London, T. McLean, 1857

Burnet, J., *Plenty & Want: A Social History of Diet in England from 1815 to the Present Day*, third edition, London, Routledge, 1989

Chesney, K., *The Victorian Underworld*, London, Penguin Books, 1991

Clegg, G., *Chiswick Past*, London, Historical Publications, 1995

Collingham, L., *The Hungry Empire: How Britain's Quest for Food Shaped the Modern World*, London, Bodley Head, 2017

Colquhoun, K., *A Thing in Disguise: The Visionary Life of Joseph Paxton*, London, Fourth Estate, 2003

Desmond, R., *Dictionary of British and Irish Botanists and Horticulturists*, London, Taylor & Francis, 1994

—— *The European Discovery of the Indian Flora*, Oxford, Oxford University Press, 1992

Dickens, C., *The Posthumous Papers of the Pickwick Club* (1837), ed. M. Wormald, London, Penguin Books, 1999

Elliott, B., *The Royal Horticultural Society: A History, 1804–2004*, London, Phillimore, 2004

—— *Victorian Gardens*, London, Batsford, 1986

Elliott, P., Watkins, C. and Daniels, S., *The British Arboretum: Trees, Science and Culture in the Nineteenth Century*, London, Routledge, 2016

Finn, E., aka 'Garryowen', *The Chronicles of Early Melbourne*, Melbourne, Fergusson & Mitchell, 1888

Flaubert, G., *Flaubert in Egypt: A Sensibility on Tour*, London, Penguin Classics, 1996

Fletcher, H. R., *The Story of the Royal Horticultural Society 1804–1968*, Oxford, Oxford University Press, 1969

Gardner Wilkinson, Sir John, *Modern Egypt and Thebes*, vol. 1, London, John Murray, 1843

Glenny, G., *The Handy Book of Gardening and Golden Rules for Gardeners*, London, Houlston & Wright, 1864

Hervey, A., *The Ocean and the Desert by a Madras Officer*, London, T. C. Newby, 1846

Hibberd, S., *The Amateur's Flower Garden*, London, Groombridge & Sons, 1871

Holway, T., *The Flower of Empire: The Amazon's Largest Water Lily, the Quest to Make it Bloom*, Oxford, Oxford University Press, 2013

Home, R. W., Lucas, A. M., Maroske, S., Sinkora, D. M. and Voight, J. H. (eds), *Regardfully Yours: Selected correspondence of Ferdinand von Mueller*, vols 1 & 2, Bern, Peter Lang, 1998 and 2002

Keynes, R. D. (ed.), *Charles Darwin's Beagle Diary*, Cambridge, Cambridge University Press, 2001

Kingsbury, N., *Hybrid: The History and Science of Plant Breeding*, Chicago, University of Chicago Press, 2011

Kinnear, J. G., *Cairo, Petra and Damascus in 1839, with remarks on the governments of Mehemet Ali*, London, John Murray, 1841

Longstaffe-Gowan, T., *The London Town Garden 1700–1840*, New Haven, CT, Yale University Press, 2001

Loudon, J. C., *An Encyclopaedia of Gardening*, London, Longman, Hurst, Rees, Orme & Brown, 1822

—— *Encyclopaedia of Plants*, London, Longman, Rees, Orme, Brown & Green, 1829

—— *Remarks on the Construction of Hothouses*, London, J. Taylor, 1817

—— *The Suburban Gardener and Villa Companion*, London, Longman, 1838

McCracken, D. P., *Gardens of Empire: Botanical Institutions of the Victorian British Empire*, Leicester, Leicester University Press, 1997

Martineau, H., *Eastern Life, Present and Past*, Philadelphia, Lea & Blanchard, 1848

Mayhew, H., *London Labour and the London Poor*, vol. IV, London, Griffin, Bohn & Co., 1861

—— and Binny, J., *The Criminal Prisons of London and Scenes of London Life*, London, Griffin, Bohn & Co., 1862

Montauban, E., *A Year and a Day in the East* (1846), London, British Library Historical Print Editions, 2011

Platt, A., *A Journal of a Tour through Egypt in 1838–39* (1841), Whitefish, MT, Kessinger Publishing Co., 2009

Poignant, R., *Professional Savages: Captive Lives and Western Spectacle*, New Haven, CT, Yale University Press, 2004

Prince, H., *Parks in Hertfordshire since 1500*, Hatfield, University of Hertfordshire Press, 2008

Pückler-Muskau (Prince), *Egypt under Mehemet Ali*, trans. H. Evans Lloyd, London, H. Colburn, 1845

Quest-Ritson, C., *The English Garden: A Social History*, Boston, MA, David R. Godine, 2003

Shephard, S., *Seeds of Fortune: A Gardening Dynasty*, London, Bloomsbury, 2003

Smiles, S., *Self-Help with Illustrations of Character, Conduct and Perseverance*, ed. Sinnema, P., Oxford, Oxford University Press, 2002

Stuart, D., *The Garden Triumphant*, London, Viking, 1988

Thompson, J., *Edward William Lane: The Life of the Pioneering Egyptologist and Orientalist*, London, Haus Publishing, 2010

Thompson, R., *The Gardener's Assistant: Practical and Scientific: a Guide to the Formation and Management of the Kitchen, Fruit, and Flower Garden…*, London, Blackie & Son, 1859

Webber, R., *Market Gardening: The History of Commercial Flower, Fruit and Vegetable Growing*, Newton Abbot, David & Charles, 1972

Willes, M., *The Gardens of the British Working Class*, New Haven, CT, Yale University Press, 2014

Wilson, B., *Heyday: The 1850s and the Dawn of the Global Age*, London, Weidenfeld & Nicolson, 2016

Notes

INTRODUCTION

A Garden to Grow Gardeners

1. Horticultural Society of London, Council Minute Book, 1804, RHS Archive

2. Horticultural Society of London, 'Statement relative to the Establishment of a Garden', February 1822, RHS Archive

3. ibid.

4. Horticultural Society of London, Preface, *Transactions of the Horticultural Society of London*, vol. 3, 1822, p.ii

5. Quoted in Elliott, B., *The Royal Horticultural Society: A History 1804–2004*, London, Phillimore, 2004

6. Horticultural Society of London, 'Statement relative to the Establishment of a Garden', February 1822, RHS Archive

7. Loudon, J. C., *Gardener's Magazine*, vol. 1, 1826, p.225

8. Horticultural Society of London, *First Report of the Garden Committee*, March 1823, RHS Archive

9. ibid.

10. Loudon, J. C., *An Encyclopaedia of Gardening*, part IV, London, Longman, 1838, p.1138

11. Bunyard, I. P., *Gardener's Magazine*, vol. 1, 1826, p.142

12. Loudon, J. C., *Gardener's Magazine*, vol. 1, 1826, p.410

13. Frazer, J., 'Reminiscences of Chiswick', *RHS Gardens Club Journal*, vol. 1, 1908

CHAPTER ONE

'The beau ideal': The Horticultural Elite

1. Horticultural Society of London, 'The Handwriting of Under-Gardeners and Labourers', RHS Archive

2. Horticultural Society of London, Garden Committee Minutes, 5 April 1824, RHS Archive

3. Loudon, J. C., *Gardener's Magazine*, vol. 7, 1831, pp.547–8

4. Appleby, T., *Cottage Gardener*, vol. 7, 1852, p.414

5. Brooke, E. A., *The Gardens of England*, London, T. McLean, 1857

6. Glenny, G., *The Handy Book of Gardening and Golden Rules for Gardeners*, London, Houlston & Wright, 1864

7. *Gardener's Magazine*, vol. 1, April 1826, p.135

8. Coats, A. M., 'Forgotten Gardeners 3: The Mangles Family', *Garden History*, vol. 1, no. 3, 1973, p.42

9. *Gardener's Magazine*, vol. 3, 1828, pp.245–7

10. Loudon, J. C., *Encyclopaedia of Plants*, London, Longman, Rees, Orme, Brown & Green, 1829

11. Loudon, J. C., *Remarks on the Construction of Hothouses*, London, J. Taylor, 1817

12. *The Gardeners' Chronicle*, 28 August 1841

13. Glenny, G., *The Handy Book of Gardening and Golden Rules for Gardeners*, 1864

14. Colquhoun, K., *A Thing in Disguise: The Visionary Life of Joseph Paxton*, London, Fourth Estate, 2003, p.154

15. ibid., p.235

CHAPTER TWO

'Much judgement and good taste': The Gardeners Who Set Standards

1. Paxton, J., *Paxton's Magazine of Botany*, vol. 5, 1838, p.255

2. W. B. B., 'Basing Park', *The Gardeners' Chronicle*, 1854, p.633

3. Fish, R., *Cottage Gardener*, vol. XVIII, 1857, pp.275–7

4. Horticultural Society of London, 'Proceedings', *Journal of the Horticultural Society of London*, vol. III, 1843, p.xv

5. Lindley, J., 'The Evergreen Berberries Grown in Great Britain', *Journal of the Horticultural Society*, vol. V, 1850, p.10

6. Loudon, J. C., *Gardener's Magazine*, vol. 1, 1826

7. Horticultural Society of London, Garden Committee Minutes, 11 October 1827, RHS Archive

8. Bailey, H., *The Gardeners' Chronicle*, 1846, pp.739–40

9. Bailey, H., *The Gardeners' Chronicle*, 1849, p.373

10. 'Nuneham Courtenay', *Penny Magazine of the Society for the Diffusion of Useful Knowledge*, 1846, p.409

11. *Oxford Journal*, 13 May 1871

CHAPTER THREE

'A great number of deserving men': Life Lower Down the Horticultural Ladder

1. Letter from 'One in the Chiswick Gardens', *The Gardener and Practical Florist*, vol. 2, 1843, p.378

2. Loudon, J. C., *Gardener's Magazine*, vol. 1, 1826, p.315

3. Horticultural Society of London, Garden Committee Minutes, 30 June 1828, RHS Archive

4. Horticultural Society of London, Garden Committee Minutes, 5 September 1825, RHS Archive

5. *The Gardeners' Chronicle*, 28 July 1860, p.694

6. *The Gardeners' Chronicle*, 11 September 1841, p.601

7. Loudon, J. C., *The Suburban Gardener and Villa Companion*, London, Longman, 1838

8. Horticultural Society of London, 'The Handwriting of Under-Gardeners and Labourers', RHS Archive

9. 'Market Gardening around London', Article 14, *RHS Botanical Tracts*, vol. 91

10. ibid.

11. 'The Londoners' Garden', *The Leisure Hour*, 1859, pp.461–3

12. Hibberd, S., 'The Pleasures of a Kitchen Garden', *Floral World*, vol. 1, 1858, p.93

13. Hibberd, S., *The Amateur's Flower Garden*, London, Groombridge & Sons, 1871

14. Calendar of the Prisoners in Her Majesty's Gaol and House of Correction at Aylesbury, January 1846

15. Mayhew, H. and Binny, J., *The Criminal Prisons of London and Scenes of London Life*, London, Griffin, Bohn & Co., 1862, p.301

16. Mayhew, H., *London Labour and the London Poor*, vol. IV, London, Griffin, Bohn & Co., 1861

17. Dr Thackrah, a Leeds physician, quoted in Harrison, J. F. C., *The Early Victorians*, HarperCollins, London, 1973

18. Dickens, C., *Nicholas Nickleby*, ed. M. Ford, Penguin Books, London, 2003, p.23

19. 'The Londoners' Garden', *The Leisure Hour*, 1859, pp.461–3

CHAPTER FOUR

'The most splendid plant I ever beheld': The Collector

1. Keynes, R. D. (ed.), *Charles Darwin's Beagle Diary*, entry: 12 May 1835, Cambridge, Cambridge University Press, 2001, p.330

2. *Gardener's Magazine*, vol. 7, 8 January 1831, pp.95–6

3. Letter from Thomas Bridges to William Hooker, 23 September 1828, Directors' Correspondence ref. DC66/6, Archives Royal Botanic Gardens, Kew

4. ibid.

5. Holway, T., *The Flower of Empire: The Amazon's Largest Water Lily, the Quest to Make it Bloom*, Oxford, Oxford University Press, 2013, p.15

6. Letter from Thomas Bridges to William Hooker, September 1829, Directors' Correspondence ref. DC66/7, Archives Royal Botanic Gardens, Kew

7. ibid.

8. Letter from Thomas Bridges to William Hooker, 24 December 1829, Directors' Correspondence ref. DC66/8, Archives Royal Botanic Gardens, Kew

9. ibid.

10. Letter from Thomas Bridges to William Hooker, September 1829, Directors' Correspondence ref. DC66/7, Archives Royal Botanic Gardens, Kew

11. Letter from Alexander Caldcleugh to William Hooker quoted in 'The Botanical Activities of Thomas Bridges' by Ivan M. Johnston, published in *Contributions from the Gray Herbarium of Harvard University* No. 81 (1928), pp. 98–106

12. Loudon, J. C., *Gardener's Magazine*, vol. 8, October 1837, p.471

13. Holway, T., *The Flower of Empire*, 2013, p.128

14. Letter from Thomas Bridges to William Hooker, 8 April 1842, Directors' Correspondence ref. DC 69/22, Archives Royal Botanic Gardens, Kew

15. Letter from Thomas Bridges to William Hooker, 3 April 1845, Directors' Correspondence ref. DC 70/9, Archives Royal Botanic Gardens, Kew

16. ibid.

17. Hooker, W., *Description of Victoria regia or Great water lily of South America*, Reeves Bros, London, 1847

18. Excerpt from a letter from Thomas Bridges to Hugh Cuming, quoted in a letter from Miss Cuming to William Hooker, Directors' Correspondence ref. DC 7024/1, Archives Royal Botanic Gardens, Kew

19. Letter from Thomas Bridges to William Hooker, 21 July 1846, Directors' Correspondence ref. DC 70/10, Archives Royal Botanic Gardens, Kew

20. Letter from Thomas Bridges to William Hooker, [n.d.], Directors' Correspondence ref. DC 70/11, Archives Royal Botanic Gardens, Kew

21. Hooker, W., *Description of Victoria regia or Great water lily of South America*, 1847

22. Letter from Thomas Bridges to William Hooker, 8 December 1846, from Bristol, Directors' Correspondence ref. DC 70/12, Archives Royal Botanic Gardens, Kew

23. ibid.

24. Holway, T., *The Flower of Empire*, 2013, p.221

25. Colquhoun, K., *A Thing in Disguise*, 2003, p.176

26. Dickens, C., 'The Private History of the Palace of Glass', *Household Words*, 1851

27. Letter from Alexander Caldcleugh to William Hooker, 30 September 1852, Directors' Correspondence ref. DC 71/48, Archives Royal Botanic Gardens, Kew

28. Letter from Thomas Bridges to William Hooker, 5 May 1858, Directors' Correspondence ref. DC 64/20, Archives Royal Botanic Gardens, Kew

29. Hall, T. H., *A Paper read before the California Academy of Natural Sciences*, 8 January 1866

30. Letter from R. E. Bridges to Joseph Dalton Hooker, September 1879, Directors' Correspondence ref. DC 199/81, Archives Royal Botanic Gardens, Kew

31. Letter sent from Miss Cuming to William Hooker, 9 March 1856, Directors' Correspondence ref. DC 7024/1, Archives Royal Botanic Gardens, Kew

CHAPTER FIVE

'Much attached to Egypt': Travelling Gardeners

1. Horticultural Society of London, Council Minutes, 4 August 1826, RHS Archive

2. Beattie Booth, W., 'Proceedings of the London Zoological Society', 1832

3. ibid.

4. Horticultural Society of London, Garden Committee Minutes, 31 March 1828, RHS Archive

5. Montauban, E., *A Year and a Day in the East* (1846), London, British Library Historical Print Editions, 2011

6. ibid.

7. Horticultural Society of London, Council Minutes, 23 April 1830, RHS Archive

8. Platt, A., *A Journal of a Tour through Egypt in 1838–39* (1841), Whitefish, MT, Kessinger Publishing Co., 2009

9. ibid.

10. Thompson, J., *Edward William Lane: The Life of the Pioneering Egyptologist and Orientalist*, London, Haus Publishing, 2010

11. Wilkinson, A., 'James Traill and William McCulloch in Egypt', *Garden History*, 39:1, p.84

12. ibid.

13. Hamdy, R. S., 'A Study of Plant Distributions in 9 Historic Gardens in Egypt', *Garden History*, 38:2, p.267

14. Bowring, John, 'Report on Egypt and Candia addressed to the Right Honourable Viscount Palmerston', 1840

15. Wilkinson, A., 'James Traill and William McCulloch in Egypt', *Garden History*, 39:1, p.87

16. Horticultural Society of London, Council Minutes, 11 March 1831, RHS Archive

17. Letter from James Traill to William Hooker, 30 April 1835, Directors' Correspondence, Archives Royal Botanic Gardens, Kew

18. Letter from Nathaniel Bagshaw Ward to William Hooker, quoted in Wilkinson, A., 'James Traill and William McCulloch in Egypt', *Garden History*, 39:1

19. Bowring, John, 'Report on Egypt and Candia addressed to the Right Honourable Viscount Palmerston', 1840

20. Letter from James Traill to John Bowring, quoted ibid.

21. Platt, W., *A Journal of a Tour through Egypt, the peninsula of Sinai and the Holy Land in 1838–39*, London, Richard Watts, 1841

22. Pückler-Muskau (Prince), *Egypt under Mehemet Ali*, trans. H. Evans Lloyd, London, H. Colburn, 1845

23. *Gardener's Magazine*, vol. 16, 1840, p.652

24. Letter from James Traill to William Hooker, 30 April 1835, Directors' Correspondence, Archives Royal Botanic Gardens, Kew

25. Hervey, A., *The Ocean and the Desert by a Madras Officer*, London, T. C. Newby, 1846, p.89

26. Pückler-Muskau, *Egypt under Mehemet Ali*, 1845

27. Martineau, H., *Eastern Life, Present and Past*, Philadelphia, Lea & Blanchard, 1848

28. *Gardener's Magazine*, New series vol. 9, 1843, pp.166–7

29. Gardner Wilkinson, Sir John, *Modern Egypt and Thebes*, vol. 1, London, John Murray, 1843

30. Letter from James Traill to Charles Lush, 17 June 1840, Archive of the Linnean Society

31. Platt, A., *A Journal of a Tour through Egypt in 1838–39*, 2009

32. Wilkinson, A., 'James Traill and William McCulloch in Egypt', *Garden History*, 39:1

33. Kinnear, J. G., *Cairo, Petra and Damascus in 1839, with remarks on the governments of Mehemet Ali*, London, John Murray, 1841

34. Letter from Edward William Lane to Lord Prudhoe, 20 November 1841, cited in Thompson, J., *Edward William Lane*, 2010, p.481

35. Flaubert, G., *Flaubert in Egypt: A Sensibility on Tour*, London, Penguin Classics, 1996

36. Lane MSS, cited in Wilkinson, A., 'James Traill and William McCulloch in Egypt', *Garden History*, 39:1, p.86

37. *Transactions of the Horticultural Society of London*, vol. 2, 1842

38. Thompson, J., *Edward William Lane*, 2010

CHAPTER SIX

'Young foreigners of respectability': Trainees from Abroad

1. Horticultural Society of London, *4th Report of the Garden Committee*, 1826

2. *Gardener's Magazine*, vol. IV, 1828, pp.76–9

3. Horticultural Society of London, Garden Committee Minutes, 15 August 1826, RHS Archive

4. Rauch, C., 'On the Construction of double roofed hot houses at Vienna', *Gardener's Magazine*, vol. VIII, 1832

5. Loudon, J. C., 'Foreign Notices', *Gardener's Magazine*, vol. XII, 1836, pp.199–200

6. Loudon, J. C., *Gardener's Magazine*, vol. I, 1824, p.269

7. Loudon, J. C., 'Foreign Notices', *Gardener's Magazine*, vol. XIII, 1837, pp.466–7

8. Loudon, J. C., *An Encyclopaedia of Gardening*, London, Longman, 1835

9. ibid.

10. Woodruff, G. W., *Memorial Service of the Reverend James Floy Nov 16 1863*, New York, N. Tibbals & Co., 1864

11. *Appletons' Cyclopedia of American Biography*, vol. 2, New York, D. Appleton & Co., 1887

12. *The Ladies' Repository*, vol. 25, issue 7, July 1865

13. Hervey, Capt. A., *A Soldier of the Company: Life of an Indian Ensign 1833–43*, London, Michael Joseph, 1988 (first abridged edition), ed. C. Allen

14. Nathaniel Wallich to E. Molong, Acting Secretary to Government, General Department, 5 November 1827, quoted in Chakrabarti, P., *Western Science in Modern India*, Delhi, Permanent Black, 2004, p.82

15. Wallich, N., 'Upon the preparation and management of plants during a voyage from India', *Transactions of the Horticultural Society* (second series), vol. 1, 1835

16. Horticultural Society of London, Garden Committee Minutes, 4 December 1829, RHS Archive

17. *Report from the Select Committee of the House of Lords to Inquire into the Present State of the Affairs of the East India Company*, 1830

18. Lindley, J., Editorial, *The Gardeners' Chronicle*, 2 September 1854, pp. 563–4

19. Rev. James Cordiner, army chaplain at Columbo 1779–1804, quoted in Desmond, R., *The European Discovery of the Indian Flora*, Oxford, Oxford University Press, 1992

20. Quoted in Desmond, R., *Dictionary of British and Irish Botanists and Horticulturists*, London, Taylor & Francis, 1994

21. Lindley, J., Editorial, *The Gardeners' Chronicle*, 2 September 1854, pp. 563–4

22. *Cape Town Advertiser*, 1845, quoted in McCracken, D. P., *Gardens of Empire: Botanical Institutions of the Victorian British Empire*, Leicester, Leicester University Press, 1997

23. Gardner, G., 'Report on the Royal Botanic Garden Peradeniya', August 1844

24. Lindley, J., Editorial, *The Gardeners' Chronicle*, 2 September 1854, pp. 563–4

CHAPTER SEVEN

'A little order into chaos': The Fruit Experts

1. Loudon, J. C., *An Encyclopedia of Gardening*, London, Longman, Hurst, Rees, Orme & Brown, 1822

2. Knight, T. A., Introductory Remarks, *Transactions of the Horticultural Society of London*, vol. 1, 1820

3. *Gardener's Magazine*, vol. 1, 1826, p.420

4. Caledonian Horticultural Society, *Memoirs*, vol. 4, 1826

5. Letter from Joseph Sabine to William McNab, 15 February 1826, in McNab Scrapbook 1, RBGE Archives

6. Horticultural Society of London, Garden Committee Minutes, 3 April 1826, RHS Archive

7. Letter from James Barnet to William McNab, 31 January 1826, in McNab Scrapbook 1, RBGE Archives

8. Byron, J., Centenary Edition, *The Caledonian Gardener*, 2009

9. Loudon, J. C., *Gardener's Magazine*, vol. 4, 1828, pp.168–9

10. Horticultural Society of London, *Report of the Garden Committee*, 31 March 1826

11. Bunyard, E. A., *The Gardeners' Chronicle*, 1918, vol. I, pp.121–2

12. Horticultural Society of London, *Fruits Proved in the Garden*, vol. 1, 1832, RHS Archive

13. Byron, J., *Caledonian Gardener*, Centenary Edition, 2009

14. Letter from James Barnet to the Secretary and Council, Caledonian Horticultural Society, 17 June 1836, RBGE Archives

15. Caledonian Horticultural Society Minutes, vol. III, p.92, RBGE Archives

16. Letter from James Barnet to Secretary and Council, Caledonian Horticultural Society, 17 June 1836, RBGE Archives

17. 'Report on certain injuries and defacements observed in the Garden Lodge of the Caledonian Horticultural Society', December 1836, RBGE Archives

18. 'Report on the general state in which the Experimental Garden has been left by Mr James Barnet the late Superintendent', 8 December 1836, RBGE Archives

19. 'Communication by Dr Neill to the Committee', 30 December 1836, RBGE Archives

20. Thompson, R., 'Some Account of the Jefferson Plum', *Journal of the Horticultural Society of London*, vol. 1, 1846, p.117

21. Bunyard, E. A., *The Gardeners' Chronicle*, 1918, vol. I, pp.121–2

CHAPTER EIGHT

'For sale at moderate prices': The Nurserymen

1. 'Report on the Progress of the Horticultural Society', *Transactions of the Horticultural Society* (second series), vol. 2

2. Advert in *The Gardeners' Chronicle*, numerous issues in the 1850s

3. *The Horticultural Register*, 1 May 1832

4. Advert in the *Sheffield Iris,* 16 May 1837

5. ibid.

6. Advert in the *Sheffield Iris*, 20 February 1838

7. 'Report on the Progress of the Horticultural Society', *Transactions of the Horticultural Society* (second series), vol. 2, p.455

8. Advert in the *Durham Chronicle*, 19 March 1847

9. Advert in the *Newcastle Daily Chronicle*, 31 October 1865

10. https://www.measuringworth.com/calculators/ukcompare

11. Advert in the *Rothesay Chronicle*, 8 October 1881

12. Harrison, G., 'On the Treatment of the *Crassula coccinea* and *Crassula versicolor*', *The Floricultural Cabinet*, vol. 1, August 1833

13. Harrison, G., 'On the Culture of the Chrysanthemum', *The Floricultural Cabinet*, vol. 1, February 1834

14. *The Floricultural Magazine and Miscellany of Gardening*, vol. 1, 1836–7

15. *The Horticultural Register*, May 1832

16. *The Penny Magazine of the Society for the Diffusion of Useful Knowledge*, vol. 7, 1838

17. *Durham Chronicle*, 10 September 1858

18. *Newcastle Journal*, 30 August 1862

19. *Durham Chronicle*, 10 September 1858

20. *Durham County Advertiser*, 2 September 1864

21. *Newcastle Daily Chronicle*, 27 August 1864

22. *Newcastle Chronicle*, 31 October 1865

23. *The Gardeners' Chronicle*, 23 February 1856

24. Advert in the *Norfolk Chronicle*, 22 November 1834

25. ibid.

26. *The London Gazette*, 19 April 1842

27. Advert in the *Sheffield Independent*, 15 June 1839

28. Advert in the *Sheffield Independent*, 5 October 1839

29. Dickens, C., *The Posthumous Papers of the Pickwick Club* (1837), ed. M. Wormald, London, Penguin Books, 1999

30. Advert in the *Sheffield Independent*, 18 November 1843

31. *Sheffield Independent*, 17 July 1847

CHAPTER NINE

'A solitary wanderer': The Australian Adventurer

1. Anon., *The Leader*, Melbourne, 2 September 1871

2. http://www.portphillipdistrict.info/C_and_F_Ports_Passenger_Lists_1838-51_114.htm

3. Finn, E., aka 'Garryowen', *The Chronicles of Early Melbourne*, Melbourne, Fergusson & Mitchell, 1888

4. Ginn, H., 'Report on the Botanical Gardens, Melbourne, from the 31st of September, 1851, to the 31st December in the same year', 1852

5. Letter from 'Hortensis' published in *The Australasian*, Saturday 8 July 1899

6. Quoted in Wilson, B., *Heyday: The 1850s and the Dawn of the Global Age*, Weidenfeld & Nicolson, 2016

7. Anon., *The Leader*, Melbourne, Saturday 2 September 1871

8. Letter from Ferdinand von Mueller to William Hooker, 3 February 1853, in *Regardfully Yours: Selected correspondence of Ferdinand von Mueller*, vol. 1, ed. R. W. Home, A. M. Lucas, Sara Maroske, D. M. Sinkora and J. H. Voight, Bern, Peter Lang, 1998

9. ibid.

10. ibid.

11. Poignant, R., *Professional Savages: Captive Lives and Western Spectacle*, New Haven, CT, Yale University Press, 2004

12. Macmillan, A. C., Letters to Byerley, 1866, archives ref: Wov/A68/26, Queensland State Archives

13. Article by 'Sketcher' in *The Queenslander*, Saturday 20 February 1904

14. Anon., *The Geelong Advertiser*, 11 May 1865

15. Letter to the Editor from 'An Older Gardener', *The Weekly Times*, Melbourne, Saturday, November 1869

16. Anon., *The Leader*, Melbourne, Saturday 2 September 1871

17. Anon., *The Weekly Times*, Melbourne, Saturday 20 January 1872

18. Letter from John Dallachy to Ferdinand von Mueller, November 1868, in *Regardfully Yours: Selected correspondence of Ferdinand von Mueller*, vol. 2, ed.

R. W. Home, A. M. Lucas, Sara Maroske, D. M. Sinkora and J. H. Voight, Bern, Peter Lang, 2002

19. Letter from Ferdinand von Mueller to George Bentham, March 1870, ibid.

20. Anon., *The Weekly Times*, Melbourne, Saturday 20 January 1872

21. Letter to the Editor from 'An Older Gardener', *The Weekly Times*, Melbourne, Saturday, November 1869

22. Pescott, R. T. M., *The Royal Botanic Gardens Melbourne: A history from 1845 to 1970*, Melbourne, Oxford University Press, 1982

23. *The Age*, Melbourne, 1 February 1868

24. Letter to the Editor from 'Veritas', *Melbourne Argus*, 8 August 1855

CHAPTER TEN

'Habits of order and good conduct': The Rise and Fall of a Head Gardener

1. *The Garden*, vol. XIII, 1878, p.199

2. Loudon, J. C., *Gardener's Magazine*, vol. 16, 1840, pp.588–90

3. ibid.

4. ibid.

5. ibid.

6. *Herts Guardian, Agricultural Journal, and General Advertiser*, Tuesday 12 July 1864

7. ibid.

8. *The Monmouthshire Merlin*, 18 June 1864

9. *Herts Guardian, Agricultural Journal, and General Advertiser*, Tuesday 12 July 1864

10. ibid.

11. ibid.

12. ibid.

13. ibid.

14. Letter to the Editor, *Herts Guardian, Agricultural Journal, and General Advertiser*, Tuesday 12 July 1864

15. Editorial, *Morning Chronicle*, 31 May 1850

16. Article XLIII, 'Report on the Progress of the Horticultural Society of London from May 1 1830 to April 30 1840', *Transactions of the Horticultural Society of London* (second series), vol. 2, 1842, p.373

17. From information supplied by Sarah Rutherford, Mentmore Landscape Analysis, 20 June 2018

CHAPTER ELEVEN

'A very respectable-looking young man': Criminals in the Garden

1. *London Courier and Evening Gazette*, Saturday 18 October 1828

2. ibid.

3. ibid.

4. Horticultural Society of London, Garden Committee Minutes, 26 October 1824, RHS Archive

5. Loudon, J. C., *Gardener's Magazine*, vol. 1, 1826, p.317

6. Letter from 'Hortulanus', *Gardener's Magazine*, vol. 2, 1827, p.105

7. Loudon, J. C., *Gardener's Magazine*, vol. 6, 1826, p.377

8. *Gardener's Magazine*, vol. 14, 1838, pp.111–12

9. *Bell's Weekly Messenger*, Monday 20 October 1828

10. *London Courier and Evening Gazette*, Saturday 18 October 1828

11. ibid.

12. Newgate Prison Calendar, October 1828, National Archives ref. HO77

13. *London Courier and Evening Gazette*, 18 October 1828

14. *The Morning Post*, 29 October 1828

15. Horticultural Society of London, Garden Committee Minutes, 24 October 1828, RHS Archive

16. Fletcher, H. R., *The Story of the Royal Horticultural Society 1804–1968*, Oxford, Oxford University Press, 1969

17. *The Standard*, 3 February 1830

18. Letter quoted in Fletcher, H. R., *The Story of the Royal Horticultural Society 1804–1968*, 1969

19. *Hertford Mercury and Reformer*, 4 July 1837

EPILOGUE

'Glory has departed': What Happened Next?

1. *Gardeners' Chronicle*, 30 August 1862, pp.809–10

2. Holloway, T., *The Flower of Empire*, 2013

3. Smiles, S., *Self-Help: with Illustrations of Character, Conduct and Perseverance* (1859), ed. P. Sinnema, Oxford, Oxford University Press, 2002

4. *Transactions of the Horticultural Society of London* (second series), vol. 2, 1842, p.373

5. Elliott, B., *Victorian Gardens*, London, Batsford, 1986

Index